TIGERS ARE OUR BROTHERS
Anthropology of Wildlife Conservation in Northeast India

AMBIKA AIYADURAI

D1502713

OXFORD
UNIVERSITY PRESS

OXFORD
UNIVERSITY PRESS

Oxford University Press is a department of the University of Oxford.
It furthers the University's objective of excellence in research, scholarship,
and education by publishing worldwide. Oxford is a registered trademark of
Oxford University Press in the UK and in certain other countries.

Published in India by
Oxford University Press
22 Workspace, 2nd Floor, 1/22 Asaf Ali Road, New Delhi 110002, India

© Oxford University Press, 2021

The moral rights of the author have been asserted.

First edition published in 2021

ISBN-13 (print edition): 978-0-19-012910-1
ISBN-10 (print edition): 0-19-012910-7

eISBN-13: 978-8-19-483163-1
eISBN-10: 1-08-19483163-6

Typeset in Berling LT Std 9.5/13
by Tranistics Data Technologies, Kolkata 700 091
Printed in India at Rakmo Press Pvt. Ltd.

For Appa,
for Jeeha Tacho,
and for my dear Idu Mishmi friends and families

CONTENTS

TABLES AND FIGURES

Tables

Figures

SELECT GLOSSARY

A list of some Idu Mishmi words and their meanings; some words are in Hindi or Assamese which are used commonly in the region.

āhū kòcī	bag made of bearskin
àkā	granary
ākrū	takin
ālā	musk deer
āmrā	tiger
āmrā la	tiger teeth
èná	observe taboo
apiya	elder person
àrhȭ	mishmi teeta *(Coptis teeta)*
ãtì	village/hamlet (*basti* in Hindi)
è. ècè	machete (*dao* in Assamese)
gaon burrah (Hindi)	village head man
īgù	shaman/village priest
kalita	medicinal root
kasturi (Hindi)	musk deer
khenyū	common term for spirits
mānjō	barking deer
nàbā	father
nànyī	mother
pà	yeast for preparing *yū*
sā	mithun
túná	lettuce (*laai-patta* in Assamese)
yū	rice beer

ACKNOWLEDGEMENTS

Many helped me personally and professionally during the writing of this book. Firstly, I would like to thank my PhD supervisor, Dr Maribeth Erb at National University of Singapore (NUS), for all her support and encouragement. She gave me the freedom to work independently, to explore new ideas. She guided me to sharpen my ideas and provided clarity to my oftenclouded thoughts. I am very fortunate to have her as my supervisor. Professor Mahesh Rangarajan (Ashoka University, Haryana, India) has always encouraged me to publish my work. Without his constant support, this work would have never materialized. Professor Sudhir Jain, the director of Indian Institute of Technology Gandhinagar, encouraged me to continue my fieldwork in Arunachal Pradesh. I cannot thank him enough for his continuous support and motivation. Drafts of this book's chapters were read by many at different stages and they provided valuable comments during my presentations made at seminars. I want to thank them all: Dr Alex Aisher (University of Sussex, UK), Professor John Kelly (The University of Chicago, USA), Dr Manjusha Nair (George Mason University, USA), Dr Amita Baviskar, Dr Rita Kothari (Ashoka University, India), Professor Brian Morris (adjunct faculty, Goldsmith College, UK), Dr Xu Xiaohong (University of Michigan, USA), Dr Medha Kudaisya (NUS), Dr Harvey Neo (Lee Kuan Yew Centre for Innovative Cities, Singapore), Dr Annu Jalais (NUS), and Romit Choudhury (Erasmus University Rotterdam, the Netherlands). Comments from Dr Emily Chua, Professor Mahesh Rangarajan, and Professor K. S. Sivaramakrishnan were valuable, and I am deeply indebted to them for that. In 2017, I received the Social

Science Research Council (SSRC) Transregional Research Junior Scholar Fellowship, during which I visited the Global Asia Initiative at Duke University, North Carolina, USA. I finalized several sections of the manuscript during that period, and I thank Professor Prasenjit Duara for his support during my time at the Global Asia Initiative.

The Rufford Small Grant for Nature Conservation and a field grant by the Firebird Anthropological Foundation were both valuable support during my research in remote parts of Arunachal Pradesh. Nandita Hazarika and Goutam Narain (Guwahati) were always there to help me out during my fieldwork with respect to accommodation, contacts, food, tickets, and transportation. Sokhep Kri helped with getting a long-term Inner Line Permit. I am grateful to Professor Sarit Chaudhuri, who hosted me at Rajiv Gandhi University, Itanagar, as visiting faculty to teach a course on environmental anthropology for MSc students. I am forever thankful to Chuko Loma for helping me with my work in the forest department. I thank Ampi for her patience in giving me access to archival documents at State Archives, Itanagar.

Nanyi Michum Mega in Koronu was my host during my initial phase of research and like a mother to me. She provided great company, and the only thing for which she was disappointed with me was for not saying yes to the shaman who proposed to me. Her children Buna Pulu and Akungo Pulu were always there to help me. Thanks to Jiten, my assistant in Koronu. In Roing, Naba Jatan Pulu's residence became my second home and his kin became my adopted family. Naba Jatan Pulu, Nanyi Yaane, Krishma, Lolly, Kimi, Tempa, Deho, Asha, Raman bhaiyya, Manmati, Sunami, and Sankar gave me company, support, and love. I miss them all. There were many in Roing who gave me their time to discuss my work: I thank Raju Mimi, Dr Rasto Mena, Dr Mite Linggi, Rezina Mihu, Jibi Pulu, Kotege Mena, Runa Pulu, Jiko Linggi, Naba Ingore Linggi, Ngasi Mena, Manaya Mena, and Eliya Tacho for the stimulating discussions about Mishmi and the culture and politics of the region.

From Anini, I am forever indebted to Apiya Jongo Tacho and Ashaya for hosting me at their house; I now feel like a part of their family. Whatever I know about the Mishmi is because of them. Apiya and I spent hours discussing farming, hunting, musk deer, and Chinese hunting stories. Sometimes I disappointed him for not supporting Prime Minister Narendra Modi and for fondly drinking *yū* (rice beer). Their children (Eha, Labi, Juhi, and Jeeha) were fun company. We watched movies together on my laptop during power cuts, played chess, harvested pumpkins, barbequed pork, and recorded animal stories. Jeeha and I went for bird watching in and around Anini. Juhi gave me the courage to bathe in freezing water and scared me with ghost stories; both were dreadful. Inge was my assistant for some time in Anini. He demonstrated to me how to restrain a pig in a bamboo basket and how to skin a frog; he was also my part-time Mishmi teacher. Krogho, Sanda, Jonti, Kano, and many others in Anini often welcomed me with food and drinks. I spent several days with the well-known Mishmi shaman Naba Sipa Melo. I thank him for sharing his knowledge with me. Apiyas Monmohan Mihu and Robert Rondo were very kind to give their precious time whenever I approached them. I learnt a lot from Ananta Meme, the great storyteller who always had exciting stories to share. From Khonsa, I thank Mishimbu Miri for sharing wonderful borderland stories. In addition, I specially thank my friends in Lohit district for their tireless support, care, and love: Bapen Kri, Dr. Kaku Gyati, Uncles Moosa (Sathyanarayan Mundayoor), and Rohinso Kri.

I am greatly indebted to Sajai Joseph for his help in reading the script multiple times and for providing valuable editorial contributions. Editors in OUP team have been very supportive all through the process.

I thank the two anonymous reviewers for their insights and comments. Names of some people have been changed to protect their identities.

Some chapters were published as journal articles in *Economic and Political Weekly* (2018), *Conservation & Society* (2016), *Asian Ethnology* (2017).

Finally, I can never adequately thank my family for giving me the freedom to do whatever I wanted to do and to go wherever I wanted to go. Thank you, Amma, Paati, Gopi, Vivek, Anna, and little Vikranta and Vanshu. They were very patient with me as weeks would go by without me being able to call them due to the poor phone network in Dibang. I am truly fortunate to be part of this family. I wish my father were here to read my book. I dedicate this book to my Appa.

TIGERS ARE OUR BROTHERS

I

INTRODUCTION

It was 26 January 2013; the sleepy town of Anini, capital of the Dibang Valley district in Arunachal Pradesh, Northeast India, was alive with an energetic buzz that day. School children in uniforms and villagers all dressed up walked briskly to the parade ground where loudspeakers blared patriotic songs in Hindi. Policemen were posted all along the road, waiting for the district commissioner to hoist the Indian national flag. It was India's 64th Republic Day. I passed by the parade ground to reach the circuit house[1] for a meeting with a World Wildlife Fund (WWF)[2] personnel from Delhi. Dr Anand from WWF was in Anini with his colleagues to map the Dibang Wildlife Sanctuary on invitation of the Department of Environment and Forests, Arunachal Pradesh (hereafter, the forest department). It was meant to be a meeting to exchange greetings before leaving for the sanctuary to start the mapping exercise. I was looking forward to meeting Anand, whom I hadn't seen in 10 years. We had been at the Wildlife Institute of India (WII) (Dehradun) together, where he was pursuing his PhD while I was a postgraduate student.

This supposedly short meeting turned out to be a two-hour-long discussion. Men from Anini, including a district council (Zilla Parishad)

---

[1] Guest house for government officials.
[2] World Wide Fund for nature, one of the leading NGOs in conservation of wildlife and endangered species.

member[3] named Athuko, slowly began to gather in the circuit house to meet the team. I wondered how the men had come to know about this meeting, which was only supposed to be between the forest department and WWF. More chairs had to be brought in to accommodate these surprise visitors. Athuko, wearing a heavy jacket and a red woollen cap, sat next to Anand. He put his hands in his pockets, tapping his feet casually. A sharp and confident young man from Anini, Athuko began to question the team in Hindi, 'What is the purpose of your visit?' Anand responded, 'We have come to see the jungle.' Athuko quickly shot back, 'You haven't come all the way from Delhi just to look at our jungle, have you?' Anand clearly did not expect such a quick-witted rejoinder from a village council member. The men began to murmur in the local dialect, which was unintelligible to the team and me. I suspected, however, that the men were concerned that WWF's visit was in response to a recent incident of the rescue of some tiger cubs. Now that it was clear that there were tigers in the forests of Dibang Valley, life for the Mishmi was likely to change and they were not happy about this possibility. Tigers are the national animal of India and a 'Schedule I' species.[4] To break the awkwardness of the moment, Anand began talking about his work in Delhi, about mapping, and the Geographic Information System (GIS) work. The men, however, started to challenge Anand again about the intention of his visit. What followed was a long discussion with an interesting show of power, strength, and verbal scoring over the knowledge of wildlife between the two parties, namely WWF and the local Mishmi. As a wildlife biologist, I had experience of such meetings in the past. As an anthropologist, however, what was now interesting to me was the way the local people challenged WWF officials, arguing that their taboos were helping tiger conservation and presenting their version of how wildlife should be managed.

The talk of tigers is inevitable whenever there is a discussion on forests in this region. During the meeting, Anand, himself a trained wildlife biologist, explained the importance of tigers as top predators in the

---

[3] Zilla Parishad Members (ZPMs) are officially elected for five years. The ZPMs' role is to provide essential services and facilities to the rural population, apart from the planning and execution of development programmes for the district.

[4] Schedule I species are protected animals according to the Indian Wildlife Protection Act (1972), which I will discuss in Chapter 5.

ecosystem and how tigers keep the herbivore population in control. He patiently explained the role of tigers and exhorted the villagers, 'If tigers are killed, the prey population will increase and destroy the forests.' This textbook-based food chain concept was demolished in a second when Athuko replied casually and confidently, 'If the deer population increases, we are there to hunt them and we will check the deer population.' Anand and his team were taken aback, since the hunting of wild animals is, in fact, forbidden. Athuko qualified his statement with pride and smiled, 'Because we don't kill tigers, the deer population is controlled by us.' Athuko grinned proudly, followed by laughter.

Athuko belongs to the local Idu Mishmi, an indigenous group in the Dibang Valley of Arunachal Pradesh (hereafter referred to as Arunachal). The Mishmi hunt wild animals and observe certain taboos. Their perception of nature conservation is different from that of WWF, which believes in preservation by not 'interfering' with the ecosystem. These officials advised the Mishmi not to kill tigers, probably not knowing that killing tigers is a taboo among the Mishmi and that they consider tigers as their 'brothers'. The Mishmi use a hands-on approach to deal with wildlife. Wild boars and barking deer are hunted to protect the crops and are pursued for meat. Hunting of musk deer yields them additional cash through the sale of musk pods.[5] Tigers, because of their kinship relations with the local people, are never hunted, unless it becomes dangerous to their life and property. Such multifaceted links to nature, in this case with wild animals, stand in contrast to a simplified notion of nature and wildlife protection held by the Indian state and science. In the last eight years, conservation NGOs from mainland India have been showing an increasing interest in remote places such as the Dibang Valley in order to survey the mountains for wildlife and for habitat mapping. Their interactions with the local people often create confusion, curiosity, and frustration for both parties. This particular visit of the WWF representatives was instigated by an incident of rescuing of tiger cubs. Discussions about the Dibang Tiger Reserve are going on, but nothing has been officially declared yet. The Idu Mishmi are demanding a reduction in the size of the existing sanctuary and for the

---

[5] The male musk deer carries a gland called the 'musk pod' (scent gland). This is in high demand in the international market (in the perfume industry) and is also used in traditional East Asian medicine.

remapping of the sanctuary to be carried out. In 2018, a meeting with the NTCA (National Tiger Conservation Agency) brought some relief when the officials convinced the Mishmi that a joint mapping exercise will be carried out with their help. The issues on the ground are far from over as tensions between the Mishmi, the researchers, and the developers have increased over the years that followed.

In the winter of 2012, a local Mishmi from Angrim Valley, one of the closest villages to Dibang Wildlife Sanctuary (Figure 1.1), reportedly killed a female tiger because of its attacks on his cattle; four orphaned tiger cubs were left to fend for themselves and started to visit houses to hunt poultry. Subsequently, the cubs fell into a dry tank and could not get out.[6] A rescue operation was carried out by a Delhi-based NGO, Wildlife Trust of India (WTI),[7] with the help of the forest department (Figure 1.2).

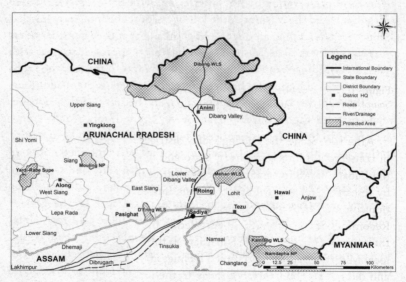

Figure 1.1   Map of Dibang Valley
Source: Dr. G. Areendran and Krishna Raj.
Note: This map does not represent the authentic international boundaries of India. It is provided for illustrative purposes only.

[6] Two of the three cubs that fell into the tank were rescued. One died. The fourth cub was not traced but there were talks of a cub roaming around the villages.

[7] WTI was helped by the International Fund for Animal Welfare (IFAW). The logistical support was provided by Arunachal's forest department.

Figure 1.2 Tiger cubs being rescued in Dibang Valley
Source: Illustrated by Gnana Selvam.

After the rescue, the Dibang Valley district started witnessing a series of conservation interventions by state and non-state actors. This made the Dibang Wildlife Sanctuary in the district a site of high-profile visits by research students, wildlife biologists, and members of the conservation community to map the tiger habitat and assess the tiger population. Recommendations from these visits led to the proposal[8] to reconstitute the existing Dibang Wildlife Sanctuary as the Dibang Tiger Reserve. The local Mishmi residents had mixed feelings about this new development and did not respond very positively to the interest shown by researchers, NGOs, and the forest department. Some even questioned the need for a tiger reserve, claiming, 'We don't hunt tigers. In fact, we protect them.' The villagers living close to the sanctuary were anxious about

[8] Following the confirmation of tiger presence by WII, the National Tiger Conservation Authority requested the forest department to send a proposal for declaring the Dibang Wildlife Sanctuary as the Dibang Tiger Reserve (letter no. F. No. 15-12/2014-NTCA, dated 28 May 2014).

what would happen if a tiger reserve was established. The fear of getting intertwined with the state's 'ever-reaching hands' and losing sovereignty was probably the chief reason behind their anxieties. There were even some who welcomed the possibility of a tiger reserve with the hope that it would create employment for their youth, who could become forest guards and tourist guides. Because of the eco-touristic potential of the region, people with entrepreneurial skills believed that Dibang would become as an important tourist location globally. The idea of a tiger reserve was welcomed by the local Mishmi, but not in the form it was presented in.

A few months after the rescue, WTI planned to release the cubs back in the 'wild',[9] but this was opposed by the Mishmi villagers, who feared that the tigers might return to the village and start attacking cattle and people. Therefore, the plan did not materialize and the cubs were shifted to the Itanagar Zoological Park, 900 kms from Anini however, this zoo does not have a good reputation.[10] The reason why it was chosen in spite of its murky reputation was the insistence of Arunachal's forest department that 'their' tigers needed to be retained in the state rather than be rehabilitated them in the neighbouring state of Assam.[11] Members of the Mishmi Students' Union, however, objected to the idea of shifting the tiger cubs to Itanagar, claiming that the tigers were *theirs*. This tussle contributed to a growing suspicion among the residents of Dibang Valley about what would follow the tigers' rescue in terms of developments regarding the wildlife sanctuary, the proposed creation of an eco-sensitive zone,[12] and the increasing interest shown

[9] 'Wild' here indicates the 'natural' home of these tigers to the Dibang Valley. The release and rehabilitation of the tiger cubs back to the wild is believed to be crucial for conservation success.

[10] In 2012, hardly a year before the shifting of the tiger cubs from Anini to the Itanagar Zoological Park, a tiger was hacked to death inside the zoo premises. In 2006, three tigers and a leopard were poisoned in the same zoo (see http://www.bbc.com/news/world-asia-india-19725397, assessed on 18 June 2015).

[11] WTI has a rehabilitation centre for rescued animals near Kaziranga National Park, Assam.

[12] An eco-sensitive zone is an additional area required by the state to effectively manage the sanctuary. A proposal from the forest department to the village councils, indicating this proposal, created an atmosphere of anxiety and confusion among the villagers.

by researchers. While the tiger cubs have ended up in the zoo, sealing their fate to eternal captivity, their habitat—hundreds of kilometres away on the Sino-Indian border—is undergoing plans to turn the wildlife sanctuary into a tiger reserve. This is being done without any serious discussion with the local residents. Suspicion about these plans, as well as the creation of the sanctuary in the past without informing the Mishmi, has led to mistrust towards the forest department and the research teams. This has resulted in mild intimidation and resistance, as well as hesitation or refusal on the part of the Mishmi to participate in the research activities. These are the differences in the perception and understanding of nature as well as its protection and conservation that I aim to examine in this book.

Nature, Conservation, and the Role of Communities

Our laws are of such a kind that every villager breaks one forest law every day of his life.

—Elwin (1964: 115)

Nature is perhaps the most complex word in the language.[13]

—Williams (1976: 219)

Natures are made and manifest through embodied activity; notions of nature work as discourse and ideology; and natural bodies are sustained through repeated material and symbolic practices.

—Moore, Kosek, and Pandian (2003: 8)

Conflicts, tensions, and misunderstandings such as those that I encountered in Dibang Valley have frequently happened across the globe since the late nineteenth century. The first epigraph in this section by Verrier Elwin, a well-known anthropologist who lived and worked with Indian 'tribals'[14] in the mid-twentieth century, sums up the mismatch and clash of interests between the ideas of conservation and the local users of natural resources. Local communities are often seen as a hindrance to conservation practices; therefore, excluding

[13] Raymond Williams is talking here about the English language.
[14] I use the word 'tribal' deliberately despite the complex meanings attached to it. I have discussed this in detail in Chapter 4.

them is considered legitimate. There is a large body of literature from the social science perspective that questions the exclusion of people in conservation both in historical and contemporary situations (Gadgil and Guha 1995; Rangarajan 1996; Kabra 2009). However, the use of violence and coercion to evict people from protected areas is still observable in many parts of the world, especially in developing countries (Peluso 1993).

The origin of the ideas of nature conservation and 'wilderness preservation' can be traced to two important historical moments. According to Igoe (2004), these two events are: (*1*) the enclosure movement of eighteenth–nineteenth-century England, which transformed common property and subsistence agriculture into private property, and (*2*) expansion of the nineteenth-century model of the United States of America of 'national parks', which captured the imagination of political elites globally. Thus began the social construct of wilderness, 'nature', and national parks. The assumption that natural resources could be protected only when converted into private property was strong. This is also articulated as the 'tragedy of the commons', where resources understood as 'open access' were seen as vulnerable to depletion unless strict rules of sustainable use were implemented (Hardin 1968). National parks are one such example of fencing forests by the state to protect these lands rather than leaving them open to people who have been dependent on forest resources for millennia and are managing the resources according to customary laws.[15] Therefore, ideas of privatization of land are against collective rights. This process resonates with 'primitive accumulation', proposed by Marx, as a process which divorces the worker from the ownership of the conditions of his own labour (Marx 1979: 875).

According to Perelman (2007), primitive accumulation can be explained in three key ways: (*1*) direct expropriation of people's means of livelihood, (*2*) forcing people to enter wage labour, and (*3*) manipulation of the division of labour. These characteristics can be seen in different aspects of contemporary conservation policies and practices,

---

[15] For this reason, resources are not really 'open access'. The notion of the 'tragedy of the commons' tends to misunderstand or ignore complex rules associated with access to land practices among locals. When the commons are taken over by non-locals, these rules and solutions are not used (Ostrom 1990).

but the catalyst is the 'expropriation'. Primitive accumulation is, thus, not just a concept of the past but very much relevant today. The kind of direct expropriation of forest lands and the forcing of people to adopt wage labour is seen as necessary to create protected areas that function as undisturbed 'wild' spaces for fauna, flora, and tourists, which Brockington (2001) coined as 'fortress conservation'. With the creation of parks, people who work for subsistence as farmers, hunters, or fisher folk (primary producers) are forcibly removed from the means of production (land, forests, rivers) in order to manufacture 'pristine nature', which Neumann (1998) appropriately calls 'imposing wilderness' for the preservation of nature.

Conservation is not just criticized for its practice but also its ideology. Some authors question the very foundation of conservation as an enterprise, which they see variously as an imperialist agenda (MacKenzie 1988), as a 'civilizing mission', and as a mandate to 'uplift the inferior races of the world' (Igoe 2004: 93). Others highlight that conservation is not as 'noble' as it is thought to be (Duffy 2010). A large number of NGOs are involved in 'teaching' people to save and care for the environment. Converting them to 'green and responsible' citizens is similar to the civilizing mission of colonialism. Local people are often seen as too ignorant to appreciate the beauty of nature (Bryant and Parnwell 1996; Argyrou 2005). Through a civilizing mission, Europeans 'developed' both nature and people (Neumann 1998). A dual mandate of colonial rule, 'the white man's burden', required control of nature and natives, both to be managed, improved, and developed for the benefit of the colony (Lugard 1972; Moore, Kosek, and Pandian 2003). This is a mandate that conservationists tend to continue to implement: control of 'nature' and control of the 'native' (Argyrou 2005).

Unpacking 'Nature'

A recurrent concern in conservation is to what extent the understanding of conservation is misaligned with the understanding of 'nature'. To understand why conservation is such a 'prickly affair' (Erb 2012), the term 'nature' has to be 'unromanticized' and unpacked. For quite some time, I have been uncomfortable with the idea that nature is 'caring' and 'nurturing'. Isn't nature also a destroyer when it takes the form of disease and 'natural' disasters such as the tsunami? Should

we embrace everything about nature? Also, 'When we say nature, do
we mean to include ourselves?' asks Williams (1976: 67). According
to Lexico (powered by Oxford),[16] the word 'nature' as a noun is 'the
phenomena of the physical world collectively, including plants, animals,
the landscape, and other features and products of the earth, as opposed
to humans or human creations'. This definition encodes for the English
speaker the idea that nature does not include human beings or their
works. Thus, the dictionary has a role in shaping our understanding of
what nature is in the English-speaking world, which is in fact, not true
universally. However, it is stated as a matter of fact, such that English
speakers come to accept this view as the one 'truth'.[17]

The uses and meanings of nature generate different ideas and feelings, as the conditions of the human world changes (Williams 1980:
85). To know nature is a complex, multiple, and highly political process
(Goldman, Nadasdy, and Turner 2011). 'Nature' is a human idea, says
Cronon (1996: 20) because of the long cultural history that led to the
various conceptions of the natural world in different ways. According
to Cronon (1996), the things, landscapes, and living beings that we call
'natural' are a manifestation of words, images, and ideas. Our notion of
nature is selective in the sense that we decide what we want to label
as 'natural'. This has left a deep and lasting impact on how policies and

[16] See https://www.lexico.com/definition/nature (accessed on 9 December
2015).
[17] The origin of the English word 'nature' comes from *naturc* (old French)
and *nātūra* (Latin) from a root of *nāscī*, which means 'to be born'. Natura means
conditions of birth, quality, character, and natural order. In the book *Keywords: A
Vocabulary of Culture and Society* (1976), Raymond Williams provides 130 keywords that have taken on new meanings and how these new meanings reflect
the political and cultural framework of past and present society in Europe. One
section is on 'Nature' (pp. 219–24). Another publication of his is *Culture and
Materialism: Selected Essays* (1980), which has a chapter on 'Ideas of Nature'
(pp. 67–85). In these works, he points out three different meanings of nature.
First is the essential quality and character of something. For example, we often
say, 'he (or she) is a good-natured person'. Secondly, nature is also understood
as an inherent force which directs the world, including humans. The third is
the material world itself, which may or may not include human beings. As an
independent noun, nature takes on new forms and uses.

laws related to nature protection are formulated, especially the use of the idea of wilderness for protecting nature.

Additionally, 'nature' needs to be 'decoded' not only at a conceptual level (the idea of nature) but also at an operational level (how nature is protected). At the conceptual level, contradictions emerge from the varied notions of nature that conservationists and communities have. The Mishmi do not seem to have a distinct word for 'nature', and their relationship with their environment is very different from how nature is promoted in conservation circles. Conservationists consider nature to be a vast landscape of wilderness, filled with endangered species, and wild, rare, and charismatic animals (Cronon 1996); such understandings often fuel what has been called 'bourgeois environmentalism' (Baviskar 2002). For this group, causes of environmental degradation are attributed to the 'poor', those such as the Mishmi who directly rely upon nature for their livelihood. But for people who live near and in the forests, nature is not only their source of life but also a world rich with symbolic meanings (Knight 2004). Western-dominated ideas about nature are increasingly capturing the imagination of urbanites across the globe and subsume 'other local versions' of nature. Such hegemonic narratives of nature do not allow for an engagement with alternative ways of understanding nature. This is true largely in urban India and is increasingly affecting people such as the Mishmi who live in remote forested areas on the borderlands.

In India, conservation of wildlife is a big challenge with large numbers of communities still directly dependent on natural resources for survival (Shahabuddin and Rangarajan 2007). The rift between people and parks is wide in many parts of India (Saberwal, Rangarajan, and Kothari 2001). Scholars such as Ramachandra Guha have been very critical of the biologists' approach to conservation. He takes an 'anti-biologist' stand to highlight the ways in which conservation is made favourable to the conservation professionals at the cost of local communities (Guha 1997). Guha calls the wildlife biologists-cum-conservationists 'arrogant and authoritarian' and accuses them of preserving species for the sake of 'science', even if it dispossesses people from their land and livelihoods (Gadgil and Guha 1995; Guha 1997). The conservation lobby refuted this claim as being 'biologically illiterate' (Gartlan 1998: 219), highlighting the contrasting opinions of social scientists and wildlife biologists on this issue.

Nature and Wilderness

The dominant narrative of conservation is that nature is 'untouched', 'virgin', and 'wild'. The term 'wilderness' is typically associated with the idea of Eden, an uncultivated and uninhabited land. American writers such as John Muir and Henry David Thoreau played an important role in shaping how nature came to be imagined in the Western world. Nineteenth-century writings professed biocentric or ecocentric views of nature, often excluding humans, especially those who were 'outside of the dominant class, race, or gender' (Naess 1989). Their writings influenced the wilderness movements and the setting up of Yellowstone National Park, which became the model for establishing protected areas globally. Thus, protecting this 'wild' form of nature required cultivating a moral right to dictate to others, especially to the indigenous peoples, not to hunt, fish, or extract anything in this 'pristine nature'.

The 'idea of wilderness' has been successfully infused in the disciplines of ecological and conservation sciences since their inception. Trained conservationists and field biologists use these ideas to advocate, plan, and implement conservation projects across the world to preserve 'wild' spaces. The problem with this approach is that most conservationists see any use of natural resources as harming nature, even when it is for the survival of poor people. Hence, people who use natural resources for their livelihood and subsistence become 'encroachers and poachers'. Argyrou says that ecocentrism 'is an extreme form of environmentalism' (Argyrou 2009: 6) because it provides justification for changing the world and changing people's beliefs, at times overriding opposing views and even ignoring the rights of the local people. The conservationists' mantra has been to evoke the idea of 'pristineness' to advocate nature preservation (Neumann 1998). Such an imagination hides the human elements and their creations. Conservationists see these spaces of wilderness as vulnerable because of the people's need for land, water, timber, and forest produce.

The conservationist notion of the vulnerability of nature is well articulated by Timothy Luke, who suggests that nature is seen as dead or dying by conservationists and global NGOs, who raise memorial sites in the world's 'last great places' (Luke 1997: 71–4) in the form of national parks and wildlife sanctuaries. He even calls these sanctuaries 'nature cemeteries'. The notion of the death of nature or the 'end of nature', to use McKibben's phrase (1989), emerges from the idea of an environmental crisis; the decline in forest cover, extinction of wildlife, rise in global temperature and sea levels project a 'doomsday'-like situation. Environmentalists and biologists speak the language of ecological emergency and crisis. For example, conservation biologists see dying nature in the form of 'empty forests'[18] (Redford 1992). Forests where wild animals have been hunted indicate an 'apocalyptic' situation. 'Endangered', 'critically endangered', or 'threatened' species are used as metaphors of dying nature. Some even say that overexploitation and depletion of natural resources is 'bankrupting nature' (Wijkman and Rockstorm 2012). Therefore, places such as national parks become living museums and natural laboratories to conserve dying species for future generations to visit and enjoy (Luke 1997; Carson 2014). A conservationist's view of nature is, thus, of preservation, which can only be achieved by separating human activities from nature.

Dominant Narratives of Hunting and Wildlife Conservation

Wildlife hunting is practised for various reasons, including subsistence and commercial reasons. The local communities are involved in hunting for fulfilling their nutritional needs as well as in commercial hunting of species such as the musk deer and black bears for their high market value. Commercial hunting in India is considered to have depleted wildlife in the twentieth century, particularly tigers, black bears, pheasants, and pangolins. Similar findings have been made in Africa and South America, where intensive bushmeat and luxury trade have visibly led to an 'empty forest syndrome'.

There are numerous studies on wildlife hunting across the globe highlighting the seriousness of this issue (Bennett and Robinson 2001). It is often the poor rural communities who are reported to be

---

[18] This term is coined by Kent Redford in reference to forests where large mammals have been removed by hunting. It is interesting to note that the term 'empty' applies to forests with no wildlife, especially mammals, and not people. Humans are acknowledged only as the destroyers of forests.

the primary consumers of wild meat (de Merode, Homewood, and Cowlishow 2004). Though urban populations are not dependent on wild meat as a source of protein, markets in Asia mainly cater to urban demands, thereby making it a luxury item (Bennett and Rao 2002). Market surveys in Africa have revealed that 'meat is being sold from a wide range of animals including large primates and small rodents' (Fa, Burn, and Broad 2002), indicating a measure of hunting pressure. Increased access to markets and the ability to travel further into the forests have changed the dynamics of hunting. For example, the number of dealers in wild pig meat trade in Indonesia increased from one dealer in 1970 to 30 in 1996 (Clayton, Keeling, and Milner-Gulland 2000). Dealers clearly profited from the road construction in remote sites, which enable them to travel from the hunting sites to the markets faster. There are relatively few studies from Asia when compared with Africa (Alvard 2000; Corlett 2007) and micro-level information on hunting by indigenous people is even more scarce (Griffin and Griffin 2000; Rao et al. 2005). In India, the emphasis of hunting studies has been on international trade of wildlife (tiger skins, ivory, and leopard parts) (Banks and Wright 2006; Menon and Kumar 1997; Talukdar 2000), and data on local and indigenous hunting in India is very sparse (Kaul et al. 2004; Kumara and Singh 2004; Madhusudan and Karanth 2002). Northeast India has witnessed only a few studies (Aiyadurai, Singh, and Milner-Gulland 2010; Datta 2002; Hilaluddin, Kaul, and Ghose 2005, Velho, Karanth, and Laurance 2012). Here, hunting by tribal populations is not just of economic concern but has a wider cultural relevance as well (Aiyadurai 2007; Nijhawan 2018). This is important for understanding the reasons why hunting is so widely practised. In my survey of hunting practices in Arunachal Pradesh, respondents talked about the population decline of certain hunted species, such as bears and musk deer. They also discussed how social taboos on hunting have helped increase the population of some species such as Hoolock gibbons and tigers in the Mishmi Hills.

Indigenous People and Nature

In contrast to the conservationists' understanding of nature, which sets humans apart from the natural environment, many indigenous people do not make that distinction. The boundary between the human world and the natural world is often blurred. Some cultures depict human relatedness to nature as a type of kinship, for example a parent–child relation, sexual relatedness, procreation, or simply just a 'namesake' relatedness (Tanner 1979; Bird-David 1990; Ingold 1996; Roy and Katsuyoshi 1996). Forests in some farming societies of India are seen as ancestors who unconditionally provide food, which Bird-David (1990) calls the 'giving environment' where forests are viewed as parents and people as children of the forests. This 'giving environment' contrasts with the 'reciprocating environment' where provision of food is conditional upon proper conduct found among hunter-gatherers such as the Nayakas (Bird-David 1990). Morris (1982) shows that among the Malaipantaram in south India, forests are an abode of ancestral spirits and forest deities which can be called upon for protection. Through the use of kinship relations with nature, indigenous people show their 'belonging and genealogical ties' with nature as a source of identity (Tanner 1979; Bird-David 1990).

Two important concepts are central to most indigenous groups— presence of 'spirits' in all non-human forms, beings, and objects (animals, trees, rivers, farms, houses, rocks) and the existence of an 'owner of the forest' (Ingold 1980; Howell 1984). There are spirits that guard farms and wild animals, and provide safety, health, and wealth to local residents. If people fail to satisfy these spirits, harvests may fail and hunts may be unsuccessful. The rituals and taboos followed in connection with resource use (harvesting and hunting) are in the context of showing respect to the forest spirits and the spirits of the dead (Howell 1982; Singh 1987; Morris 2000). Forests and animals have owners, therefore, people do not claim ownership of these animals, but instead seek permission before hunting or farming. Another key belief among some indigenous peoples is that there is an exchange of a vital force between humans and spirits through the sacrifice of domesticated animals and the reverse via hunting. Ingold (1980) calls ideas such as this as supporting a 'world renewing process', thus contributing to the regeneration of life. Therefore, human–nature relations among indigenous people involve a constant engagement of humans with the various elements of nature and the spirits. This differs from conservationists' perspectives, and the basic difference is that they consider humans and nature as separate, while indigenous people such as the Mishmi do not see this separation.

Nature and Neoliberalism

Recent participants in the domain of conservation are those forming the neoliberal lobby, who claim to be able to fix environmental problems through the market economy. This lobby sees nature as a commodity to be traded and which is constructed as a 'world currency' (McAfee 1999b). Natural resources are appropriated from local people and a price tag is put on nature for capital creation. Market-based solutions are often aligned with profit-driven corporations, disregarding local cultural values and uses. The belief continues to be that they need to 'sell nature to save it' (McAfee 1999b: 97). Fletcher rightly points out that over the last few decades, conservation has become 'infused with a neoliberal economic philosophy' (2010: 172), resulting in the creation of capitalist markets for natural resource use and consumption. Ecotourism has been criticized for targeting new frontiers in nature and for packaging nature for global consumption (Laudati 2010). The spread of protected areas, the faith in ecotourism, the infusing of conservation into developmental agendas, and the creation of community conservation programmes are clear indications that conservation is increasingly intertwined with, or has become an outgrowth of, capitalism. This raises questions of ecological equity and justice, especially when different actors with different capacities seek cooperation and collaboration from each other.

When multiple partners are involved in the practice of conservation, collaborations are formed through negotiation. Afiff and Lowe (2008) suggest that projects of 'nature-making' have always involved collaborations of the sort where local people become field assistants in research projects, or guides, porters, and suppliers of local knowledge of the unfamiliar landscape. The way decisions are taken as to whom to partner with and what types of partnerships to form is a kind of 'political mobilization' (Brosius, Tsing, and Zerner 2005: 9). Collaboration with different groups seems to be a socially equitable process of knowledge and skill sharing, but collaboration is rarely ever a 'simple sharing of information' (Tsing 2005: 13). This kind of association creates new interests where not everyone benefits, as these collaborations have their own limitations. Sometimes the idea of 'collaboration' also takes the form of helping 'an occupying enemy' (Erb and Acciaioli 2006: 144).

These collaborations can be said to be taking place in 'contact zones'. Pratt (1991) defines these as 'social spaces' where cultures meet, clash, and grapple with each other, often in contexts of asymmetrical relations of power. What often ends up happening are a series of negotiations, promises, and compromises where communities are gently, or sometimes forcefully, coerced to agree to the ideas offered by more powerful actors (Peluso 1993). Marginal communities who are already weak and vulnerable are pushed further to the periphery. Although community-based conservation (CBC) projects intend to provide an equitable platform for people's participation, in hierarchical societies such as India, there are groups (the poor, the landless, the Dalits, and the indigenous) whose voices are suppressed and who consequently participate only minimally, or not at all. The inequalities inherent in caste-based societies are part of a larger socio-economic and political process which conservation projects often ignore. Paudel (2005) argues that lack of representation from these groups is a common feature in all rural development programmes. These inequalities have been aggravated by conservation projects leading to a 'double marginalization' of vulnerable groups (Kothari 2003). For example, in India, dominant Hindu nationalistic ideas have become crucial rallying points for environmental movements (Sharma 2012). Certain ideas of conservation are deeply Brahmanical as they marginalize Dalits by condemning their meat-eating practices as dirty, inferior, and not environment friendly, and coerce them to turn vegetarian. One such thought-provoking work is by Mukul Sharma (2017), which has added another layer to demonstrate the complexity of environmental issues and discourses. He captures the relationship between Dalits and the environment. Nature and caste are rarely seen together in discussions around environmental movements. For decades, environmental narratives—whether local, national, or regional—have rendered the voices of the Dalits silent. The new generation of environmental activism and writings has begun to pay more attention to the hitherto unseen and unheard people of India. The politics of caste in the domain of environment conservation has been a 'blind spot' (Sharma 2017: xix). Sharma explores environmentalism through the lens of various Dalit conceptions; such as a particular caste's access to nature, Dalit thought, writings, discussions, histories and memories, and activism. His book argues most powerfully and appeals that rather than looking for conventional environmentalism in conventional conservation movements, we should rather locate strands of it in Dalit political and social traditions.

Nature of 'Community' Participation

The term 'community', therefore, is not a simple word and has multiple layers embedded in hierarchy, power, and politics. Conservation workers who implement projects are usually urban-educated and do not share the same cultural values and pragmatic concerns as the local people. They have limited knowledge about the landscape, social realities, and local customs, and tend to see 'community' as a singular unit (Agrawal and Gibson 1999). However, class, clan, religion, ethnicity, and caste divide communities. Communities in conservation projects are treated as a 'small spatial unit' or as a 'homogenous structure', which is misleading. Agrawal and Gibson (1999) appeal for a reconsideration of the definition of community as constituting multiple sets of actors who have different interests. Communities have tensions and structural inequalities within their domain, which conservationists are often ignorant about or fail to grasp (Ghimire 1992).

For a long time, conservationists struggled to keep people out of protected areas, but in the last two decades, there has been a serious attempt to bring people and nature back together (Adams 2004). This turning point came during the 1992 Convention on Biological Conservation opened at the United Nations Conference on Environment and Development (the Rio 'Earth Summit'). It was also the International Year of the World's Indigenous Peoples, when the 'experts' formally recognized the rights and knowledge of indigenous people. This inclusive model provided the platforms for collaboration between indigenous communities and NGOs. Many organizations, local and regional, adopted 'community' in their project plans, and the expression 'community participation' or CBC became the new buzzword. CBC is seen as a 'politically correct' way of doing conservation, but the ground reality suggests that it is overrated and has raised doubts about the naivety surrounding real situations, socio-economic dimensions, and differing intentions (Agrawal and Gibson 1999; Tsing, Brosius, and Zerner 2005).

From the local communities' point of view, conservation brings to the community benefits such as health care, additional sources of income, employment opportunities (as tour guides, research assistants, porters), and access to new technology. Many NGOs believe that it is important to gain the goodwill of poor communities who are in need of basic civic amenities such as schools and hospitals, which they help build with the aid of donors. Communities may get civic facilities such as roads, schools, and hospitals, and, in turn, may show substantial participation in conservation projects. However, Heatherington (2012) suggests that these initiatives are in fact a form of structural adjustment, which lead to the overall development of the area but do not particularly result in the conservation of resources or equal participation. While the stated intent of CBC projects is to empower people, some see this as a coercive way of diffusing the ideas of global partners such as funding bodies and international NGOs, and as a way of controlling local resources (Peluso 1993). The expectations of local people towards NGOs and vice versa often do not match, and it often appears as if they are speaking different languages (Brown 1998; West 2006). NGOs sometimes have opposing agendas, which leads to disappointment for both the parties (West 2006). The vision of conservationists to protect nature is seen only as a management issue unrelated to the rights of the local people (Alcorn 2005), whereas local communities aim to gain some employment and income through conservation projects (West 2006). Community-based projects are part of a larger process in which multiple actors, institutions, and discourses define, contest, re-interpret, and enforce claims over resources, making it a complex political process (Paudel, Budhathoki, and Sharma 2007).

Imagining Nature and the Nation

Nature is not just about the natural world but the human cultures that lend meaning and moral imperatives to that world.

—Cronon (1996)

Dibang Valley is a particularly fascinating place to study tensions over conservation because it is a 'borderland' between India and China. Thus, the area has attracted attention from various national and international actors, not just because of its rich biodiversity and endangered animals, such as tigers, but also because of the geopolitical location of the Dibang Valley, as it is crucial for national security. This has resulted in the setting up of infrastructure in these border regions by the Indian Army. Because of its proximity with China, defence forces and intelligence staff patrol these borderlands to keep a check on Chinese activities, for which the knowledge of the Mishmi becomes crucial. Various state players are also investing in Dibang Valley for development, conservation, and nation building.

The boundary of Dibang Valley forms the international border with China, with whom India fought a war in 1962. Prior to that, the British were interested in this frontier region because of commodities such as tea and for its strategic location (Mitchell 1883). The British feared that if this region was left alone, the Mishmi would become 'Chinese subjects'. The relationship of the state with the border communities, such as the Mishmi, therefore, was often ambiguous. The movement of people between India and China for trade and to maintain kinship ties decreased with the creation of nation states and with the subsequent war with China. Nation states and the drawing of borders create categories of 'citizens' and 'foreigners' (Van Schendel and Abraham 2005). Such categories are born even within communities which get partitioned because of the borders, in spite of sharing similar cultures. While the local people negotiate and continue to cross the border, the borders define the identity of people living within a national territory. Mountains, animals, and birds within the border are also given national identities such as 'national animals', 'national birds', and so on. The appointment of these animals as mute ambassadors reflects eco-nationalism or eco-regionalism, a theme that Adrian Franklin explored in detail in Australia, where native animals are given more importance than the introduced/exotic or alien animals brought along by colonial Europeans (Franklin 2006). Animals, especially native animals, and the places to which they belong inculcate feelings of people's belonging to the land, their connection to their motherland, their origins, and their histories. Therefore, preserving nature takes a particular form of nationalism, 'ecological nationalism', where national identity is entangled with the concerns of nature and its association with cultural pride, belongingness, regional identity, and struggle for resources (Cederlof and Sivaramakrishnan 2007). Rangarajan articulates the idea of 'ecological patriotism', providing the example of tigers in India (Rangarajan 2009). Around 1972, he writes, the Bengal tiger began to be referred to as the Indian tiger to link nationalistic emotions to the animal, a few years after India's Independence. Therefore, to see nature only as an ecological resource is too simplistic, nature also becomes a 'nationalistic enterprise' (Rangarajan, 2009: 303). This 'perceived' bond between nature and nation is often based on what Armerio and Von Hardenberg call the 'foundational myths', which grow around the issues of frontiers that are used in nationalist and patriotic discourse to justify environmental policies (2014: 4). Conceptions of national identity and state-making, therefore, are linked to nature (Schwartz 2006, Rangarajan 2015). Nation building involves construction of identity and an 'otherness', where one form of 'native' nature becomes more important than those that are not native (Armerio and Von Hardenberg 2014). 'Nativity', combined with rarity of species, is prioritized for conservation, and this is at the core of contemporary conservation (Dooren 2015).

Wildlife and nature do not recognize such borders and nation states as people do. The issues in Dibang Wildlife Sanctuary are fascinating for wildlife sciences and conservation because of its linkages to nationalism. After rescuing the tiger cubs, biologists were anxious to find out whether these cubs were 'Indian' or 'Chinese' tigers. Blood samples from the cubs and a DNA test ultimately confirmed their identity (Gopi, Qureshi, and Jhala 2014: 32). For both the tigers and the Mishmi, borderlands become a place of 'anxiety' about national identity and where one belongs. One can learn a great deal about 'nature', politics, and power by examining 'nature's role in nationalism' (Songster 2004). Songster shows that the giant panda as a national icon of China emerged only in the twentieth century as it came to be linked to nature protection and nationalism. It was after founding the People's Republic of China (PRC) that the new government embraced science as a means of strengthening China. The panda became a national symbol because of its scientific peculiarity and for being a uniquely Chinese indigenous species (2004: 51). One way of demonstrating the integration of 'nationalism and nature' is in the protection of nature, especially 'native' forms of nature. Loving 'native' nature becomes synonymous to loving one's country. The 'nation, according to Williams, is a term closely connected with "native"' (Williams 1983: 180).

According to Schwartz, many groups, large and small, see the soul of their nation reflected in their native landscapes (2006: 3). Nevertheless, we know that nations are 'imagined communities', that is, socially constructed entities imagined by the people who perceive themselves as part of that group (Anderson 1982). Nature has often played an important role in the invention and management of the concept of nation through symbols and concepts (Armerio and Von Hardenberg 2014).

People feel connected to these symbols and are brought together by the image of their communion. Local people such as the Mishmi use elements of nature to claim an identity and also the rights to their lands. Such claim-making also emerges from the way the Mishmi are imagined by 'others' as inferior and primitive. Such stereotypes for people such as the Mishmi stem from 'imaginaries'. Imaginaries have been conceptualized as socially shared, unifying core conceptions, fantasies or illusions created in response to a psychological need (Salazar 2012). Using the example of tourism, Salazar defines imaginaries as 'socially transmitted representational assemblages that interact with people's personal imaginings and are used as meaning-making and world shaping devices' (2012: 864). Conservation imaginaries, I argue, similar to tourism imaginaries, construct the ideas of 'pristine nature', 'paradise-like forests', or 'edenic gardens', as well as 'indigenous people living in harmony with nature'. These imaginaries have been constructed and circulated across the globe via the nineteenth- and twentieth-century European writings. Imaginaries are reproduced on visible platforms such as the media, photographs, websites, postcards, travelogues, guidebooks, and brochures. In nature conservation, such imaginaries play a powerful role in circulating and perpetuating one particular form of nature or one kind of indigenous peoples, with meanings attached to each. For example, images of nature are often represented as 'paradise', making this a 'master image' of a desired form of nature. Conservation actors reproduce such stereotypical images through setting up of protected areas and promote these areas as 'natural' and 'wild' by erasing local histories. 'Green fantasies', according to Foale and Macintyre (2005), are created through photographic representations of 'idealized nature', excluding the realities of local people and mystifying their relationship with nature. Such images are produced for Western consumption where nostalgia for the past drives the creation and recreation of these imaginaries and becomes institutionalized as a dominant narrative of how nature should look. The practices and ideology of conservation actors continue to recreate such imaginaries that often shape conservation policies.

The borderlands of Dibang Valley witness the intertwining of humans and animals as well as the encounters between humans and spirits. Places such as Dibang Valley merge the social and natural worlds to create more 'contact zones' (Pratt 1991) and inter-species encounters (Kirksey and Helmreich 2010). In such meeting spaces, cultural meanings of nature are created and recreated resulting in a multi-species ethnography. Earlier works looked at the impact of humans on nature and how natural processes influence human societies, where only humans were treated as agents (Peet, Robbins, and Watts 2011). Multi-species ethnography differs from earlier studies in that it focuses on mutual dependencies of humans and non-humans (Faier and Rofel 2014). The interface between humans and non-humans allows hybrid ontologies to emerge, enables a deeper exploration of how human life arises out of encounters and entanglements with other species, and reframes human identity through inter-species relationships (Tsing 2012).

When the Mishmi and the conservation actors, state, and capitalists meet, both see the other through the stereotypical lenses of the imaginaries they hold of each other. The ideas of nature and people are constantly constructed in new ways. In this book, I try to uncover how these varying visions of nature are contested, claimed, and counterclaimed through the tiger research projects in Dibang Valley. I use tiger conservation as a central theme to explore 'human–animal relations' in Dibang Valley. These relations are ever changing with the transformation of human societies, as is the case for the Mishmi. My research attempts to uncover the various understandings of nature, conservation, and the role of communities. I draw on how scholars theorize nature and why nature conservation is a sensitive issue, especially during the implementation of conservation projects and in the context of 'national security' and identity formation. My aim is to understand how indigenous peoples express their relationships with nature, which is connected to their social, economic, political, spiritual, and ecological contexts. My research combines pieces of my observations of different actors who visited Dibang Valley for various engagements in order to protect tigers and their habitat through science and mapping, and of the local Mishmi residents, their culture, and their social interactions with their natural habitat.

Themes and Chapters

The chapters that follow explore in detail what I have highlighted in the previous sections. I begin by discussing the site and what made me choose this topic. Chapter 2, 'My Journey in the Land of the Rising Sun' collates my day-to-day observations of the Mishmi through interviews with officials in the government of Arunachal, NGOs, and scientists from research institutes. I also examined documents of the British administration preserved at the State Archives in Itanagar and in The British Library, London. I discuss at length my positionality during the fieldwork and how my respondents expected me to be a 'form-carrying' researcher with a research team. The biggest challenge for me was facing the expectations of the Mishmi to 'write the right things about them'.

In Chapter 3, 'Mishmi Social Worlds: Animals, Humans, and Spirits', I provide an account of the Mishmi's relations with animals (both domesticated and wild). I highlight the role of animals in the lives of the Mishmi from a cultural, commercial, and conservation point of view. The symbolic interaction of the Mishmi with the mountain spirits and their reciprocal engagement is crucial during farming, hunting wild-life, or the slaughtering of domesticated animals. I discuss the tensions between the subsistence-related hunting and the wildlife protection laws that see hunting as illegal.

The geopolitical location of Dibang Valley and its inhabitants are discussed in Chapter 4, 'The Thin Red Line: Living on the Sino-Indian Border'. I provide a historical account of the Mishmi Hills and the state of Arunachal. As the Mishmi live on both sides of the Sino-Indian border, I attempt to elucidate the relation of the border communities with the state and with their subgroups living across the international borders. On the one hand, the Mishmi are employed as porters and guides by the military, but on the other, they are occasionally looked upon with suspicion by security forces because of their kinship with the 'Deng Mishmi' who live in the Zayul Valley of Tibet. I used sources collected from the State Archives in Itanagar to study the activities of the Mishmi crossing the border for trading and those associated with working for the Chinese government in the past. This chapter tells stories of how the border has shaped the Mishmi's lives post the Sino-Indian war.

In Chapter 5, 'Mithun Out and Takin In: Shifting Ecological Identities.' I show how and why the Mishmi elite are fostering and shaping their ecological identity in response to local and global envi-ronmental concerns. Through acts of symbolism, the Mishmi are claiming an 'ecological identity' by using elements of nature as objects of identification. I narrate the reasons why the Mishmi redesigned their society's emblem by replacing 'Mithun', a cattle used for ceremonial slaughter, with 'Takin', an endemic and endangered species. I argue that 'rare' and 'wild' forms of nature are privileged over 'domesticated' nature by the urban, elite Mishmi. Rarity of animals enhances people's feelings of respect and responsibility towards them. I discuss that there is a conscious effort by the urban Mishmi to redefine their identity through a wildlife conservation ethos brought in by wildlife scientists and conservation NGOs from mainland India.

Chapter 6, 'Tiger Conservation' and Its Predicaments', concentrates on the diverse human–nature relations in Dibang Valley, especially the Mishmi's relationship with animals. Locally, people see tigers as their brothers and take credit for tiger conservation as they follow the taboo against hunting tigers. Using their notion of a sibling relation with tigers, the Mishmi question the state's decision to propose converting the Dibang Wildlife Sanctuary into a tiger reserve by contesting and even blocking scientific surveys on tigers and the mapping of their habitat. The state's view of tigers as national property and the biologist's view of tigers as an endangered species are notions of nature as becoming extinct, which stand in opposition to the local interpretations of nature that see it as an intrinsically connected part of human life.

Finally, the last and seventh chapter summarizes my research. Two observations that I make on the story of wildlife conservation in Dibang Valley are the deficit of the 'social' in understanding conservation and the need for an interdisciplinary approach in nature conservation. Using these, I will reflect upon some practical implications of my research.

2

MY JOURNEY IN THE LAND OF
THE RISING SUN

There are serious reasons why I was drawn to Arunachal and why I decided to conduct my field research there (see Figure 2.1). My first trip to Arunachal was in 2003 to investigate human–animal interactions in the Itanagar Wildlife Sanctuary, not as an anthropology student but as a wildlife biologist. My first project in Arunachal was assigned to me by the NGO Wildlife Trust of India to conduct a survey on why the local Nyishi[1] killed dholes.[2] I was assigned this job not only because of my background in wildlife sciences but also because I wrote a master's thesis on Asiatic jackals. After completing an intensive two-year training programme in wildlife sciences at the prestigious WII, I took on this assignment enthusiastically.

I went to the Itanagar Wildlife Sanctuary with a colleague, Surendra Varma, of the Asian Nature Conservation Foundation (ANCF), Bangalore, and our guide Nabam, a Nyishi from a nearby village, to carry out a survey of human–animal conflicts (Aiyadurai and Varma 2003). After several hours of trekking inside the sanctuary, we failed to see any wild animals except a bird of prey, which Nabam was aiming to shoot. I requested him not to. He replied, 'Madam, *sirf khaane keliye*' (only to eat).

[1] Nyishi are the local indigenous people living in and around the Itanagar Wildlife Sanctuary.

[2] Dholes are Asiatic wild dogs (*Cuon alpinus*) and are enlisted as endangered species.

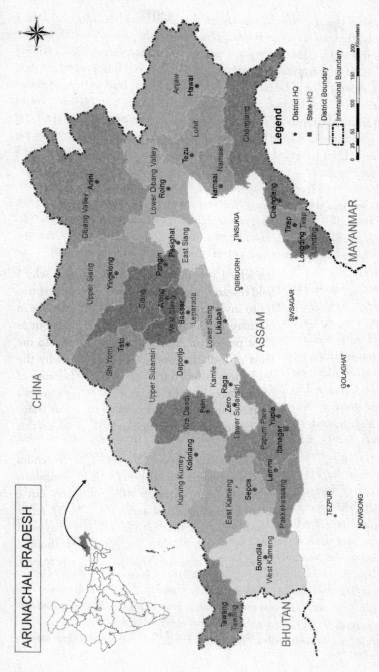

Figure 2.1 Arunachal Pradesh

Source: G. Areendran.

I insisted that he should not shoot that bird and he did not. Later, I realized that my act of preventing him from shooting was a selfish act, the response of a wildlife biologist working for a conservation NGO. Killing wild animals is a crime according to the Indian Wildlife Protection Act. I was afraid I would be party to it if he killed that bird in my presence! Mine was an emotional and instinctive response, but Nabam would have shot that raptor if I was not around. At the time, I thought I did the right thing in asking him not to shoot, but later I felt very guilty for stopping him. I carried that guilt for years, asking myself what right I had to stop him.

Part of that study was to conduct a social survey in the Nyishi villages around the sanctuary. We were surprised and disturbed to see that the 'wild' animals that we searched for in the forests were instead inside people's houses in the form of skins, skulls, and bones. Animal skins were used as mats and animal skulls were hung in a corner. While we were there, a boy returned home with a dead red-vented bulbul (a bird), which was thrown into the fire and consumed within a few minutes. Seeing the remains of wildlife in the villages instead of live animals in the forests had an overwhelming impact on me and I wondered why wildlife protection laws did not work in this region. Was there something wrong with the law, the implementers, or the people? This prompted me to do a survey of indigenous hunting practices across Arunachal in 2005–6 with the support of Nature Conservation Foundation, an NGO based in South India (Aiyadurai 2007). The survey highlighted that people hunted not only for consumption or the market, but because they felt a cultural compulsion: for example, hunting during festivals and the need to offer wild meat during weddings. This was the key result of my survey, which highlighted the cultural aspects of hunting practices (Aiyadurai, Singh, and Milner-Gulland 2010). This was my first piece of research that dealt directly with people's lives, livelihoods, and cultural practices. As a wildlife biologist, conducting such social surveys was considerably challenging because I felt quite clueless about it.

For a trained wildlife biologist, attempting to study 'what people do' was at first strange and awkward. I felt guilty that I was interviewing people without having received adequate training in the social sciences, both at WII and subsequently in the NGOs where I worked. In India, no serious effort has been made to expose natural science researchers to methods focussed on social surveys or doing interviews; these are absent from conservation biology as well as wildlife management courses (Saberwal and Kothari 1996). This is a critical issue since conflicts between local people and the state have increasingly come to occupy, as Saberwal and Kothari (1996) put it, the 'centre stage' in conservation debates. Anthropologists and political scientists have begun to point to the absence of a 'social' component in nature conservation. According to Mascia et al. (2003: 650), 'Conservation is a human endeavor: initiated by humans, designed by humans to achieve a socially desired objective of conservation of biodiversity.' Bridging the gap between conservation biologists and social scientists is essential for an effective understanding of conservation (Agrawal and Ostrom 2006; Brosius 2006; Adams 2007).[3] At that time, without adequate training, I felt I was doing injustice to the research and to the people from whom I was seeking information. Armed with a structured questionnaire, without any training in social skills or methods, I felt like an interloper trying to know their personal affairs, especially when it came to hunting; a question I included was how often people ate wild meat. A paper, a pen, and a series of questions not only made people uncomfortable but also made me feel awkward. At a personal level, intruding and probing into the eating habits of people to prove or reject my hypotheses was extremely uncomfortable. The approach was problematic for me because there were times when people were reluctant to answer the questions, but gave other interesting socio-economic information that was not necessarily part of the questionnaire. It was required for a wildlife biologist to reduce the usefulness of data collected from people into a numeric framework, but it devalued the rich information about human experience that they provided. The 'fixation' with sample size made the fieldwork look like a 'sampling' race to meet as many people as possible at the expense of the quality of the information, thereby treating people like data suppliers. Such rapid surveys do little except 'bombarding people with questions' (Aiga 2007: 823), resulting in fatigue for both the respondents and the interviewer. The limitation of a structured questionnaire was a big disappointment for me, but at that time this was the only way I knew of getting information from people.

[3] These are among the few works that have attempted to bring together biologists and social scientists to understand the biodiversity crisis in Asia.

Questionnaires have their advantages, but for my work a structured questionnaire proved counterproductive. In my earlier experience, people were bemused by my questions, found them hilarious in fact, and gave me answers that were entertaining to them. Here are some of the answers I received for questions assessing the wealth of a household (Aiyadurai 2007):

AA: How many mithuns[4] do you have?
Respondent: We don't have any mithuns, instead we have many children (laughed aloud).
AA: Do you have any goats, if yes, how many?
Respondent: Goats! I have none but my neighbour's goats enter my farm and damage my crops. Why don't you do something about it?
AA: Do you have a radio?
Respondent: Yes, but it does not work. Do you know how to repair it?

Conversations such as this are an indication of how people responded to some of my questions. In general, the 'quality of data' proved unfit for analysis, but the information I got from outside the framed questions was valuable. By this I mean the descriptive field notes (the notes I jotted down at the end of each day in my personal diary) which I never used in analysis as it seemed unfit to run any statistics on it, but which provided insights into what I aimed to understand.

It was only at University College London, (2008–9), when I began to learn about social methods for my master's in anthropology, environment and development, and later at the National University of Singapore (NUS; 2011), where I did my PhD, that I began to fully realize the necessity and importance of social science in conservation research and practice. Often my writings were considered descriptive, journalistic, and 'unscientific' by my biologist colleagues. To be considered 'scientific', I needed numbers, tables, graphs, statistical values to answer hypotheses, and write texts in third person in a detached impersonal language. My training in anthropology changed my thinking and style of writing. I shifted my methods of inquiry, asking fewer questions and listening to people more. While I felt that ethnography was better at capturing the nuances and sensitivities of social reality, it was not that simple. Marcus and Cushman (1982) point out that ethnographic

---

[4] Semi-domesticated cattle (*Bos frontalis*).

description is by no means a 'straightforward, unproblematic task but a complex effect achieved through writing and dependent upon the strategic choice and construction of available detail' (Marcus and Cushman 1982: 29).

Ethnographic writing has its own baggage of contradictions and engages the researcher in dilemmas of subjectivity–objectivity, insider–outsider, native and non-native anthropologist, and so on. Because of my prior experiences as a researcher, Arunachal was familiar to me in many senses compared to other parts of India, however culturally different it may be. Prior experiences, according to Narayan (2012: 100), are like the 'pull of the past'. From an ethnic point of view, I am native to India, which makes me a native anthropologist, but a non-native to Arunachal. The different identities have made it complex for me to define my position. Narayan (2012) challenges the assumption that 'native' anthropologists can represent an unproblematic and authentic insider's perspective. Factors such as education, gender, class, race, or even duration of contact outweigh the simplistic dichotomy of the identity of the researcher as an insider or outsider (Narayan 2012). Narayan argues, 'we all belong to several communities simultaneously', which she calls 'multiplex identity' to indicate that there are threads of culturally tangled identities and many strands of identification available (673). Crisscrossing of identities in our everyday lives, as Rosaldo (1989) suggests, is created around sexual orientation, gender, class, race ethnicity, age, politics, dress, and food or taste.

I may be seen as a native researcher but my being an Indian studying an 'Indian' community did not help for many reasons. India is a large and complex country with multiple languages, castes, tribes, classes, and religions. I am an insider only as an Indian national and all my other identities make me a complete outsider to the Mishmi community, a state of being which Kirin Narayan would call the 'halfie-anthropologist'. My background in science and the subsequent shifting to anthropology added another level of academic complexity to my identity, which not only debated whether I was an insider or an outsider, but also whether I could truly be considered an anthropologist? In University College London, one of the faculty members introduced me as a 'convert'!

I did my master's fieldwork in Anjaw district. For my PhD fieldwork, I sought a site within the Mishmi Hills where some kind of conservation intervention existed. My deliberate attempt in choosing a village or a cluster of villagers near or inside a protected area reflects my ideological standpoint and the methods I planned to use. I was conscious of the fact that my position as a researcher would be laden with power. The freedom, knowledge, and resources that I had in my hands to choose where to go and whom to contact had already given me much power. With generous funding from the Rufford Foundation and other organizations, I had plenty of options to select the study site. It was not at random that I chose Dibang Valley as the core site of my inquiry.

I had initially avoided focusing on tigers as part of my research; I did not want my research to centre on a high profile, highly 'political' animal as well as a sensitive issue in India. However, during my exploratory visit to Koronu village, adjacent to Mehao Wildlife Sanctuary, in 2012, I heard stories about the rescue of tiger cubs in Dibang Valley, which I referred to in Chapter 1. I was shown a letter from the forest department that pleaded for help from the villagers in providing information about the tiger-killing incident. The letter had become a sort of joke and the villagers ridiculed and questioned the naiveté of the forest department expecting the villagers to identify the killer of the tiger. People told me about visits by scientists and NGOs to Dibang Valley. I had contacts among the faculty of WII, with whom I had studied earlier. One of them visited the mini zoo in Roing to assess the zoo's infrastructure and capacity to accommodate the fast growing tiger cubs. As I began to assess the situation, I felt that Dibang Valley had all the features that I intended to research: the interest of NGOs and scientists, the imposition of state authority, human–wildlife conflict, and a very vocal community, the Mishmi. I carried out my research in two districts (Lower Dibang Valley and Dibang Valley) with the Idu Mishmi (Table 2.1).

Going beyond Questionnaires

It was clear to me from the beginning of this research that I would avoid doing any formal or structured interviews, because of my past experiences. I was open to casual conversations beyond questionnaires, discussions, and informal meetings, which enriched my experience as a researcher. I wrote regularly and at length about what I felt, what I heard from people, about the weather, the food, and the place.

Table 2.1 Study sites at a glance

Features	Lower Dibang Valley	Dibang Valley
District headquarters	Roing	Anini
Borders	North: Dibang Valley	North: China
	South: Assam	South: Lower Dibang Valley
	East: Lohit and China	East: China
	West: East and Upper Siang districts	West: Upper Siang district
Population*	54,080	8,004
Number of villages	314	108
Population density (per sq. km.)	14	1
Demographic	Idu Mishmi, Adi, Mishing, and Galo	Idu Mishmi
Number of towns	1 (Roing)	1 (Anini)
Circles	7	5
Nearest railway station	Tinsukia, Assam (113 kms away)	Tinsukia, Assam (303 kms away)
Protected areas	Mehao Wildlife Sanctuary	Dibang Wildlife Sanctuary

Source: Author.

Note: *Population data has been taken from the Department of Economics and Statistics, Arunachal Pradesh.

I audio-recorded discussions after asking for permission. I played back the recording, which created an atmosphere of fun and joy. Older people who were hard of hearing were most curious, and laughter followed when the volume was increased. One man asked if the recorder could translate Mishmi to English or Hindi, in addition to recording. These discussions were pleasant icebreakers, and so recording interviews and discussions was very useful. All my interviews were informal. They were held in people's homes, sitting next to the fire, in shops, in farms, and sometimes inside a vehicle during the long 12-hour journey from Anini to Roing. I was offered home-made rice/millet beer (*yu*), which is regularly offered to guests, and I accepted with pleasure. Discussions lasted for about an hour or slightly more, but sometimes, with evening drinks and dinner, such discussions went on until late in the night. Hanging out with men and women during their drinking sessions became regular, fun, and insightful. Women drinking alcohol is not seen as immoral here, as in other parts of India. I learned how to prepare *yū*, which is brewed locally at home: a good Mishmi wife is one who can brew good *yū*. Women don't prepare *yū* during menstruation, and I was always asked if I was menstruating before I could start helping them prepare *yū*. Women generally did not cook during menstruation either, instead their husbands or sons or any other family member prepared the meals at that time. There being no taboo surrounding talking about menstruation was sometimes embarrassing for me. Once Kahito[5] asked me, in front of her 16-year old son, 'When did you have your menses, I forgot mine. Wasn't it at the same time for both of us?' I was very embarrassed and looked at her son to check whether he had heard. He did not show any reaction and continued weaving the bamboo basket.

I was often invited to important village events such as celebrations, funerals, and get-togethers. This gave me a lot of opportunities for casual interactions with people who were at leisure during such events. I was also invited when there had been a successful hunt, and I documented what was hunted and what restrictions were followed. Such occasions gave me a window of opportunity to learn about the taboos related to the cooking of wild meat (such as men having to cook the wild meat in a separate room or outside the house). Women do not eat any wild meat, except fish (*āngā*), rats (*kācēnggō*), and birds (*prā*) because they believe that something unfortunate will happen if they consume it. I personally don't have any food-related taboos, and it was one of the things that enhanced my fieldwork. When it involves cooking wild meat (mammals, birds), it invariably had a taboo attached to it. A Mishmi school student took interest in my work and became my part-time assistant. He took me around for bird hunting and frog catching. Later, I also jotted down recipes of Mishmi dishes, how the frogs are cooked, how to make *pahu*[6] chutney, and stories about *Khəpā*[7] who also loves eating frogs! It took some time for me to understand taboos related to gender and space in relation to hunting as these overlap with the role of spirits. In my previous trips as a wildlife biologist, I accepted only the

[5] My host in Anini.

[6] A species of water-beetle found under the rocks on a riverbed during winter. These beetles are either eaten raw or made into a chutney. T. T. Cooper in 1873 wrote about a group of Mishmi villagers collecting edible beetles.

[7] One of the forest spirits.

meat of domesticated animals and not wild meat. I made excuses so
that I wouldn't hurt people's feelings but I missed out a lot because in
doing so I distanced myself from their daily activities. As a researcher of
anthropology, I got over the guilt of a wildlife biologist, and this opened
new doors for me into the world of the Mishmi. My stay in Singapore
and my earlier stint in Arunachal had helped me be more open to tast-
ing all kinds of food. Kahito found it surprising that I had adjusted so
well and remarked, 'non-tribals never like our food which consists of
boiled vegetables, and prefer only *masala-wala* food' (food with spices).
A Mishmi man in Chaglagam, Anjaw, in 2008 said to me, 'Hindus do
not eat beef, Muslims do not eat pork. Mishmi eat both and we also
drink, so we are like foreigners!'

In addition to trying new food, a reason for my easy acceptance in the
village was my knowledge of the Hindi language. Hindi is not my native
language but I learned Hindi while growing up in the Hindi-speaking
states of central India (Madhya Pradesh and Chhattisgarh) and later in
Gujarat. My mother tongue is Tamil, but I speak Hindi well and so do
people in Arunachal (Chandra 2014). We had mutual admiration for
each other's linguistic skills because Hindi is not the native language for
either party. The Mishmi are multilingual, most of them speak Hindi,
Nepali, and Assamese; those with some school education speak English
very well. The present lingua franca of the Mishmi is, in fact, Hindi, and
many of the younger generation are losing their ability to speak Mishmi.[8]
One of the concerns of the Mishmi is the increasing disappearance of
the local language and the quick adoption of Hindi. Roger Blench, a
scholar from Cambridge, was invited by the Mishmi society to prepare
an Idu alphabet chart and a reading and writing book of the Mishmi
language (Blench 2018). This book was released during the 50th anni-
versary of the Reh festival in February 2018. While someone from Tamil
Nadu being fluent in Hindi is not common, being a Tamilian was an
added advantage. There is a general feeling that south Indians have
better intentions than Hindi-speaking people from the north Indian
states of Delhi, Uttar Pradesh, and Haryana. Thus, my communication

---

[8] The language predicament among the Mishmi is obvious, as the language
has no script, it is neither practised at home nor is it taught in schools. Moreover,
the risks of this language disappearing is so high that it is considered endangered
(Lewis, Simons, and Fenning 2013).

with the local residents was easy and effortless. My attempt to learn Mishmi, however, did not move beyond the basic greetings and sentences related to food, hunger, and drinks. I learned the names of animals and birds very quickly, which helped me when discussing issues around forests and wildlife. Learning more of the Mishmi language was frustrating, however, and I stopped making the effort when I failed to find someone to teach me on a regular basis.

Getting There and Starting Work

I started my fieldwork in June 2013 and continued until May 2014. Anini in Dibang Valley was my core field site, but I did make trips to Roing, Itanagar, and Guwahati. However, before reaching Dibang Valley, I had to go to Itanagar, the capital of Arunachal, to procure a long-term Inner Line Permit (ILP),[9] which is required by Indian nationals in order to stay in Arunachal. In addition to the travel permits, I also needed a research permit from the forest department to carry out my research, something that is always difficult and uncertain, especially for foreigners or even for Indian scholars registered with a university outside India.

One has to pass through Roing in order to reach Anini, my chosen field site. In Roing, I had the opportunity to stay with Naba Tana, a well-respected member of the Mishmi community and one of the first generation of his community to receive formal education. He had served in the government as a language officer, publishing several articles about Mishmi customs. Considered a mentor of the Mishmi (Idu clan), he was a founder member of Arunachal Pradesh Vikas Parishad (Development Board) and chairman of the Idu Mishmi Cultural and Literary Society.[10] There, I received advice as to who to contact in Anini, the district capital of Dibang Valley. One of Naba Tana's daughters, Krina, suggested that I contact Angeche, who is knowledgeable about the mountains and who makes frequent trips to hunt. She suggested Angeche because he is well respected; moreover, he does not drink or smoke, something that is rare

[9] The inner line permit (ILP) is required because Arunachal Pradesh is considered a restricted area and is a border state. I will discuss more about the ILP in Chapter 4.

[10] The Idu Mishmi Cultural and Literary Society (IMCLS) is the apex body of the Idu Mishmi and its objective is to preserve the Mishmi culture and address the issues of the people.

in Dibang Valley. As a lone female researcher, Krina thought, it would be safe for me to stay with Angeche's family. In addition, since they lived in a bamboo hut (*chang-ghar*) on a farm, I would learn a lot about the Mishmi's way of life.

My ultimate goal was to reach Anini. As the capital of Dibang Valley district, it was the best place for me to centre my research activities. Dibang Valley is one of India's largest and remotest districts, with its northern boundary forming the international border with Tibet (Figure 2.1). Named after the river Dibang, the district is home to around 14,000 members of the Idu Mishmi community. The rugged mountainous landscape has left most parts of this district uninhabitable. The weather conditions are fairly harsh, and the mountain tops are permanently under snow or frost. Dibang Valley district has the least human density in India (1 person per square kilometre) because of unfavourable living conditions and the lack of basic infrastructure such as reliable roads or hospitals. Largely dependent on land for swidden farming, the Mishmi, who are the majority population of Dibang Valley, have a difficult life, as the land is largely unsuitable for any kind of agriculture, especially on higher altitudes. Lately, the Government of India has been investing in developing this area, which is rapidly re-shaping the region. Anini has a population of around 3,000 local Mishmi, who constitute the only ethnic group here; the remaining 4,000 are non-Mishmi migrants who work as labourers, government staff hailing from all over Arunachal, shopkeepers, and some Assamese who run small businesses; people from Uttar Pradesh, Bihar, the Indian Army, and the Indo-Tibetan Border Police (ITBP)[11] make up the rest of the population.

Many Mishmi in Roing discouraged me from going to Anini. People said all sorts of things about this town—bone-chilling winters, frequent road blocks, landslides, road accidents, and even spirits (*khényu*) on the road that overturn vehicles! It is logistically a difficult place to live in and is at a distance of 250 kms from Roing, which takes 12 hours of backbreaking road journey to cover. I was also discouraged because of my gender, but I received sympathy and concern. When I heard about the proposal for a tiger reserve from one of the forest officials in Itanagar, shifting to Anini became even more compelling for me.

[11] Indo-Tibetan Border Police (ITBP) is a specialized mountain force; it was raised in the same year as the Sino-Indian war to guard India's border with Tibet.

because the tiger cubs' rescue had started a chain reaction towards the conservation of tigers and the protection of the landscape in this area.

Travelling from Roing to Anini is an event in itself. There is no public transport available. Private vehicles, all jeeps, that charge exorbitantly high prices are the only option. One has to book tickets in advance if one wishes for the front seat. It is sensible to avoid taking a back seat because of the nasty, bumpy ride on bad roads. When I set out for Anini, it took an hour to settle all the luggage on top of the vehicle; the two men in charge of fastening the luggage did their job so efficiently that boxes, beer cases, sacks of rice and vegetables, small tables, even chickens in cages were neatly tied up on the top of the jeep. A blue tarpaulin covered the top. 'Can't trust the rain here,' said one of the men. A passenger with a tray of eggs looked up at the roof of the vehicle and asked, 'Can you also tie this on the top?' 'Keep it on your lap, you mad fellow,' shouted the driver.

When the vehicle was about to start, a Nepalese man from the agricultural department in Anini started chanting Sanskrit mantras with his ͗olded and his eyes tightly shut. A teacher from Manipur, posted
                ͘ng next to me and told me that he b ͗ ͘ ͗͘
                         ͗͘ not their first time ͗

movement. There are around 15 gates between Roing and Anini. The passenger who sits in the front opens and shuts the gate every time the vehicle approaches one. Drivers are careful not to leave the gates open. Ryanli, which is about 140 kms from Roing, is where the vehicle usually stops for lunch; a small shop sells biscuits, snacks, cigarettes, and beer. Apart from this, there are no shops on the road all the way till Etalin. Cricket fans catch up on the scores here on TV. After Ryanli, Anini feels closer but takes another three hours to reach. Phones begin to catch networks near Amboli, just before Anini. There is no phone network until then; and phones are reduced to working as mp3 players and clocks.

I reached Anini at 6:30 p.m., by which time it was already pitch dark. I had been given the contact of Angeche's family in Kongo village, which is 3 kms from the town. When I arrived, I found Kahito, Angeche's wife, and Bilaa, one of their four children, sitting around the kitchen fire and cooking. Sitting next to the fire was a relief as it was getting terribly cold. Angeche is in his mid-forties. He loves to talk, which is good for an anthropologist. When I asked Angeche how I should address him, he replied, 'Just call me Apiya,' which means 'brother' in Mishmi. Hiju is the only daughter out of their four children. All the children stayed in a hostel, so there was plenty of room for them to accommodate me; in fact, they were happy to have me in the house. Pishi, their ever hungry and lazy cat (*mēkārī*), was always around the fire and a pig (*ìlì*), named Maharaj, stayed in a pen next to the granary (*àkā*), a few metres away from the house. When I returned in 2017 to thank them after defending my thesis, Maharaj had to be sacrificed for the party.

Staying in Apiya's house benefitted me as I got familiar with the Mishmi way of living by contributing to the household chores, cleaning utensils, sweeping, cutting vegetables, engaging in some farm work and cooking, fetching firewood, and learning how to weave. In winters, firewood has to be replenished and refilled on the bamboo tray (*ātò*) hanging above the fire. I felt guilty sitting next to the fire and writing most of the time, using up their firewood reserve, so I joined the women who went into the forests to bring in more firewood. Preparing tea for guests was a non-stop activity. Once, a group of teachers came in to meet Apiya, who is an important member of the local school community. He called out for me, 'Ambika, *chai banao* [prepare tea]', with a tone of authority. The teachers laughed at how he ordered me to make tea. Apiya said, 'She is now one of us, let her prepare tea, so what?' I smiled and felt glad to hear it.

Figure 2.2 Fieldwork in Kongo village (Anini)
Source: Author.

Apiya's house had two rooms, was made of bamboo, and stood on stilts. The first room was the living room with a TV in a corner; the kitchen, an attachment to the common room. Beautiful cane chairs lined the wall, facing the fireplace in the middle. I was given room in one corner where I had all my things: rucksack, bags, laptop, camera, books, and notebooks (see Figure 2.2). I never had to keep any of my things locked up. The floor was made of bamboo and was covered with cane mats. An RCC (reinforced cement concrete) house was ready by the time of my second visit and I shifted there during my subsequent stay, but I preferred the bamboo house because of the fireplace and because it provided space for socializing.

As one walked, the bamboo floor made creaking noises with every step. The walls were made of flattened bamboo stems, which let sunlight filter in, especially the morning sun, and bright rays of smoke filled the house. Nights, however, were bitterly cold. A takin skin was my sleeping mat; there was a mattress and a sleeping bag above that, and yet the nights felt unbearably cold. Apiya and Kahito were very concerned and enquired every morning whether I had slept well the previous night. Bearing with that cold was the most difficult part of my fieldwork.

Living among the Mishmi: Debunking Stereotypes

For many from the mainland, Northeast India stops at Assam and the region beyond, until recently, was a land of 'wildness' and 'fear' because of the mainland's lack of familiarity with the people there as well as the military insurgency. Ramjee Nagarajan, a friend of mine from Tamil Nadu, declined a government job in Dibrugarh (Assam) in the 1990s because his father, a bank manager, told him that there were 'cannibals' in 'that part' of India. An engineering student from India studying in NUS was so surprised to learn that I was working in Arunachal that he was keen to visit my field site to 'discover an untouched tribe!' He believed that there could be un-contacted tribes in Arunachal, similar to the ones said to be found in Brazil, popularized by Survival International. The father of a friend of mine was disappointed to see pictures of the Mishmi. 'Look at them, they wear watches! They wear pants, they have TV! There is electricity! Oh, they are very modern,' he said with disappointment. Such reactions are common, an indication of people's imagination of 'the tribe'. Indigenous people are always stereotyped for their colourful dresses, dances, bows and arrows, and their warrior image and strange beliefs. These portrayals are reproduced in tourism manuals, magazines, television advertisements, movies, museums, and government policy documents (McDuie-Ra 2012). It is expected that 'tribes' must wear traditional attire, stay in jungles, and look 'exotic' and 'primitive'.

McDuie-Ra (2012) provides us with a complicated view of people from Northeast India. They are not as isolated as many people think and, indeed, are even migrating out of the region to Delhi and many others parts of India for education and for work. Except the extremely remote places on mountaintops and on the borders of Arunachal, the rest of the state is more or less connected to the outside world through media, phones, and roads. Visitors to Arunachal not only expect the local people to behave in a certain way but also patronize and discriminate against them.

I stumbled upon a website 'themishmis.com', which had interesting postings by historians, anthropologists, and Mishmi scholars. 'Are you on Facebook [FB]?' asked many respondents in Roing and in Itanagar. Among the Mishmi in Roing, FB is very popular. I was not on FB at that time and was tempted to get on it only to see what issues the Mishmi discussed. I had not made up my mind to join FB until I heard that the logo of the IMCLS was uploaded on FB to get the opinion of people on it (see Chapter 5). Now I have an FB account which continues to create links between me and my 'field'.

'Where Is Your Team?': Stereotyping the Researcher

Many surveys and censuses have been conducted in Anini, largely by government organizations (development agencies and health workers). Such organizations have a team and their visits last for a few days. For this reason, people often asked me, 'Where is your team? Where are the other members?' Research is often understood as a 'survey', which the villagers are used to. Government officials (teachers and staff from the health department) and researchers come in teams, aboard a four-wheeler (mostly a jeep). I was not taken seriously in the beginning, not only because I was a lone researcher but also because I did not have a 'survey form' to fill out. When university students or government researchers visit, they are always in a team, they stay at the circuit house, and have a jeep. The Mishmi see more of such research teams than a single anthropologist and tend to associate research with a group of 'form-carrying people', not sole individuals (further still, a lone female).

During my fieldwork, a small team (four persons) from Khonsa visited Anini for three days to study the material culture of the Mishmi.

They used a long questionnaire and asked questions about the things people used and their textiles. Another researcher, a PhD student from the University of Delhi, was there on fieldwork for two months to investigate the increasing incidents of suicide among the Idu Mishmi.[13] He stayed in the circuit house. The researcher collected blood samples and studied the physical attributes of the Mishmi, in addition to seeking answers to a long list of questions. This is what one of the villagers had to say about this researcher, 'He asked so many questions, he is such a good researcher!' Asking questions, doing surveys from house to house, and writing the information down in a form are seen as the markers of a good researcher. I was initially thought to be a TV journalist because I was filming a ceremony. 'Why is Singapore University interested in the Mishmi?' was a recurring question. These impressions changed as I stayed there for a longer period of time and had opportunities to explain myself and my research.

Challenges during Fieldwork

My fieldwork proceeded without hiccups until I met Akola in Angrim Valley, the village from where the tiger cubs were rescued. Angrim Valley is 22 kms north of Anini. This village was a key site for me and I had plans to talk to the people there about the tiger cubs and the tiger attacks on mithuns. I went to meet the *gaon burrah*, the village headman, where I met Akola, the headman's son. There was a casual gathering of a few men, and Akola was the most curious to talk to me and ask about the purpose of my research. 'So many people come here and don't know what they are doing,' he said; he told me that there had been a group of Japanese researchers there and he didn't know what research they did. When he said, 'People come here and go, we get exploited,' I realized he was serious. 'What is your research about?' he asked. I explained, 'I am here to study the Mishmi and their relationship with nature and how it has changed with the growing government interest in forest conservation.' Akola shook his head, smiling with disagreement. Bluntly, he asked, 'This is a known fact, what is the use of this research?' I felt like I was defending my thesis proposal once

[13] For more information on suicides in Dibang Valley, see Mene (2011, 2013) and Singh, Singh, and Biswas (2013).

again. He offered me *yū*, which I politely declined because it was eight in the morning. He insisted and asked, 'What kind of anthropologist are you? You should follow our culture, it is our culture to offer *yū* to our guests.' The men started to discuss *āmrā* (the tiger). I understood that they were talking about tigers and the discussion grew serious and a bit heated. A local lady who had accompanied me signalled to me that it was better to leave. Akola stopped me, 'Madam, please sit with us.' But I excused myself abruptly. The men laughed, looking at the way I was avoiding Akola, because he was drunk.

In the evening, he came to meet me again, carrying an *īcīphrú*.[14] The first thing he asked me was: 'What is your research about and why are you not talking clearly?' I did not know whether to engage in a discussion with him or not as he was drunk again. He started to quiz me about my knowledge of the Mishmi culture, and asked me if I could name the mug he was holding in his hand. I said, '*īcīphrú*.' 'What is the meaning of animal skulls in homes?' he asked again. As I started to explain, I noticed that he was not interested in my answer. He shook his head with a cynical smile, 'You are an anthropologist? What did you do all this while, you should know all about the Mishmi culture by now.' My dilemma was understanding whether he was joking or seriously accusing me of not learning enough about the Mishmi culture.

As I was about to leave, Akola turned to me and said, 'You are an anthropologist, you should not sleep early. It is only 10.30 p.m.' He smiled. Before going to sleep, I finalized my plan to visit Dibang Wildlife Sanctuary with my host. At this, Akola jumped in and asked why I wanted to go to the sanctuary. He got very suspicious and asked, 'You are an anthropologist, you should be in the village', shaking his head and smiling while staring at the floor. I got a bit nervous to see him disagreeing with whatever I told him. 'Did you get permission from the district collector, do you have it?' he asked. I answered that I had spoken to the district commissioner about going to the sanctuary. 'No one will allow you. They don't allow us. We have to enter our names, then how can they permit you?' he asked. I sensed that Akola was glad to see me in trouble and enjoyed throwing hurdles at me. To my surprise, he wanted to join us the next day at the sanctuary. 'I will get my gun! I will shoot animals inside the sanctuary in front of you, what

---

[14] An *īcīphrú* is a bamboo mug specifically used for carrying *yū* (rice beer).

can you do? Can you stop us?' he mocked. Perhaps Akola thought that I was part of the forest department or a wildlife scientist, which is why he appeared unfriendly towards me.

'You can do whatever you want inside the sanctuary, how can I stop you? But shooting inside a sanctuary is illegal,' I replied. I regretted responding to him in this way. Akola's laughter that followed was irritatingly loud at this point. His joy was to show me that he knew the rules and he would break them in front of me, regardless. Later that night, I heard Akola discussing with my host about me: 'If she is an anthropologist then she should stay in the village, what is the point of going to the sanctuary?' Later, I came to know that Akola repaired rifles and fixed guns, which is not legal, and this was probably why he was rude to me. On the one hand, I could easily dismiss Akola's concerns as the blabberings of a drunken man, but I could not help but wonder if these were the sentiments of many others in the village, which they didn't express in front of me. What if researchers had actually exploited them in the past? And even if they had not, the impression of researchers as exploiters was disturbing.

This small village saw a lot between December 2012 to 2014: the tiger cubs' rescue, visits by NGOs, and the stationing of a WTI staff in Dambeun for a few months. Akola reminded me of my moral responsibility as a researcher, and I will not forget the points he raised for a long time. I met Akola twice again, but he treated me like a stranger. Later, I saw him in a meeting with a WWF team at the circuit house, where he was very silent and again did not seem to recognize me.

Writing the 'Right' Things? Expectations of the Mishmi

In addition to being curious about how the book will be received by my colleagues and the anthropologist community, I am also anxious about how the Mishmi will feel about it. The expectations of the Mishmi from me are high. I tried not to get influenced by these expectations and have tried to give an account of what I observed and understood. My intention here is not to speak for the Mishmi because they are already expressing their views for themselves. This will be evident later, in Chapters 5 and 6.

All through my fieldwork, people took a lot of interest in my work. They helped me understand the meaning of Mishmi terminology and their customs. A school teacher in a village once asked, 'What have you found about the Mishmi, tell me?' People wanted to know what I had found and what I was writing. Those who could read and write English were especially very curious to see me writing most of the time. While talking about hunting, people requested me to write about their taboos and conservation practices. 'You write good things about us,' said a resident in Roing. This expectation burdened me initially, but I got used to the questions later. I feel certain, however, that many in the Mishmi society will read my book and my subsequent publications. During my visits to Dibang Valley, I shared copies of my papers, articles, and reports with the residents of Anini and Roing. They will be some of the primary consumers of my work. In some ways, they already are. One of my articles published in 2009 was uploaded on an FB page called 'voiceofmishmi' and has been commented upon. My work will not only be read but also be scrutinized.

Unlike the anthropologists of the nineteenth and twentieth centuries, anthropologists today have a greater responsibility towards the local communities that they do research among. One of the senior leaders based in Roing told me, 'You should show your PhD thesis draft first to us and then submit.' Now I have reviewers in the field too, I thought. Though he was joking, he qualified it by saying, 'There may be some mistake which we can point out.' One of the concerns the Mishmi have is 'whether I am writing the "right" things about the Mishmi'.

I wrote a story published in 2019 in *Current Conservation*, about Ajaimai Yun, my field assistant during my MSc fieldwork in 2010. She died due to cerebral malaria in Anjaw. Ajaimai was related to Sokhep Kri (a senior officer in the Arunachal government) who emailed the following after reading the draft about my field assistant:

> Great to have an enthusiastic scholar like you who is more interested in knowing people by heart, from whom I belong. You have seen the Mishmis with your own eyes and felt it very closely, which I being a Mishmi couldn't for sometimes. You are the ambassador of our people abroad and back home as well. (email from Sokhep Kri, in English, on 17 March 2012)

On the one hand, it is heart-warming to feel accepted by the Mishmi, but on the other hand, it is concerning to see what they expect from me.

A newspaper article published in a well-known English daily is a good example to elucidate this. One of the indigenous people of

Arunachal, the Apatani,[15] challenged a scientific paper (Selvan et al. 2013) published by some researchers from the WII through an article (Sethi 2013) about wildlife hunting. According to the Apatanis, the paper painted their hunting practices in stereotypical colours (Sethi 2013). The community strongly reacted to this research paper that showed that the indigenous people predominantly engage in subsistence hunting of rare and threatened animals, which was building pressure on the mammals in the region. The Apatani challenged the researchers not only for their findings but also their methodology! Nitin Sethi, author of the newspaper article, writes:

> [A]ssertive communities are now able to engage with the language of the academia; careful about how they are portrayed, they have begun to question not only the methods, the findings but also the stereotypical prescriptions often dished out too often. The Apatani fight back is one good example of the communities that no more accept being treated as merely 'objects' of scientific studies.

For local communities, especially the indigenous people, portrayals in publications are increasingly becoming a contentious issue. As information technology becomes more accessible to all sections of the society, it becomes an equal playing field, especially on social media platforms. People who did not have access to written material earlier now have access to the internet, and they are now able to read how their cultures are being written about. Online platforms give communities a space to mobilize and form networks with other like-minded groups to voice their views. Marginal voices will only become louder in the future, questioning the authority of researchers and government officials.

Likewise, implementing wildlife conservation projects and engaging local communities is becoming increasingly problematic in Arunachal and probably in other parts of India as well. In the past, it was convenient to declare protected areas without taking into account the local people's opinions, and sometimes they hardly knew that they had been living next to a protected area. Lately in Arunachal, there have been incidents of local people threatening the research community and stopping researchers from carrying out their work. A recent example comes

---

[15] Apatanis are from the Ziro valley of the Lower Subansiri district of Arunachal Pradesh.

from Namdapha Tiger Reserve (Arunachal) where researchers and forest officials were assaulted and even shot at (Rina 2012). In Chapter 6, I will show how researchers from WII were not permitted to survey the forests for tigers. Local leaders were not convinced about the research project and the team had to leave.

Producing Texts

When I started to write my book, I was careful not to be too self-indulgent. The challenge was how to meaningfully position myself in the text. How much do I want to write about myself and reveal myself in the text? What aspects of my background do I need to write about and how do I voice my experience? I found Kirin Narayan's advice of bringing in an 'I' useful. According to her, one can set the 'I' rolling and unfurling as a long thread, a thread that can be used to stitch and weave diverse experiences and insights (Narayan 2012). How accurately I will write about the Mishmi is something I cannot say. How authoritatively can I or should I write, and can I do justice to the people about whom I am writing? These are some questions that linger in my mind. What I produce in this text is just a glimpse of what I observed and understood of people's perceptions about conservation issues in the Mishmi Hills.

The principal methods, among several approaches I used, were participant observation and interviews. The materials used in this book originate from my day-to-day observations, my field-cum-personal diary, transcribed interviews, archival material, audio and visual documentation, and oral histories. I also use information from the previous research work that I carried out in Arunachal as a wildlife biologist, which shaped my theoretical framework and the methods I chose to adopt for this book. I interviewed officials in the forest department in Arunachal, NGO staff, and scientists from research institutes. My positionality during the fieldwork played an important role in generating information about conservation in Dibang Valley from multiple viewpoints. I was aware of my status at that time as a woman from Singapore and that it was a privileged position. Initially, the flexible approach during my field research was not taken seriously, as my respondents expected me to be a 'form-carrying' researcher with a team. My methods were diverse, which helped me to not confine myself to one particular approach. This was liberating for me and I was free to modify the methods in the field, when necessary. I was adaptable with my methods, which helped me absorb information in whatever form available (scientific or folk-based). My background training in wildlife science came handy when I joined the tiger researchers (narrated in Chapter 6). I have anonymized all my respondents in this book, except the names of places and institutions or the people whose names appear in published material. I use the broad term 'Mishmi' for the Idu Mishmi for the sake of convenience, and I indicate the names of other Mishmi subgroups where necessary.

I am in touch with my respondents through email, phone calls, sms, and Facebook, and clarified my doubts through these channels. Dr Rasto Mena (from Roing) wished me well on Facebook as I was close to my PhD thesis submission in 2015 and said, 'All luck for the thesis … that's not yours alone. … Defend it well. All luck' (Facebook, 27 November 2015). Dr Mena's claiming of my research as the Mishmi's research is both overwhelming and encouraging. What I present is just a tiny snapshot of the Mishmi's relations with nature and their perceptions of biodiversity research and conservation projects.

3

MISHMI SOCIAL WORLDS
Animals, Humans, and Spirits

Similar to many indigenous people, the Mishmi do not make a distinction between the human world and the non-human world; all nature is 'one', including the world of spirits. The Mishmi constantly engage with animals and spirits during farming, hunting wildlife, or slaughtering domesticated animals. The Mishmi[1] believe that spirits take care of domesticated animals (*mītūsì pà*) and wild animals (*ngōlō*). This belief is so strong that spirits are often talked about as if they are people; the Mishmi are respectful towards and fearful of them. For example, when I asked an old woman in Anini what would happen if women ate wildmeat, she told me, '*ngōlō humko maarega*' (*ngōlō* will beat us), and that *ngōlō* watches over people from afar.

Shamans (*īgù*) play an important role as mediators between these worlds, which gives them a central role in the religious practices and beliefs of the Mishmi society (Dele 2017; Chaudhuri 2008). *Igu* are respected for their services during funerals, births, farming, hunting, and slaughtering of domestic livestock. The Mishmi acknowledge the

---

[1] Most of the information in this chapter comes from the Mishmi living in Anini and the villages nearby. The Mishmi's belief in spirits is common but taboos are followed strictly mostly by the Mishmi living in the villages and less in Roing.

spirits for all their life events and believe that their lives are ultimately governed by spirits, both benevolent and malevolent. Therefore, the Mishmi are expected to act in accordance with the obligation to give, to receive, and to pay in a reciprocal way through a dense network of exchanges that exist between the animals, the spirits, and themselves in a 'nature–man–spirit' complex (Vidyarthi 1963).

The Mishmi's social world is a network of their associations with humans and non-human beings (animals, rivers, birds, and spirits) (see Figure 3.1). The presence of several spirits (Appendix 1) in farms, homes, forests, and mountains as well as the significant roles of these spirits is reflected during harvesting, healing rites, funerals, and birth ceremonies.

The role of animals among the Mishmi is crucial from cultural and commercial perspectives. The Mishmi's relation with animals becomes particularly interesting from a conservation point of view, as Dibang Valley has been witnessing many conservation-related activities since the tiger cubs' rescue operation that took place in 2012. I provide a brief account of the wildlife law in India that prohibits all forms of hunting, and conclude with a brief discussion on the impact of this law in Arunachal.

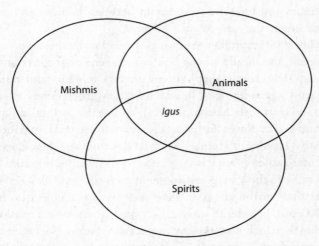

Figure 3.1 Thematic representation of the Mishmi social worlds
Source: Author.

I do not wish to speak of the Mishmi as one entity because they are not. The Mishmi living in Roing and Anini have different social positions; there are many different forms of the Mishmi life, namely urban and hill dwelling, elite and non-elite, and male and female. I aim to present the world of the Mishmi as complex, and its culture as not stable or intact but as changing with time.

Humans and Animals

There are various ways of perceiving human–animal relationships (Manning and Serpell 1994; Morris 2000; Knight 2004). From hunter-gatherers, pastoralists, and agriculturists to industrial societies, the relationships between humans and animals have changed tremendously over time. Animals are worshipped or considered as kin; they are also loathed as evil spirits, and are often slaughtered for food or offerings (Manning and Serpell 1994; Knight 2004; Govindrajan 2018). The human perception of animals in the contemporary world is also complex, where animals are employed as entertainers in circuses, objects to gaze at in zoological parks, research subjects, and also recipients of considerable care and concern as pets (Franklin 2002; 2006; Bouissac 2010). I find Ingold's work useful to discuss the role of animals in hunting societies and how the relationship between humans and animals changed among the agro-pastoral cultures.

Ingold (2000) examines the changing relationship between humans and animals, specifically among hunter-gatherers, pastoralists, and agriculturalists. His claim is that hunter-gatherers' relation with animals is one of trust and reciprocity, in which hunter-gatherers feel a sense of kinship and trust with the animals, while among the pastoralists, animals are considered as slaves. In his article 'From Trust to Domination: An Alternative History of Human–Animals Relationship', Ingold explains that hunter-gatherers are basically collectors of whatever nature has to offer (similar to the 'giving–environment' of Bird-David 1990) and that they see their surroundings as 'alive' and inanimate objects as having life (2000: 50). In order to survive, they have to maintain a relationship with animals, which is marked by respect and due consideration. Using an example from northern Canada, he shows how the Cree Indians believe that animals intentionally present themselves to the hunters to be killed. The hunter, in return, must follow a certain behaviour so that the soul of the animal is released to become another animal, which the Cree Indians see as a 'rite of regeneration' (2000: 67). Similarly, with regard to reindeer hunting among the Yukaghirs of Siberia, it is believed that animals offer themselves to the hunter (Willerslev 2007). When animals come to the traps, they are being 'given' or 'offered', but when they are chased and killed, for example by hunting with guns, it is equivalent to 'taking' without permission. The Cree Indians, writes Ingold (1986), believe that animals intentionally present themselves to the hunter to be killed. He also writes that observing the proper and respectful procedure during hunting and post hunting (butchering, consumption, and disposal of bones) is important among indigenous societies (Tanner 1979; Ingold 1986).

If proper conduct is not followed, animals will not return to the hunters in their subsequent trips. This notion of reciprocity between humans and animals, Ingold believes, is because hunter-gatherers depend on non-humans for food, and these exchanges between humans and non-humans are integrated into a 'cosmic economy of sharing' (2000: 44). On the contrary, the relationship of pastoralists and farming communities with animals is not of trust but of domination, says Ingold (1994). Herdsmen and farmers control their animals using whip, spur, and hobble to inflict pain on them and force them to behave in a certain manner. Therefore, domesticated animals are like 'slaves' under the control of humans (Ingold 1994: 17).

According to Oma (2010), the basic assumption of Ingold is that hunter-gatherers look at animals not as individuals but as animal groups. Knight (2005) also makes this point that the relations of hunters with animals are not at an individual level and they do not get familiar with animals in the manner that farming and pastoral societies do, who have feelings attached to and connections with individual animals. In agro-pastoral societies, the daily association with individual animals gives rise to mutual familiarity and trust with the animals, whereas hunters do not get a chance to familiarize themselves with any particular animal. Therefore, although one may understand that hunters have a relationship of 'trust' with animals, they do not, in fact, get a chance to build that trust. Trust-building is possible only with domesticated animals, which results in these animals becoming docile and cooperative, in return for which humans provide them with labour, companionship, food, shelter, and care. Because of this reciprocity, says Oma, animals give up their autonomy for humans to take charge of their lives. Oma, in fact, turns Ingold's argument around to say that hunting to husbandry is not signified as a shift from 'trust to domination' but instead from 'domination to trust' (Oma 2010: 177). She suggests that human–animal relations can be seen as a 'social contract'. The idea of a contract is used to examine human–animal relations as terms of 'engagement' where there are a variety of roles, duties, responsibilities, and obligations that people follow to maintain this relation. This point is made very well by Brian Morris (2000), who observed among the people of Malawi (who have an ambivalent attitude towards animals) that contrasting approaches towards animals can coexist. On the one hand, farmers see wild animals as destroyers of crops and as competitors; on the other hand, wild animals serve as a source of meat, medicine, various materials (for example, skins used as mats), and as subjects of cosmological significance (Morris 2000).

Among the Mishmi, trust and reciprocity seems to be more prevalent than domination. In the absence of herding or pastoral practices, Mishmi relations with animals are limited to the hunting and trapping of wild animals. The semi-domesticated cattle, called mithun, which takes a central position in the lives of the Mishmi will be discussed in detail in this chapter.

Mishmi: A Brief Introduction

The Mishmi form one of the 26 major 'tribal' groups of Arunachal. There are four subgroups recognized within the Mishmi (Idu, Digaru, Miju, and Deng). According to the Mishmi, they address the members of other Mishmi groups as their brothers and recognize each other as belonging to the common major 'tribe' of the Mishmi. Each subgroup has several clans that are known to inhabit areas along rivers and tributaries. The Mishmi see themselves as a separate ethnic group from their neighbours, the Adi, who belong to the Tani group. The Tani group consists of the Adi, Nyishi, Apatani, Tagin, and Hill Miris tribes of Arunachal.

A senior Mishmi told me that Idu, Miju, Digaru, and Deng are all different 'tribes', whereas another Mishmi scholar who did his PhD on the Idu Mishmi claims these groups to be 'sub-tribes'. In literature, however, the Mishmi are reported to be divided into 'clans' without any reasons for labelling them as clans (Mitchell 1883). The Mishmi themselves, however, recognize separate apical ancestors, hence the term 'clan' does not seem appropriate. Idus and Digarus share language similarities, but Digarus have a larger affinity with Mijus and Dengs in the sociocultural aspect.

All Mishmi are believed to have migrated from Burma, following the course of the Lohit river (Bhattacharjee 1983). However, there are different claims about their migration routes; according to Baruah (1988), the Idu Mishmi migrated from Tibet. Constant fighting and feuds separated them from each other. The Miju Mishmi believe that they migrated from Burma. I will discuss more about the geographical location of the different Mishmi subgroups and its significance in Chapter 4.

Wildlife Hunting

Hunting among the Mishmi[2] is part of an ancestral way of life and a cultural practice. Men undertake hunting for subsistence, trade,[3] and for crop protection. Shifting cultivation results in the burning of forest patches on mountain slopes. This opens up the land to be cultivated and facilitates the growth of new plants, which attracts animals. During shifting cultivation, villagers are on a constant lookout for animals that raid crops. Villagers lay different types of traps around the farm boundary to protect the crops. Maize (*àmbó*) and millet (*yàmbā*) are the major crops grown in these plots, along with a variety of vegetables (*anapra*). Bears (*āhū*), wild boars (*àmē*), and monkeys (*àmē*) are reported to raid crops during the harvest period (June–July).

---

[2] This is not true for all Mishmi, as hunting has decreased over the years. The Mishmi living in Anini largely hunt on a regular basis. My information on hunting among the Mishmi comes from the men who live in Anini and the villages beyond that. People in Roing often suggested that I should speak to people in Anini about animals and spirits, as they are more 'culturally rooted' than the people in Roing.

[3] Species such as musk deer and black bear are hunted for musk deer pod and gall bladder, respectively. These are in demand in the international market for their use in traditional Chinese medicine.

Long-distance hunting trips, especially the ones undertaken for musk deer (*ālā*), takin (*ākrū*), and other ungulates, are often carried out in the mountains. Hunters in Dibang Valley move uphill and cross the mountains towards the Sino-Indian border for hunting musk deer. Barking deer, wild boars, monkeys, and bears are some of the animals commonly hunted closer to the villages or when they raid crops, especially during the harvest of maize (see the list of animals found in Dibang Valley in Appendix 2). Hunting is carried out alone, in small groups, or with trusted partners[4] (other village men). Long-distance hunts, especially to the snow-covered areas for musk deer, usually involve groups of two or more. Hunting up in the mountains is a risky activity, prompting hunters to form groups for safety. Sometimes, hunters die in accidents such as land or snow slides, or by falling off cliffs, or they get injured from animal attacks. Such accidents during hunting periods are attributed to the curse/wrath of the forest spirits, such as *ngōlō*, usually as a result of not observing taboos properly (Nijhawan and Mihu 2020).

According to hunters, winter (November to February) is the preferred season to hunt, as the vegetation on mountain tops gets covered by the snow and the high-altitude[5] mammals are forced to move to lower altitudes or near the foothills. Hunters prefer this season also because they need not travel very far to look for animals. Hunting in winter is not only relatively less tiring but also allows for more time for trekking and camping as there is no substantial farm-related work during this season.

Dibang Valley district is known for the Alpine musk deer, *Moschus chrysogaster*. The scent glands of the male musk deer, called musk pods, are in demand in the international markets because of their use in

---

[4] Some hunters develop trusted partnerships with other hunters and tend to carry out trips only with them. For example, Angeche and a medical doctor (earlier posted in Anini, and now based in Roing) made several successful trips together. Compatible working relations and mutual trust help in planning the trip as both have the knowledge of the routes and know each other's strengths and weaknesses. Another resident of Kongo village said he often went hunting with his father-in-law.

[5] The altitude in Dibang Valley varies from 1,700 m to 2,000 m with highly undulating terrain.

perfumery. One way of searching for musk deer is to smell the rocks. The rock would smell of musk if a male animal (only the male deer have these scent glands) had rested on it. The smell of musk is strong and remains on the rock for hours. One of the hunters said that this animal carries 'gold', by which he meant the musk pod, which fetches a high price both in local and international markets. The cost of these pods is around INR 20,000–30,000 (USD 300–450) per *tola*.[6] Meat is consumed and musk pods (*ālāpi*) are sold quickly. The pods are not used locally but are often sold to either Lamas[7] or Marwaris,[8] who then export them illegally to international markets. Another animal that is hunted for trade-related purposes is the black bear. It is targeted for its gall bladder from which bile is extracted and used in traditional Chinese medicine. It is sold locally for INR 5,000 (USD 75) per *tola*. The demand for soft and waterproof otter skins is high in international trade and each skin is sold for INR 8,000–10,000 (USD 120–150) to buyers from outside the region, sometimes even from Myanmar.[9] The duration of the hunting trip varies with the species targeted. For musk deer, takin, and black bears, hunters camp for around 10 days or longer, including travel time and search time.

Hunting Methods

Hunters use traps, guns, and catapults (largely used by young boys and occasionally by adults) to hunt and trap wild animals. Traps are made from bamboo, cane, plant fibres, and small rocks. In addition to that, metal wires bought from the market are used. Boys frequently use catapults to hunt birds, squirrels, and sometimes bats, whereas frogs are manually captured from ponds. Serrated leg-hold metal traps are used

---

[6] *Tola* (10 grams) is a unit to measure gold, and musk pods are also measured using the same unit. This cost is perhaps higher today.

[7] Lamas are Tibetans who migrated to Dibang Valley from Tibet in the1960s after fleeing Chinese persecution.

[8] Marwaris are traders from Rajasthan who run businesses in Arunachal and other parts of Northeast India.

[9] In Anjaw district, the Mishmi reported that men from Myanmar provided leg-hold metal traps to the local people for trapping otters.

for capturing otters and are set on the riverbanks in the evening. These traps are left there overnight and are checked the following morning. There are special traps (*adrapo*) set around granaries for capturing rodents that come to attack the grain. Canopy traps (*adradri*) are set for capturing small birds and mammals in the canopy; other traps are designed for ground-dwelling birds such as pheasants and for large mammals.

Bows and arrows (*ilìprá-īpūtà*), crossbows (*rèkā*), and poison-arrows (*mràla*) were commonly used in the past. Paste from a tuber of a high-altitude herb, *Aconitum ferox* (*mrà*), would be applied to arrow tips, making them powerful enough to kill a large animal. The paste would be prepared away from the house for the safety of family members. Care would be taken not to touch the paste with fingers, and poisoned arrows would be placed high up near the ceiling, out of the reach of children.

In gun hunting, which is a commonly used method, animals are searched and pursued. Guns are both locally made and bought in the market, usually purchased from Tezu town (the capital town of Lohit district) and sometimes from Dibrugarh and Tinsukia (Assam). In Dibang Valley, the types of guns used include the double-barrel breech loading gun (DBBL), single-barrel breech loading gun (SBBL), rifles, and shotguns. The government of Arunachal Pradesh began issuing gun licences in the 1950s for protecting crops and for personal safety against wild animals. However, the arrival of guns in Arunachal goes back to the British administration. Guns were given to village headmen as 'political gifts' by the British for their assistance and alliance (Bailey 1912b; Mainprice 1945). The local Mishmi blacksmiths then replicated these guns, resulting in the proliferation of small arms.

Dogs are also taken as companions on hunting trips to chase the prey. Hunters have to be alert and follow the dogs. Once the prey is spotted, the dogs bark and chase the prey towards the hunters, who shoot the prey.

Hunting Rituals and Taboos

The Mishmi do not take hunting (*ānjī*) casually. Hunters (*ìrhùnyi*) equate hunting to a spiritual activity with many taboos (*èná*) that need to be observed carefully. Taboos are observed before, during, and after hunting. Hunting kits that contain essential items, such as rice, dal, salt, and bedding (Appendix 3), are prepared. These materials are useful both for subsistence during hunting and for performing rituals. Women are forbidden from touching the kit (see the section on 'Women and Wildlife Hunting').

Hunters leave very early in the morning, before sunrise. *Ambu*, a type of generic ritual, is performed to pray for success and safety in any endeavour, especially if it is related to hunting. Once they reach the hunting grounds, a spiritual gate (*lahrō*) is prepared facing the direction of their movement. Made with thin bamboo strips on the ground; the gate is symbolic of the boundary between the two worlds, i.e. world of the humans and the world of the spirits. It is a reminder that the area beyond this gate does not belong to them, but the spirits, where the hunters must be careful of their behaviour. A short prayer is chanted by one of the hunters before crossing this symbolic gate. They offer *yū* to the spirits associated with forests and the ancestral spirits, and pray for a good hunt. Leaf cups filled with *yū* and fixed to a stick are carefully placed either near a tree or on a rock. A piece of brass is held over this and is scratched by *dao* (machete). This piece of brass metal is the most important item that hunters carry. In general, the base of the cartridge is used for the ritual. In the olden days, hunters were said to carry brass spoons from China, which were tied to the bag permanently. Only brass (*tamba*) and no other metal such as iron, copper, or aluminum is used. This ritual is called *yū chi āphū* or *yū āphū* (ritual where alcohol is offered).

The gate is a symbolic boundary between the village and the hunting zone (Guite 2014). Crossing the gate indicates the beginning of the hunt, which requires the hunters to follow certain rules. This is seen as the beginning of a 'spiritual' journey in which hunters engage with forest spirits and animals. It is a kind of ritual where the Mishmi enter into a 'social contract' with animals and spirits. It is based on the Mishmi world view, wherein hunters are believed to have certain duties, responsibilities, and rights towards animals and spirits, founded on terms of engagement that depend on trust, reciprocity, and mutual assistance. Hunters share food and drinks with the spirits symbolically (a piece of meat or a leaf cup filled with rice beer) as one would share with other people. Both animals and spirits are seen as socially equiva-'ent and are believed to have feelings like people. Therefore, rituals similar to those that people conduct at home are performed for animals at the hunting ground. Rites always form a part of hunting trips as a mark of respect and reverence towards animals. This relationship is one of ambivalence, embodying both respect and fear. Offerings are made with the expectation that the spirits will be pleased and, in turn, will provide more animals in the subsequent trips, similar to the reciprocal relations observed by Ingold and Bird-David.

Spirits are considered to be active agents, and wild animals in the hunting zone are believed to be owned by the mountain spirit *ngōlō*, the most important spirit for hunters, which is believed to live on the high mountains and in thick forests. People believe that *ngōlō* is the one who 'supplies' animals to hunters. Thus, after a successful hunt, an offering has to be made to *ngōlō*. If not, *ngōlō* gets angry, annoyed, and could cause accidents to both hunters and consumers of the hunted animal, or cause severe illness to either the hunter or his family members. Hunters have duties, responsibilities, and rights that need to be followed to have *ngōlō* offer animals to them. One of the duties is to address the animals in a proper way, with special code names. Wild animals have two names: one is the Mishmi name that is used in the village, while the other is the name that is used by hunters and is used during the hunt.

Code Names for Animals

During the hunting trip, hunters follow a 'moral code' of conduct: for example, getting angry, abusing, cursing someone, as well as swearing is strictly avoided. Hunting is considered a very risky activity, therefore cracking jokes or ridiculing someone is against the rules. If proper conduct is not followed, hunters believe, they could face accidents or suddenly fall sick during the trip. There are unique code names for animals which only hunters seem to know and use during hunting, especially in the high mountains (Table 3.1). It is important for hunters to have the knowledge of these codes; not knowing them would have negative consequences. Hunters who do not know these code words are advised to remain silent and not call out incorrect names, which could enrage the spirits. For example, *ālā* (musk deer) is called *tambe aaroku-chi*, which means 'meat of the high mountains'. These code names for animals are part of a hunter's knowledge. They also indicate the kind of

Table 3.1 Code names for animals used exclusively by hunters

English names	(Idu) Mishmi names	Hunters' code names
Red goral	*àmí*	*Àjùshù chi* (the one on the rocky slopes)
Takin	*ākrū*	*ambeka chi* (the one with big meat; *tambe*: meat, *kachi*: big)
Musk deer	*ālā*	*tambe aaroku chi* (meat of the high mountains; *tambe*: meat, *aaro*: high mountain, *ku*: place)
Wild boar	*àmē*	*enàmbòn lon* (the one with long nose; *enambo*: nose, *lon*: long)
Barking deer	*mānjō*	*tambre-shu* (the one with small meat; *shu*: small)
Serow	*māạy*	*aazo-chi/ama-dro* (*ama*: tree name, *dro*: two horns)
Asiatic Black Bear	*āhū*	*ikku-zongon**
Monkey	*àmē*	*aadichi* (the one who lives on the trees; *aadi*: above)
Satyr tragopan	*pebá*	*apipa-chi* (the one who lives near leaves; *apipa*: leaves)
Sclater's monal	*pidi*	*aaron chi pra-a* (bird of the mountains; *aaron*: mountain)
Himalayan monal	*chēndá*	*kaanei* (colour)*
Blood pheasant	*cheekhoo*	*brunshu* (the one with red legs; *brun*: leg, *shu*: red)
Tiger	*āmrā*	*ketrebo* (stripes)
Snake	*tàbù*	*kanlon* (long)
Elephant	*ātà*	*enonohoya imina gila/chunlaa* (the one having tails on both sides; *enonohoya*: both sides, *imina*: tail)

Source: Author.

Note: *meaning not clear. This information is being published with the permission of Apiya and other elders of the village, and they confirmed that this is no secret.

habitat and forest types in which the animals are found, reflecting the hunter's knowledge of the landscape.

After a successful hunt, the hunter performs a ritual (*āphū aangi*), making a symbolic payment in the form of meat and a piece of metal to the spirit *ngōlō*. '*Hum ko daam dena padta hai*' (We have to pay the price), said a hunter. A small part of the hunted animal's ear, inserted into a fork made from bamboo, is planted on a nearby tree or on the ground. Using a dao, the hunter scrapes the piece of brass metal *aaphundi* over the dead animal and recites a chant, which roughly translates as follows:

> This animal has been killed. When I come again, please give more animals. One who rears the animals, let more animals be produced. Give us more animals whenever we come again. We have given you the payment, do not disturb or harass the one who eats this meat and the one who hunted this animal. The restrictions will be observed and do not follow us and watch us, whether we did the right thing or not. Do not disturb us.

Fresh meat is carried back if the hunters are within a day's trek from the village, but if they are far away, the meat is smoked. This is done over a makeshift platform in the forest. Fresh meat is heavy and smoking helps to make it lighter and, therefore, easier to carry. Smoking also prevents the meat from rotting and allows it to be stored for longer periods of time.

When a hunter returns home, there are restrictions on the things he can or cannot do for five days, but only if he has had a successful hunt. There are taboos on eating onion (*élōmprà*), garlic (*eloni*), mushroom (*ākūpi*), a herb called *marsana*, and fermented soyabean (*àdùlù ci*). Men stay in a separate room for this period and sex is forbidden. They are not allowed to receive water or tea prepared by women who are menstruating. Hunters also avoid attending funerals and washing clothes. Wild meat is cooked in a separate room, or in a separate shed outside the house. Only men participate in cooking wild meat, using separate utensils. Animal skulls are mounted on the walls of men's rooms. Displays of wild and domesticated animal skulls are a common sight amongst the Mishmi (Figure 3.2). Wild boar, takin, serow, goral, and the Asiatic black bear are some of the animals whose skulls, mounted on a neatly made bamboo frame, are found in almost every rural Mishmi house. Animal skulls and jaws are symbols of hunting and sacrificial rites. They are carefully arranged on the skull board. Skulls remind hunters of special events related to the hunting or slaughtering of animals.

Figure 3.2 Display of wild animal skulls in an Idu Mishmi house
Source: Author.

There is a spatial separation between the skulls of domesticated
animals and wild animals displayed on the trophy boards. Two
wooden poles (*àmūnyī*) separating the skulls of wild and domesticated animals are believed to house a spirit (*àsú àndrō*, benevolent
spirit of the home), which keeps an eye on people's behavior and
the observation of taboos. Animal blood collected during slaughter is
applied on the skulls, making them appear black over time. Men take
pride in their skull boards and maintain the skulls by cleaning and
applying animal blood on them. Women are forbidden from touching
these skulls. They are not even permitted to be near the board. As a
practice, menstruating women take a detour around the hearth to go
to the next room rather than walk past the skulls. Women's menstrual
blood is considered the blood of life, as opposed to the blood of death
spilled during hunting (Morris 2000). Therefore, contact with each
other is prohibited, also indicating a separation of the spaces of men
and women, domesticated and wild animals, and domesticated animal
meat and wild animal meat.

The Mishmi observe a separation between the notions of the domesticated and the wild. The spirit that owns wild animals is different from the one that owns domesticated animals. Mithuns roam freely between forests and villages, but their skulls are displayed separately from wild animal skulls. Mithuns are associated with male power and men take care of them. They are slaughtered during ceremonial sacrifices. The relationship between animals and the male identity is prominent among the Mishmi. This is displayed in the way men maintain the skulls of wild animals and of mithuns. While the hunting of some animals is permitted, provided one follows the taboos, there is a restriction on the hunting of animals such as tigers and Hoolock gibbons. These are *misu* (forbidden to kill) animals. Killing a tiger is the worst crime someone can commit, and a strict taboo on this matter is observed not only by the hunter and his family members but also by the entire village.

Women and Wildlife Hunting

Women[10] are forbidden from wildlife hunting, but they indirectly follow certain regulations and observe taboos to ensure success in the hunting attempted by men. Hunting is avoided when one's wife is menstruating. The day the men leave for hunting, the women of their kin eat only in the evening, when the men would have reached their destination. Eating food earlier than this is believed to lead to failure in hunting. While the hunters are away, no rituals are held at home. Performing a ritual would mean the slaughter of a chicken, and hence the spilling of blood. Similarly, since no blood should be spilled at home while the hunters are away, men avoid going hunting when the women in their house are menstruating.

There are some general rules that women follow with respect to hunting. They are not permitted to touch guns and arrows when they

[10] Only older women and women living in villages have the knowledge about taboos. Some even ridicule these taboos and call them superstitions. Many living in Roing feel that they are modern and educated and, therefore, believe that the Mishmi way of living should be changed. Women whose husbands are hunters follow these taboos very strictly.

are menstruating. Women are prohibited from eating wild meat, mostly large mammals and pheasants. However, I was offered wild meat. Since I am not a Mishmi, I was exempted from these prohibitions. The only wild meat that Mishmi women are permitted to consume comes from fish, birds, and farm rats. If women eat the meat of mammals or pheasants, they observe taboos (*èná*) until the new moon phase. These taboos usually include not washing clothes and not eating garlic, ginger, and mushrooms. However, many younger women do not follow these restrictions seriously, reflecting changes in the local cultures due to a modern lifestyle and conversion to Christianity.

A strong link to menstrual blood is expressed through these taboos that segregate all aspects of hunting (hunting trips, weapons, food, and animal remains) from menstruation and sexual activities. The taboos place the blood from menstruating woman and the blood of hunted animals opposite each other. Mixing of these bloods is seen as very dangerous, therefore the contact of menstruating women with weapons is prohibited.

Although wild animals and domesticated animals are seen as separate, their worlds are interlinked in Mishmi society. Wild animals are believed to be offered by the spirits. In return, the Mishmi are obliged to offer domesticated animals to the spirits. Chickens, pigs, and mithuns are slaughtered during rituals (for example, healing rituals and funerals) in the family or at the village level. Animals in the Mishmi world serve as an important link in creating social relations. Spirits also enter into social relations with human beings. Mithuns are offered as bride wealth during marriages and during births. Domesticated animals are slaughtered during funerals. Live chickens and piglets are buried with the deceased, along with other belongings. Mishmi funerals are elaborate,[11] and it is believed that once the deceased reaches the 'other world', he/she needs these animals to rear in the new world. Therefore, association with animals continues even after death for the Mishmi.

---

[11] A small hut-like structure is prepared in the burial site where the deceased is laid on a bed, covered with a blanket. A small shelf is filled with food, alcohol, clothes, utensils, lantern, matchbox, salt, torch, rice, millet, and other things that will be required for the deceased to start a new life. I have seen live chickens and piglets in a bamboo cage buried along with other items such as rice and meat.

Domesticated animals that are reared by the Mishmi include pigs, mithuns, and chickens (*ètō*). They are reared for meat, for selling locally, and for ceremonial slaughtering. Pigs are always stall-fed in a separate section either below the bamboo house standing on stilts or adjacent to the house in pens (*ilì apa*). Mithuns are never stall-fed but are let out into the nearby forests to roam freely. There are gates to prevent them from entering other villages. Chickens are kept in a compound attached to the house. The Mishmi's engagement with domesticated animals (mithuns, chickens, and pigs) and their subsequent slaughter during rituals is part of a complex system of their association with certain spirits. Of these domesticated animals, mithuns are considered most important and play a vital role in the local cultures of the Mishmi as well as among other indigenous groups of Northeast India.

Mithun: A Ceremonial Cattle of the Mishmi

A mithun *(Bos frontalis)* is a semi-domesticated cattle and a descendent of the gaur, the Indian bison (*Bos gaurus*). Mithuns are not found truly in the wild, though some animals have become feral and can be found roaming in the wild. They belong to the bovine family and are widely distributed in the hilly areas extending from the Arakan Hills and Chin Hills of Burma to the Chittagong Hills of Bangladesh, Northeast India, and Bhutan. In northern Yunnan, they are called *drung, dulong*, or *gayal* (Simoons and Simoons 1968). A mithun is a highly prized and culturally valued domesticated animal, not only for the Mishmi, but for all other cultural groups of Northeast India.

Reared for slaughter during ceremonies (marriages, funerals, and political gatherings), mithuns have also become a surrogate for fine payments. Interestingly, people do not rear them for milk or ploughing. The National Research Centre on Mithun in Nagaland was set up in 1988 to preserve, conserve, and propagate superior quality mithun germplasm for better nutritional and socio-economic support to the farmers. Mithuns are not stall-fed but are left out in the forests to be reared under free-ranging conditions. They play a crucial role in the exchange of wealth between relatives (during marriages and conflict resolution), during ceremonies for the dead, and in the propitiation of spirits. The slaughtering of a mithun as an offering to the spirits is considered the most significant form of exchange possible between humans and spirits, which renders it the sacrificial animal par excellence (Aisher 2005). During the Reh[12] festival, shamans chant hymns (*sācha*) when a mithun is sacrificed. These hymns describe the origin of mithuns and are believed to help lead the soul of the slaughtered mithun to its place of origin. After the sacrifice, mithun skulls with horns intact are placed on the sacred skull board in the first room, similar to wild animal skulls. For a ritual such as *amrase* (to cure illness, for protection of the family, and overall peace and prosperity), pigs and chickens are usually slaughtered, which are less prestigious as sacrificial animals than the mithun.

Mithuns indicate the status of the owner and are used as bride wealth during weddings. These are valuable animals economically, each costing around INR 40,000–50,000 (USD 650–750). The wealth of a person (usually a man) is gauged by the number of mithuns he owns. Wealthy Mishmi men can afford to give more bride wealth and have more wives.[13] According to customary law, wilful killing of a mithun, similar to killing tigers, is a serious crime, equivalent to murder, and a heavy fine of three to five mithuns is imposed on the accused (Chaudhuri 2008). When needed, mithuns are used to pay fines and settle disputes. Mithun heads were used as currency for bartering in the nineteenth century (Cooper 1873: 190). An owner of mithuns constantly maintains contact with the animals by providing them with salt.[14] Men walk into forests or the periphery of their village with a bag of salt and call out: 'Ho! Ho! Ho!' One by one, mithuns appear from the forest and lick the salt from their owner's hand or from the pile of salt left on the rocks

---

[12] The Reh festival is celebrated to worship Nanyi Inyitaya. All Idus are believed to be the children of Nanyi Inyitaya. Reh celebrations are held in a personal capacity and at the village level as well. Nowadays, the festival has become institutionalized and is celebrated from 1–3 February. At a personal level, Idus believe that a Reh ritual should be carried out once in a person's lifetime to get Nanyi Inyitaya's blessings.

[13] The Mishmi men are allowed to have more than one wife.

[14] Cattle, both wild and domesticated, have a strong appetite for salt. In the wild, the locations of salt-licks are permanently imprinted in their memory and they return to these locations when they require salt. Mithun calves are fed with salt by the owners when they are born, and as adults, mithun either return to the village for salt or the owners frequently visit them in the forests to feed them salt. It is also a way of creating loyalty and bonding between owners and mithuns.

Figure 3.3   Mithuns being fed salt by their owner
Source: Author.

(Figure 3.3). Owners identify their mithuns by slit marks made on their earlobes. Each mithun is given a distinct ear marking. Salt is offered to mithuns frequently to inculcate loyalty. This resonates with what the Mishmi remark about purchasing salt from China, which I will talk about in Chapter 4. Salt, in both the cases, is a metaphor for 'being loyal' to the provider of the salt.

The Mishmi's Relations with Animals

The relationship between humans and spirits is acknowledged through rules and regulations in the form of fear and respect, and is mediated by blood. This fear is manifest in the way wild animals, their meat, and their skulls are treated. As mentioned before, there is a strict physical separation between wild and domesticated animal skulls on the trophy board. Mixing of wild and domesticated animal meat is also seen as a taboo, and therefore the two are never cooked together.

Similar to what Bird-David (1990) says about Nayakas, there is a reciprocal 'process of exchange' between the spirit and the human world among the Mishmi. *Ngōlō* is the most important spirit for long-distance hunts, such as those for musk deer, and is believed to be the caretaker of wild animals (the animal master). *Ngōlō* should be respected so that it continues to provide wild animals to hunters. In exchange, hunters make a payment in the form of a piece of metal and a small piece of meat from the dead animal. Like *ngōlō* there are other spirits that offer good health and wealth for an exchange. For example, Àsā is the spirit that looks after large trees and the forests near villages. Cutting these large trees is believed to annoy these spirits. In general, large trees are not cut down unless they are required for house construction. People cover the stumps of a chopped tree with mud and trees to prevent *āsā* from seeing it. There are trees that should not be cut without performing certain rituals.

The Mishmi act in accordance with the obligation to give, to receive, and to pay. For example, an act of reciprocity is followed when meat is shared. The person who shoots the animal gets the head. The rest is shared with others. The Mishmi have strong ethics when it comes to sharing both domesticated and wild animal meat. During the Reh festival, meat is widely distributed among relatives and guests; similarly, sharing of meat between villagers is crucial during weddings and funerals. Therefore, wildlife hunting and slaughtering domesticated animals are taken very seriously. A complex network of exchanges exists between these two worlds, in which the slaughtered domesticated animals and the hunted wild animals form part of the exchange process. This resonates with Ingold's work (1980) among the Cree Indians; slaughtering and hunting activities are seen as important to maintain the 'world renewing process' and continue the circulation of energy. If certain taboos are not observed, there could be a disruption in the circulation of energy, causing illness, death, bad harvest, and hunting failures.

The relations of the Mishmi with animals are undergoing transformation because of the changes in their socio-economic situation. Cultural taboos, which were instituted to prevent the over-hunting of animals, are eroding due to changes in the belief system. The Mishmi who convert to Christianity do not follow hunting taboos. For example, those who have converted do not display animal skulls in their huts and have abandoned the ritualistic ways of worshiping spirits. However, they continue to hunt without necessarily following the rules. The Mishmi who are inclined to the Hindu belief system have stopped slaughtering mithuns, while some have even stopped eating meat (more on this in Chapter 5). Those who have converted look down upon the traditional Mishmi beliefs as 'primitive' practices. The changing Mishmi–animal relations also need to be seen in the light of wildlife conservation practices brought in by conservation NGOs and the government.

Wildlife Conservation

Wildlife hunting is an age-old practice in Arunachal. For people who live in and around forests, wildlife is an important resource for food and additional income, and plays an important role in their cultural practices. Hunting in Northeast India is also a traditional leisure activity for various tribal communities as well as politicians and bureaucrats who take part in modern-day hunting (Aiyadurai 2011). I have met doctors, engineers, and school teachers, not only of the Mishmi community but also from among other indigenous people in general in Northeast India, who participate in hunting.

However, the Indian Wildlife Protection Act, 1972 (GoI 1994), prohibits the hunting[15] of virtually all large wildlife. The main objectives of the Act are: (1) prohibition of hunting of wild animals, birds, and plants; (2) setting up and management of national parks and sanctuaries; and (3) control of trade and commerce in wildlife and wildlife products. The Indian Wildlife Protection Act is a comprehensive law for protecting India's biodiversity and prohibits the hunting of any species or their trade in the form of trophies, animal parts, and their derivatives. A complete ban on the hunting of wildlife species has affected the livelihoods of many communities in India (Dutt 2004; Gadgil and Malhotra 2008). The law was created in response to the rapid decline of India's wildlife and the international pressure to conserve forests and wildlife. With the creation of protected areas, the subsistence activities of the local people were deemed illegal. For example, according to

---

[15] Hunting here means capturing, poisoning, snaring, or trapping of any wild animal.

India's Wildlife (Protection) Act, 1972, Chapter III: 'Hunting of Wild Animals:

> No person shall destroy, exploit, or remove any wildlife from a National Park or destroy or damage the habitat or any wild animal[16] or deprive any wild animal or its habitat within such National Park except under and in accordance with a permit granted by the Chief Wildlife Warden and no such permit shall be granted unless the State Government, being satisfied that such destruction, exploitation, or removal of wildlife from the National Park is necessary for the improvement and better management of wildlife therein, authorizes the issue of such permit. No grazing of any livestock shall be permitted in a National Park and no livestock shall be allowed to enter except where such livestock is used as a vehicle by a person authorized to enter such National Park.

In remote areas of Northeast India, however, hunting still continues, largely due to its linkages with local customs (Aiyadurai 2011; Roy 2018). The awareness of these laws on the ground is extremely low. Even in places where people are aware of this law, hunting continues because people do not see it as unlawful and take pride in it. This is due to the absence of effective implementation of the law and also because of cultural compulsions (Aiyadurai 2018). The northeast region of India was cut off from the rest of the country for decades. Lack of road connectivity and basic infrastructure made this region immune to active governance for a long time. Therefore, implementation of laws has been rather weak. In addition to this, due to the lack of economic alternatives for sustaining livelihoods in the region, people continue to hunt and trade wildlife parts to earn some extra cash (Hilaluddin, Kaul, and Ghose 2005, Aiyadurai, Singh, and Milner-Gulland 2010). Setting up of protected areas has been one of the major approaches to conserve wildlife. Arunachal's forest department has set aside large tracts of land for conservation in the form of national parks and wildlife sanctuaries. There are 11 wildlife sanctuaries and two national parks in the state, which are also designated as tiger reserves. The forest department's engagement with the local communities for wildlife conservation

---

[16] Wildlife refers to non-domesticated animal species, and includes all plants, fungi, and other organisms that grow or live wild in an area without being introduced by humans. 'Animal' includes mammals, birds, reptiles, and their young ones, and in case of birds and reptiles, their eggs.

has been slow, and it was not a priority for the government for a long time. NGOs (World Wide Fund for Nature, Wildlife Trust of India, and Nature Conservation Foundation) have played an active role in the conservation of wildlife in protected areas, namely Pakke Tiger Reserve and Namdapha Tiger Reserve. There has been little or no social assessment or analysis of these projects to examine their impact on the local communities, and how these interventions are perceived by the local communities.

Commentary

Over the last few decades, wild animal extraction and research that indicates that hunting is leading to the extinction of wildlife populations have become serious causes of concern globally. (Bennett and Robinson 2001; Velho, Karanth, and Laurance 2012). Places such as Arunachal have recently been subjected to a growing academic interest from ecologists and conservationists. Wildlife research has increased in the region partly because of its inclusion in the Eastern Himalaya[17] 'biodiversity hotspot' (Myers et al. 2000). Conservation laws and NGOs consider the local people to be harmful to wildlife species in their area and their extraction of natural resources to be unsustainable, resulting in the decline of forest cover and wildlife population (Hilaluddin, Kaul, and Ghose 2005; Datta, Anand, and Naniwadekar 2008). Community-based conservation projects have been implemented in Arunachal to wean hunters away from hunting. Schools are being set up and awareness and health programmes are being conducted to encourage local communities to participate in conservation projects (Datta 2007). In places such as Arunachal, the local people are dependent on wild animals and forest resources for subsistence, and have complex relations with the animals. Any successful conservation measure needs to take into account the locals' attitude towards natural resources and, especially, people-animal relations. New sociological studies on community-based conservation are

---

[17] Eastern Himalayas is the geographical region from central Nepal in the west to Myanmar in the east, including south-east Tibet in China, Sikkim, north Bengal, Bhutan, and Northeast India. Conservation International has declared this region as one of the Global biodiversity hotspots.

now emerging from Northeast India (Aiyadurai and Banerjee 2019; Nijhawan 2018; Aisher 2005; Roy 2018).

How the local people react to the conservation efforts of the state, NGOs, or biologists depends on their relations with the animals themselves. The cultural linkages of the Mishmi to the natural world and their subsistence-based livelihood place them in opposition to contemporary conservation practices (Aiyadurai and Velho 2018). The following chapters will highlight how the Mishmi use the knowledge and practice of taboos and their kinship with tigers to raise questions about the state's and science's way of conducting conservation.

4

THE THIN RED LINE
Living on the Sino-Indian Border

Only after 1947, we came under Indian territory. Earlier, we were not with the Bharat *sarkar* (Indian government), we were on 'no man's land'.

—an Idu Mishmi resident in Anini

The location of the Dibang Valley district on the Sino-Indian border makes it crucial in geopolitical terms. Changes on the border, both in military and political terms, have affected the lives of the Mishmi. The drawing of the McMahon line in 1914, the Sino-Indian war in 1962, and the subsequent administration of the Indian government have shaped the Mishmi's relations with the state tremendously. The British presence in the Mishmi Hills from the early nineteenth century left a lasting impact on how these borderlands and the Mishmi were imagined. This chapter[1] aims to provide a broad understanding of the Mishmi's association with the Sino-Indian border and to discuss the lives of communities who live along the international border. I travel back in time to provide an overview of British writings on the Mishmi and their perception of them as 'wild' and 'barbaric'. These impressions continue to shape the views of visitors even today.

The relationship of the state with border communities is often ambiguous. As a political construct, national borders have different

---

[1] The title of this chapter was suggested by Rahul Barkataky.

meanings for different groups and their practical consequences are often quite different. However rigid the borders may be, people find ways to cross them to access services or products that may not be available within their country. Baud and Van Schendel (1997) focus on how peoples' strategic access to the control of resources is negotiated with various officials of the state. Border regions have their own social and historical dynamics. In general, the state's views and issues of security have constituted most of the scholarship in borderland studies, while the local communities are ignored or appear as 'footnotes'. For example, the China–India borderland is treated as an 'uninhabited space' (Guyot-Rèchard 2017: 26). Over the last two decades, studies have focused on the social realities and the social and cultural impact of people living on the borders, in addition to the matters of politics and economics (Van Schendel and de Maaker 2014). Borders reveal the territorial definition of a state, as a line that divides citizens who have rights and duties from 'aliens' or 'foreigners' (Baud and Van Schendel 1997). Inclusion and exclusion of people and the contestation of rules is central to all border dynamics, but political borders often do not coincide with natural and cultural divides. Borders create categories of 'citizens' and 'foreigners' and people are re-categorized as 'Indians', 'Pakistanis', or 'Burmese' (Van Schendel and Abraham 2005).

Borders often cut through populations, such as the Mishmi, who have similar ethnicity, dress, language, or culture. When boundaries are drawn or contested by states, little attention is paid to the networks of economic trade, kinship relations, and any sociocultural or political institutions that exist among such trans-border communities (Asiwaju 1985). While the local people may continue their trade on the other side of the border, their exchanges with the other side are resented by the authorities, who often try to suppress such movements. However, for many people living at the border, these areas continue to provide both opportunities and barriers (Eilenberg 2012).

The overlapping of political, geographical, ecological, and historical domains makes the borderland of Dibang Valley with China a space to understand the relations between the Mishmi and the state. Dibang Valley helps us understand state–society relations that can enhance the state's view of trans-border communities such as the Mishmi and provide insights on how the Mishmi associate with the state in relation to the issues of the Sino-Indian border.

I provide two stories from Dibang Valley to show this ambiguous relation. Both stories are spread over a period of 50 years. One is that of Yaaku Tacho, a Mishmi woman who went to China in the 1950s and worked there for a few years. I met her daughter who shared a few pages of her mother's personal diary written in Chinese. In her diary, Yaaku writes as a Chinese patriot and praises Chinese officials for being helpful in providing education and jobs. People's movements across the border was common in the past and traders brought back stories of better living, education, and material conditions in China, which attracted the Mishmi to that country. Even now, the Mishmi talk of better infrastructure on the Chinese side of the Sino-Indian border. When the Indian administration made its presence felt in Dibang Valley in the year 1950, the Mishmi men and women who returned from China were looked upon with suspicion.

The second story is that of Apiya, my host in Anini. He is concerned that Chinese hunters are entering deep into the Indian territory and hunting wildlife indiscriminately. He and others claim that the trips they (the Mishmi) make to the border for hunting in a way help in the protection of India's territory and in keeping a check on Chinese intrusions. I find it interesting how the Mishmi assert their right over land through hunting practices, despite knowing that hunting is illegal. It is a fact that military agencies use their services, skills, and knowledge during patrolling and intelligence gathering. This dual and contradictory position of the Mishmi in relation to the state provides fresh insight into the state–people relations on the borderlands.

As state (the forest department, the Indian Army, the administration) and non-state agencies (NGOs, corporations) compete over for this space for national security, development, and increasingly for wildlife conservation, the Mishmi's role becomes complex. While the intelligence and military units seek the Mishmi's services for information gathering and as porters-cum-guides, the forest department sees hunters as lawbreakers and aims to regulate their hunting trips to the border. How the state agencies see the Mishmi must be viewed against a historical canvas, starting with the community's trading trips to China and their relations with the British, the arrival of the missionaries, and the presence of the Indian administration, the army, corporations, and conservation actors.

The Mishmi: A Border Community

Arunachal is a frontier state of Northeast India, also known as the 'land of the rising sun'; it shares an international border of 1,126 kms with Tibet, which is claimed by China. The state had largely been cut off from mainstream economic and infrastructural development until recently. The government of India, in its national policy, imagined the region to be 'backward' due to the lack of infrastructure and connectivity (Baruah 2003). China's claim over Arunachal made it a disputed territory, which led to a war between India and China in 1962 (Guyot-Rèchard 2017). There are several indigenous communities on either side of the border. The Mishmi are one among them. They have three subgroups (Idu, Digaru, and Miju) who reside on the Indian side, namely in Lohit, Anjaw, lower Dibang Valley, and the Dibang Valley districts, broadly called the Mishmi Hills, while one subgroup, the Deng Mishmi, live on the Chinese side, in the Tibet Autonomous Council's Zayul county (Table 4.1). There has been little or no connection between the Deng Mishmi in Tibet and the other sub-groups since the war in 1962. The movement of the Mishmi across the border has been restricted, thus impacting the social ties and trade-related activities between these communities.

Table 4.1   The Mishmi and their subgroups

Mishmi	Sites	Country	Population* (approximate)
Idu	Dibang Valley and Lower Dibang Valley, East Siang	India	12,000
Miju	Lohit and Anjaw	India	—
Digaru	Lohit and Anjaw	India	—
Deng	Zayul Valley	South Tibet (China)	1,300

Source: Author.

Note: *There is no tribe-specific population data available for the Miju and Digaru. It is estimated that the Mishmi population in India, including all three districts, is 50,000 (Kri 2008). According to the census of 2001, there were 9,076 Idu Mishmi, while by the census of 2011, their population had risen to 12,000 (Sarma 2015). According to Blench (2018), the 1971 census recorded 7,700 individuals identifying themselves as Idu Mishmi. The most recent figure could be approximately 14,000 (Nijhawan and Mihu 2020).

Since the time of the British, the area that constitutes the present day state of Arunachal Pradesh has been seen as a threatening 'backward frontier'. The Mishmi Hills went through a series of administrative adjustments, including naming and renaming of administrative units, from the colonial through the post-colonial era. In 1919, the British declared the three frontier tracts of Balipara, Sadiya, and Lakhimpur as 'Backward Tracts'. In 1936, these were renamed as 'Excluded Areas and Partially Excluded Areas'. By 1948, these frontier tracts came to be known as frontier divisions: the Sadiya Frontier Tract was made into Siang Frontier Division and Lohit Frontier Division, while the Balipara Frontier Tract was split into Kameng Frontier Division and Subansiri Frontier Division. After India's Independence in 1947, all the frontier divisions were grouped together to form the North-East Frontier Agency (NEFA) and were administered by the Ministry of Foreign Affairs with its headquarters in Shillong. The outpost (administrative office) in Anini was set up in 1950 (it is now the district headquarter of the Dibang Valley district). In 1965, the frontier divisions were renamed as districts (Kameng, Subansiri, Siang, Lohit, and Tirap). In 1967, NEFA was separated from Assam, and in 1971, the government of India passed the North Eastern Areas (Re-organizing) Act, which changed the status of NEFA to a union territory. In 1987, the territory was granted full statehood and its name changed to Arunachal Pradesh.[2]

Geopolitical Significance

Arunachal is strategically important for both China and India. There exists much scholarship on issues related to security and political debates (Vertzberger 1982, Basu and Miroshnik 2012, Jacob 2011), but anthropological and sociological research on the local communities living on the borders is lacking (Guyot-Rèchard 2017). It was only after the war in 1962 that India began to focus on building infrastructure in Northeast India and the region entered a new nationalist discourse aimed at the 'nationalization of the frontiers' (Baruah 2003: 8). This process has made regions such as Northeast India financially dependent on the central government, as there are no industries or production of goods within the state. Since then, there have been tremendous

---

[2] Arunachal Pradesh means 'the land of the rising sun' (in Hindi).

demographic and sociocultural changes with 'significant social, environmental and political costs' (Baruah 2003: 917). So far, development policy in Arunachal has been shaped largely by a concern for national security. Therefore, Baruah has argued, it is only in a cosmetic sense that Arunachal has witnessed development.

Across the border, western China has invested huge funds to develop its own frontier regions. China is increasingly engaging with and controlling border disputes by strengthening its defence and border security (Sharma 2014). There have been talks about developing the border regions for mutual benefit, but the reality is different; China has even gone to the extent of preventing a multilateral development loan[3] meant for Arunachal. China wanted the word 'Arunachal', the name used by India, to be removed from the policy document as it claims the entire state as its own. China opposes the idea of any further infrastructure development on the border and sees this as a threat. In addition, China was concerned that Japan was helping India with infrastructure development in Arunachal. Japan's statement that Arunachal belongs to India was a source of friction between India and China (Reuters 2015).

India is increasingly investing in military infrastructure and development in the Northeast region, which it had neglected for years. The state building projects have intensified in the last decade and the government continues to expand its infrastructure and military facilities in Arunachal. The government of India is building a 2,000 km all-weather road along the border with China (Kumar 2014). Arunachal's first passenger railway service was started in 2014 (Singh 2014) and a special Mountain Strike Corps was set up along the border by the Indian Army (Pandit 2014). To fortify defences along the China border, 54 new Indo-Tibetan Border Police (ITBP) posts were planned in Arunachal (*Times of India*, 2015). The region is currently witnessing the construction of several hydroelectric projects (Dutta 2008). One of them is the 3,000 MW Dibang Multipurpose Project, which got cleared by the Ministry of Environment and Forests in 2014. The latest is a major controversy over the Etalin Hydropower Project in Etalin, Dibang Valley (more on this in the epilogue). To raise the

[3] A USD 60 million loan from the Asian Development Bank (ADB) for watershed development projects (that is, flood management, water supply, and sanitation) for Arunachal.

socio-economic profile of the region, the government's 11th Five Year Plan (2007–11) assigned funds of USD 19 billion for Northeast India (Kurian 2014). The latest development was the Dhola-Sadiya bridge (also called the Bhupen Hazarika Setu) over Lohit river, claimed to be India's longest bridge (9.15 kms) connecting Assam to Arunachal, which was inaugurated by Prime Minister Narendra Modi in 2017. The bridge will not only improve trade in Arunachal but, more importantly, provide quick and easy connectivity for the military to reach the international borders or to facilitate the numerous hydroelectric projects (Saikia and Gogoi 2018). There have been concerns that these projects are not inclusive in nature, especially for the local inhabitants who may be left behind as 'doubly marginalized under the weight of such fast-paced development goals' (Rahman 2014, 2017).

Other than military and infrastructural developments in the region, ideas of development are reflected through the creation of national parks and biosphere reserves within the framework of 'green development' and 'ecological modernization' (McAfee 1999a; Yeh 2009, 2012). Biodiversity conservation can be seen as a new 'development' project. West (2006), for example, uses the phrase 'conservation-as-development',[4] by which she means that rural people see biodiversity conservation as a new form of economic development. While some local people welcome these developmental activities, environmental activists, NGOs, and civil groups within and outside Arunachal are concerned about the unplanned development in this geopolitically, ecologically, and culturally sensitive region (Bhaumik 2009; Rahman 2014).

From the Chinese Side

The Chinese name of Arunachal is 'Afunaqiaerbang' (transliteration of Arunachal in Chinese) or 'zangnan diqu' (the region of South Tibet).

---

[4] In her book *Conservation Is Our Government Now: Political Ecology of Papua New Guinea* (2006), West shows that when NGOs talked to the local people about conservation, people thought of 'earning cash' and participating in the market, so that they could access goods. Local people were trained to do small businesses, to work with biologists (as wage labourers, guides, porters), and for monitoring the wildlife population. The first two are related to development and the latter two are for conservation.

The Mishmi community in South Tibet is called Deng, which is one of the 55 officially recognized minority groups officially recognized by the government of the People's Republic of China (Li 2008).

The Deng are known by other names[5]—Deng, Dengba, Darang, Geman, Kaman, Mishmi, or Miju. They live mainly in the south-east part of the Tibetan Autonomous Region in Zayul County in the forest areas of the Hengduan Mountains at an elevation of 1,000 metres. According to Lang and Qianghaduogi (2000), Deng people live on the border between south-east Tibet and Myanmar. Known to be divided into at least two groups, Darang and Geman, the Deng are related to the Miju subgroup living in the Arunachal province in India. Fei Xiaotong, one of the founders of early anthropology and sociology in China, states that the status of the Tibetans of Pingwu County and Sichuan Province, and the Dengs in Zayu County in the south-eastern part of the Tibet Autonomous Region is not yet established (Fei 1980). The Deng, like the Mishmi, speak a language derived from the Tibeto-Burman language.[6] From the limited resources of images on the internet, the material culture of the Deng looks similar to the Digaru and the Miju Mishmi. During my field trips to the border villages (Chaglagam and Taflagam) in the Anjaw district in 2006–8, the Mishmi would often talk about their relatives on the other side of the border.

The British and the Mishmi: Imagining and Shaping People and Territory

Arunachal was never brought under any formal administrative control by the British government.[7] Arunachal, was administered as part of Assam during the British rule. To prevent the possibility of violent rebellion, the British adopted a policy of minimal interference in the region, which Guha calls 'shadowy suzerainty' (Guha 1999: 579). Later

[5] Its Chinese name is *Dengren* 僜人 (Deng people) or *Dengbaren* 僜巴人 (Dengba people). They can be known as Idu Mishmi (Idu Lhoba), Digaru tribe (Taraon, Darang Deng), or Miju Mishmi (Kaman Deng).

[6] Because of lack of information, I cannot confirm whether the Deng speak the same language or dialect as the Mishmi.

[7] The British came to Assam during the Anglo-Burmese war of 1824–6 and the region came under their rule during this period (Bose 1979).

on, British officials started visiting the Mishmi Hills more frequently for mapping and surveying, but also for the occasional punitive expedition. The British saw these border regions as promising areas for trade (tea, timber, and ivory) and thereby focused on maintaining the law and order here to maximize economic gains and to control territory.

Historically, there has been constant friction between the hill people of Arunachal and the 'civilized' valley dwellers of Assam. People in Assam would traditionally pay tolls to the hill people for the collection of wood or any other forest produce. The Mishmi (Miju) collected tolls from the Hindu pilgrims who visited the Parasuram Kund (Anjaw district) as well. Raiding by the Mishmi prompted the British to set up an armed outpost to keep a check on the movement of the hill people.

In 1873, the British enacted a regulation, known as the Inner Line Regulation of 1873, with the aim of controlling interactions between Assam and the populations that lived beyond that. This prohibited anyone residing in Assam or passing through the districts of Assam from going beyond without a pass (ILP). The pass constituted a written permission from the designated authorities and was meant to prevent poachers, moneylenders, woodcutters, traders, and missionaries in the valley from exploiting the hill people. Arunachal continues to be a restricted area and an official permit is required for all except the native residents of Arunachal to enter the state. The ILP has been an impediment to the economic development of Arunachal and continues to be a burning issue there. The first ever railway service, which began in 2014, was suspended for some time due to huge protests by the Arunachal Pradesh Students' Union against the mass entry of non-native Arunachalis from outside the state (Gao 2015).

British relations with the Mishmi and other hill people were guided by a payment system called *posa*.[8] For greater efficiency of administration, the British created a special post of 'political officer'. These

[8] *Posa* (blackmail tribute) is money or goods offered to the hill tribes by the Ahom kings of Assam to prevent them from raiding the villages in the foothills and plains. *Posa*, in the form of clothes, salt, and iron, was valued a lot by the hill people (Singh 2010). For every 10 houses in the foothills, the hill people were entitled to receive a set of cloths, one *dao* (machete), 10 heads of horned cattle, and four *seers* of salt. *Seer* or *sihr* is a traditional unit of mass and volume (1 *seer* = 0.944 kg).

political officers were required to be intelligent in their instinct, quick in their sympathies, and needed to have the ability to learn vernacular languages (Bose 1979: 175). These officers, in a short period of time, attained some influence over the frontier people and opened friendly communication to start commerce. The British policy with regard to the hill people was generally of non-interference, unless in the case of attacks on British subjects, violations of the 'inner line', or any aggression towards the people in the foothills and Assam. These hills were surveyed for mapping on their exploratory missions, and even for punishing the hill tribes as punitive missions (Guyot-Rèchard 2017).

For the British, Assam and the adjoining hills, including the Mishmi Hills, were important for expanding trade and promoting their commercial interests (Bhattacharjee 2002), which, in turn, required control over the frontier population. The British needed to conquer and subdue the inhabitants to further their economic interests, for example, planting of tea in Assam (Baral 2009). Defining the frontier was a key step towards identifying the people who were to become British subjects (Robb 1997). Maintaining peace in the region was crucial for the promotion of trade, as there were conflicts not only between the hill tribes but also between the Mishmi and the Tibetans over incursions into the territory and hunting. Stopping feuds between these groups was a major challenge for the British. One of the ambitious ideas of the British was to start a rail link from Sadiya (Assam, India) to Batang (Sichuan, China) through the Mishmi Hills, but this never materialized due to the fear that it would facilitate the entry of Chinese troops into Indian territory (Bose 1979). During that time, the British controlled the territory up to Zayul Chu, a Chinese outpost near Rima. At the local level, however, trade was practised between the Mishmi Hills, China, and Burma using the historic trade routes.

Another strategic reason to manage this frontier area was that the British were concerned that if they did not take an interest in this region the Mishmi would end up becoming 'Chinese' subjects. By 1911, China had expanded its claim on the Mishmi area, and flags were found planted in Menilkrai, south of Walong (Guyot-Rèchard 2017). To win over the local native people, the British carried with them tea and cigarettes as 'political presents' (Routledge 1945). F. P. Mainprice, the assistant political officer of Lohit Valley in 1945, had a long list of political presents that included iron and steel for making *dao*s (machetes), black thread for making coats, salt, tea, rum, red lamp cigarettes, and opium (Mainprice 1945).

Tobacco leaves were gifted to Tibetan coolies, while wristwatches, safety razors, torches, soap, and towels were presented to the Tibetan officials in Rima. Even guns were presented to the local village headmen with the expectation that they would cooperate with the British. In 1909, Noel Williamson, the assistant political officer of the time, presented six Mishmi (Miju) men each with DBML (Double Barrel Machine Loading) guns for assisting him in an expedition in 1907–8 (Williamson 1910). The headmen who cooperated with the British and those who checked the existing feuds were presented with red coats (Routledge 1945).[9]

These political officers had multiple duties: they were naturalists and anthropologists, in addition to being administrators and surveyors Appendix 4. Acquiring knowledge about people and places was an integral part of the colonial enterprise. As Monahan (1899) puts in his letter[10] to the secretary of the foreign department of the Government of India: '… acquiring as far as possible, an accurate knowledge of the country and of the haunts and habits of the people, and, of impressing definitely on these savage marauders that they cannot raid on our frontier, or murder, rob, and carry off unoffending British subjects with impunity.'

Acquiring knowledge about the people and landscape was not the only aim of the British in reaching out to these frontier people; the idea was to gain control over the local people. For example, the murder of Noel Williamson (a political officer) and Dr Gregorson (a tea planter and doctor) changed the approach of the British from non-interference to direct confrontation. There were several incidences of British troops extracting fines, arresting 'criminals', and even destroying Mishmi villages. An expedition was carried out in 1853 after two French missionaries, Father Nicolas Michael Krick and Father Augustine Etienne

[9] Village headmen were given woollen red coats by the British to signify the authority of the person and to represent the administration of the area concerned. Red coats are still widely used by village headmen during official meetings and functions.

[10] F. J. Monahan was the secretary to the chief commissioner of Assam. Assam Secretariat Proceedings Foreign 'A', November 1896. Report by Assistant Political Officer Sadiya, on the relations with the frontier tribes for the year 1895–96. Report no. 12 by J.F. Needham, APO Sadiya, dated 2 March 1896.

Bourry, were killed by a Mishmi headman named Kaisha in Anjaw district (Heriot 1979). Kaisha was arrested later and hanged in Dibrugarh. This account was vividly retold by the poet and journalist Mamang Dai in a book titled *The Black Hill* published in 2015. One of the best known expeditions into the Mishmi Hills in 1911 was the 'Mishmi Mission' led by W. C. M. Dundas, the chief political officer, to subdue and settle three groups: the Abor (Adis), the Mishmi, and the Miri, particularly to punish those who had murdered British officials. The military strength of this mission was 750 troops, made up of 350 Naga Hills military police, 150 Dacca military police, 200 sappers,[11] as well as 1200 Naga coolies who acted as porters (Hamilton 1912).

In addition to practising trade and maintaining law and order, earlier European visitors were intrigued by the magnificent landscape and fascinating wildlife. A junior officer named Ronald Kaulback, a British explorer and geographer, wrote several letters to Francis Kingdon-Ward, the well-known British botanist and explorer, asking for his advice so that he could visit this region. Kaulback later took up the position of an assistant for Ward's botanical survey (Kaulback 1935). Kingdon-Ward, who visited this region, came to be known as the last of 'the great plant hunters' (Lyte 1989). William Griffith, a British doctor and naturalist-cum-botanist, travelled up to the Lohit river to explore the natural history of the area.

Writings by these visitors created an image of 'untouched' hills waiting to be explored. These explorers saw the frontier Himalayas as a natural laboratory for documenting plants, insects, mammals, and birds. On the one hand, their writings extolled the natural heritage of the region, the majestic mountains, rivers, and waterfalls, while on the other they wrote about the hill people and their behaviour, cultures, and customs as 'dangerous' and 'barbaric', starkly contrasting with the mesmerising beauty and magic of the landscape. The British perceived the Mishmi as dangerous, dirty, unfriendly, and wild. The views of these earlier visitors about the Mishmi were often negative, and they were not sympathetic at all towards understanding the people. In 1882, the Mishmi were seen

---

[11] Sappers were soldiers who performed a variety of military engineering duties, such as bridge-building, laying or clearing minefields, demolition, field defence and general construction, as well as road and airfield construction and repair.

as 'untouched by any civilizing influences' (Waller 1990: 138). Not only the Mishmi, the description of natives 'as less than human and abominable' is common in the Northeast's colonial ethnography (Baral 2009).

The Mishmi controlled the trade in the area between Tibet and Assam and refused the entry of outsiders into their territory. They were, thus, seen as a 'ferocious tribe' (Stewart 2006: 79). Mishmi country was reported to be dangerous and because it was not properly explored until the early twentieth century, it was seen as 'a place not for an outsider' (Stewart 2006: 79). F. M. Bailey, a British intelligence officer, wrote: 'I found Mishmi difficult to manage, but luckily, had some opium with me, for which drug a Mishmi will do a great deal' (1912a). According to Kingdon-Ward (1913: 1), '[T]hough they would not ordinarily murder an intruder, they would willingly leave him stranded without food and porter.'

Hamilton[12] observed that the tribesmen were of uncertain temperament and frequently at war among themselves. After 1826, intense fighting among the Mishmi prevented the entry of visitors from outside the region for around five years (Hamilton 1912). T. T. Cooper reported that the (Idu) Mishmi were 'war-like and predatory', and that at one time they were such trouble that they were forbidden to visit Sadiya (1873: 180–1). The Mishmi in Lohit Valley were reported to be 'uncooperative with each other and of strangers they have an abiding dislike and mistrust' (Mills 1952: 1). In describing the Mishmi houses, Cooper writes: 'The interiors of the Mishmee houses more resemble a cowshed than human habitation, while from the outside they might be mistaken for fowl house. The most striking feature of the interior is the number of skulls of mithuns, bullocks, buffaloes, tigers, bear, deer, monkeys and takin' (1873: 189).

In spite of the European visitors' skewed representation of the Mishmi, their writings left behind a rich source of information about the material culture and lives of the community. For example, J. P. Mills, administrator-cum-anthropologist, gave a detailed account of the Mishmi of the Lohit Valley (Mills 1952). But one has to be careful when reading what the Europeans wrote about the Mishmi, given the prejudice and unequal relations of the colonial administration with

[12] A fellow of the Royal Geographical Society, Angus Hamilton gave an account of the British army's expeditions in the Mishmi Hills in 1911–12.

the local Mishmi. Elwin (1959) was probably one of the few scholars who had positive views about the Mishmi as being friendly, colourful, and beautiful. He was surprised by the negative views of the previous visitors and said that they seem to have something wrong with their eyesight. He wrote in his autobiography:

> All the previous travellers had stressed how 'difficult' the Mishmis were and how unpleasant and unattractive. I can only say I fell in love with them at once. Our first village was inhabited by Digaru Mishmis and the men wore their hair tied in a knot on the top of the head and the women had theirs in a fantastic piled up style which would attract admiring attention anywhere. (1964: 274)

Books[13] on the Mishmi by scholars from mainland India were largely written by administrators who were posted in Arunachal. There is new scholarship emerging from Dibang Valley (see Mene, T and S. K. Chaudhuri (2019). Mishimbu Miri has written a book on the Mishmi tales (2010)). Diaries written by missionaries and anthropologists provided information about the native people's way of life for effective local administration. In the absence of any text prior to the British period, one is dependent on colonial ethnography, but one should be critical of how these texts were produced and for what purposes. The British saw the Mishmi as 'backward', 'uncivilized', and 'primitive'. Similar terms were used to describe several groups in India by the colonial state. The term 'tribe' emerged as a distinct category in colonial times, which continues to be used until today by bureaucrats, scholars, and by the Mishmi themselves. Among the Mishmi, like other groups in Northeast India, the term is internalized and used in identity discourses as a source of pride (McDuie-Ra 2012).

'Making Up People': Tribes, Scheduled Tribes, and Indigenous People

Categorization and creating new classes of people has consequences for the ways in which we conceive of others and think of our own possibilities and potentialities.

—Hacking (1990: 6)

---

[13] *The Idu Mishmi* by T. K. Baruah (1988), *The Idus of Mathu and Dri Valley* by T. K. Bhattacharjee (1983), and *A Tryst with Mishmi Hills* by D. S. Negi (1996).

The word 'tribe' is hugely debated among Indian scholars (Beteille 2006; Xaxa 2010). The official definition of the term in India is not clear and it is often associated with 'primitiveness', 'isolation', and 'animism', leading to confusion and vagueness surrounding it. Derogatory connotations (uncivilized, backward and/or primitive) attached to the term continue to be a concern among scholars (Karlsson and Subba 2006). However, in the Northeast ethnographic texts, the term 'tribe' was used for hill people to distinguish them from the people of the plains or the valley of Assam. The Mishmi, in fact, take pride in calling themselves 'tribal'.

The term 'tribe' is contested globally due to its roots in colonialism (Baral 2009), however, in India, the word 'tribal' is used freely and has multiple meanings academically, politically, and socially. British administrators-cum-researchers described 'tribes' as being different from caste groups and living in isolation from the rest of the population. Therefore, in India, the category of 'tribe' is a colonial one, influenced by the colonial discourse designed for administrative convenience to govern people in British India (Bèteille 1998; Misra 2012).

The 1901 census of India defined 'tribes' as those who practised animism and were viewed as 'primitive societies' dependent on forests for shifting cultivation. In South Asia, the term 'tribe' is very vague. Often, non-Western people see the hill societies as 'backward and child-like, [who] therefore need to be protected, educated, and disciplined ... by those who are more advanced socially' (Van Schendel 1992: 103). In some cases, the physiognomy of the colonized subjects became an important principle for describing 'tribal' people as 'specimen of discovery like bird or animal species' (Baral 2009). The description of 'tribe' by the Indian government is not very different from the definition provided by the British. In 1965, the official criteria for the Scheduled Tribe status was established by the Lokur Committee, which reflects the ambiguity in their understanding and definition of a 'tribe'. According to the committee, indications of primitive traits, distinctive culture, geographic isolation, shyness, and 'backwardness' define a 'tribe'. These criteria do not have a rationale or any nuance of meaning.

Scheduled Castes[14] (SCs) and Scheduled Tribes (STs) are official designations given to various groups in India on the basis of their

[14] The Scheduled Castes are sometimes referred to as Dalits, former Untouchables. According to the 2011 census, the Scheduled Castes and Scheduled Tribes comprise 16.6 per cent and 8.6 per cent of India's population respectively.

historical disadvantage. They have been eligible to receive special benefits since 1950 and compete for reserved positions in educational and
government institutions. Hence the term 'tribe' became closely linked
to political considerations and was used for affirmative action. Recent
global attention on the concerns of indigenous people (Bèteille 1998)
has also helped to raise the status of being 'tribal'.

The other term that has had a similar trajectory is 'Adivasi', often
associated with the 'tribes' located in eastern and central India.
Adivasi[15] is a term coined in the 1930s during a fight against the
colonial government and moneylenders (Hardiman 1987). In central
India people often use the term Adivasi, but in Northeast India the
use of this term is limited (Karlsson and Subba 2006). Local people
in Arunachal and the rest of Northeast India call themselves 'tribals'.
The term 'indigenous', which has come up only in the last few decades,
is widely used during political struggles and conflicts over the rights
to lands and forests. The term 'indigenous' continues to be viewed as
being linked to an international framework, and the Government of
India has been reluctant to accept this term, claiming that it does not
apply in the Indian context. According to the government, it is impos-
sible to distinguish any group as 'indigenous' because of the complex
historical movements of people and mingling of cultures. In that sense,
everyone in India could be considered 'indigenous' (Erni 2000).

The criteria of being 'indigenous' was first formulated in the
The Indigenous and Tribal Populations Convention, 1957, of the
International Labour Organization (ILO). This was the first attempt
to codify the international obligations of governments with respect to
indigenous people and was adopted by the ILO at the request of the
United Nations. According to ILO, 'indigenous people' have a distinct
identity from the dominant group, and identify themselves as the 'original inhabitants of the land'.[16] The idea of indigeneity is tied to the ideas
of land and territory. It became controversial in India and opinions are
divided due to its applicability (Bèteille 2006: 19). The term continues

---

[15] Adivasi is a Sanskrit word (*adi*: first or original and *vasi*: inhabitant), refer-
ring to tribes or Scheduled Tribes.

[16] Draft Universal Declaration on the Rights of Indigenous Peoples for rati-
fication by the UN General Assembly. The draft declaration was produced by
over 7,000 indigenous people and states that indigenous people have the right
to identify themselves as indigenous and be recognized as such.

to be used widely in people's land rights movements against the depre-
dations of the state and corporations.

   The ambiguity surrounding the people on the borders and the mar-
ginality of their status according to the Constitution of India become
apparent in the case of the Mishmi. Their physical features, linguistic
affiliation, and religious beliefs set them clearly apart from mainland
Indians and affiliate them more closely to Chinese minorities and
south-east Asian cultures. The Mishmi could be considered marginal
in several ways: in the sociocultural aspect (their status as tribal/indig-
enous), demographically (they are a small group numerically), and
linguistically (they speak a language that is considered as endangered).
The Mishmi's geographic location and past trade links across the border
create multiple, complex, and overlapping stories of people in these
borderlands, as elucidated by the story of Yaaku Tacho.

The Story of Yaaku Tacho

I interviewed[17] a Mishmi lady, also a government official, posted in
Khonsa (Tirap district), whose parents lived in China for 9 years in
the 1950s according to her. This is the story of her mother Yaaku, who
received free school education in China and was later reported to be
employed by Chinese officials. Yaaku and her husband went to China
with a small group of people from Dibang Valley, and many of them
received education there for 8–9 years. They found the Chinese to be
very kind and believed that communists were nice people. They spoke
of the Chinese army as being good. Yaaku's daughter remembered what
her parents had told her about the time they reached China: 'When we
reached, we were welcomed. It was very nice. We were taught patriotism for China. We were told that China is the best. Boys and girls were
kept in separate hostels. We were kept in a military school. We were
always trained by military officers and we received weapons training'.

   Pages from Yaaku's diary[18] reflect that the Mishmi were well treated
and taken care of by the Chinese. They were influenced by the Chinese

---

[17] Interviewed in Hindi and English. Yaaku wrote her diary in Chinese and
it was translated to English by Claire Lee (Inha University, South Korea).

[18] The diary and other notes were not maintained properly, and only a few
pages and a certificate were available for research.

propaganda that painted India as their 'enemy' and China as their good friend. Along with education, the Mishmi received weapons training. Some of the Mishmi even participated in the 1962 Sino-Indian war and were reported to have fought against India. Based on Yaaku's writings, it seems that the Chinese Liberation Army aimed to liberate the Mishmi from India. Yaaku wrote: 'Uncles—The Liberation Army on the border is defending our motherland, please liberate Luoda region! … I am one of China's sons and daughters.'

The meaning of 'motherland' (*zuguo*) in her diary refers to 'China' and not 'India'. This feeling is reflected in Yaaku's diary (Figures 4.1 and 4.2).

A certificate (Figure 4.3) of 'ethnic harmony' was issued by the Government of China in December 1960 to Yaaku Tacho. It has a picture of Mao Zedong at the top with the flag of China on either side and an official seal. The text in the certificate reads: 'This is to certify that Yaaku Tacho (student from Aidabo village, district …, Luo Yu ethnic group,[19] 20 years old) has graduated from the Mandarin class four in department two.'

The Sino-Indian war broke out in 1962, and both Yaaku's husband and brother-in-law[20] fought with China in Kibithoo against Indian soldiers; this is now a legend in Anini. After the war, the Indian officials at the border arrested them, imprisoned them, and reportedly tortured them for several days. The story of their escape from the Tezpur prison is popular in Dibang Valley even now. Even after they returned to their respective villages, I was told that the security officials in India continued to monitor their activities to check if they retained links with China.

These stories evoke the ambiguities of the border spaces before and since. Independence and the creation of the nation state, made people such as Yaaku Tacho and others who went to China at that point of time, 'for all practical purposes, [of] both Indian and Chinese nationality' (Baruah 2003: 936). For the security forces, such ambiguities of identities and geographic spaces are seen as dangerous. Therefore,

[19] Indian ethnic groups are known to have different names in China. Luo Yu is probably one of the names the Chinese use for the Mishmi.

[20] A newspaper article in *Assam Tribune* (2000) carried a story of Yaaku's brother-in-law. He lives in Anini now, where I met him during my fieldwork.

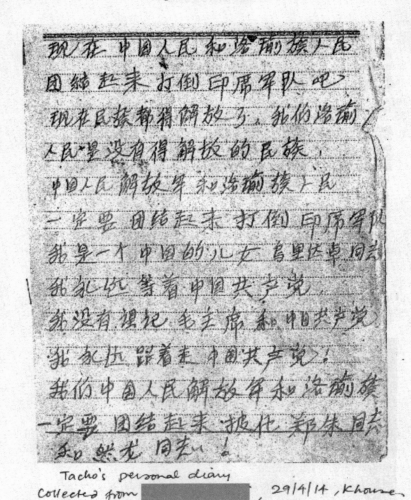

Figure 4.1 Yaaku's personal diary
Source: A Khonsa resident.

nationalizing such spaces becomes urgent and crucial for the government. Although the government turned its focus to the frontier region only after the war, the ambiguities of the border regions continue to be evident, as reflected in the next story, that of a Mishmi hunter.

(Original in Chinese)

现在中国人民和洛瑜族人民团结起来打倒印度军队吧。现在民族都得解放了，我们洛瑜人民是没有得解放的民族，中国人民解放军和洛瑜族人民一定要团结起来打倒印度军人。我是一个中国儿女乌里达卓同志。我永远等着中国共产党，我没有望（忘）记!毛主席和中国共产党，我永远跟着走中国共产党！

(In Chinese pinyin by Claire)

Xianzai Zhongguorenmin he Luodazu renmin tuanjie qilai dadao Yindu jundui ba. Xianzai minzu dou de jiefang le, women Luoda renmin shi meiyou de jiefang de minzu. Zhongguo renmin jiefangjun he Luoyu zu renmin yiding yao tuanjie qilai dadao Yindu junren. Wo shi yi ge Zhongguo erny Wuli Dazhuo tongzhi. Wo yongyuan dengzhe Zhongguo gongchandang, wo meiyou wangji Mao zhuxi de he Zhongguo gongchandang, wo yongyuan genzhe zou Zhongguo gongchandang!

(In English)

'Let us Chinese and Mishmi peoples, unite and overthrow the Indian army. Now all the other minorities have been liberated, but we Mishmi have yet to be liberated. The Chinese Liberation Army and the Mishmi people should unite to overthrow the Indian Army. I am one of Chinese's sons and daughters. Yaaku comrade [referring to herself] will wait for the Chinese Communist Party forever. I will never forget Chairman Mao and the Chinese Communist Part. I will always follow the Chinese Communist Party'

Figure 4.2 Translation of Yaaku's diary
Source: Claire Lee.

Figure 4.3 Certificate given to Yaaku by Chinese officials
Source: A Khonsa resident.

The Story of a Hunter on the Border

Apiya Angeche, in whose house I stayed for my research, is a well-known musk-deer hunter in the area; he has stopped hunting because of his age. He is never tired of telling the story of how courageous he was to fire at the Chinese during one of his hunting trips when he encountered Chinese troops close to the border. While he and his hunting team were inside a cave (*èpò*), they heard gunshots. Initially they wondered if the sound had come from a falling tree. The second shot confirmed that it was indeed a gunfire. Apiya said, 'I wanted to go out and shoot at them. There was another shot *dishkiiaayoon*,[21] from the Chinese.' Apiya and his team left the site, but after walking for a few minutes he found that his lunch box was missing, so he went back to the camp. 'Why should I leave the box for the fear of the Chinese?' Apiya asked. That was a way of showing his courage and his challenge to the Chinese. He said, 'They were showing *dadagiri*,[22] showing off as if it was their territory. I knew by which route they had come, I should have ambushed them.' Later, he shot back at the Chinese. After this, the Chinese did not fire back and Apiya and his team moved to another site. Many have heard this story as Apiya repeats it whenever there is talk of China, the army, and border patrolling. Speculating how vulnerable the Indian Army is, he continued, 'In this day of computers, if there is a war, India *nahi sakega* [will not be able to manage]. Our children can go up to the borders because they know the route, but the army cannot go without our help.' The reliance of the Indian Army on Mishmi knowledge gives him a sense of importance and he takes pride in this. Similarly, Mishmi knowledge of the wildlife and the trails up in the mountains make wildlife researchers completely dependent on the Mishmi's support.

The stories of Yaaku and Apiya are from different periods, set apart by more than half a century, and relate to the border differently. Yaaku's trips across the border were facilitated by Tibetans who helped her group meet the Chinese officials who, in turn, provided them with access to education, trade, and jobs. Fifty years later, however, movement in the border regions is restricted to just hunting, patrolling, and

[21] Apiya imitating the sound of gunfire.
[22] Hindi word for a big bully.

surveillance. Yaaku seems to have been unaware of her citizenship.[23] It was only after the establishment of the Anini outpost in 1950 that the restriction on people's movement was implemented. The last post is in Dambeun and anyone (except the natives of Dambeun and Acheso) going beyond this post need to inform the authorities.

After the war, the border was militarized as army bases were set up at Walong and Kibithoo (key sites in Anjaw during the war). Dibang Valley has had the Assam Rifles[24] and the ITBP since the 1950s and other Indian Army units too have now set up infrastructure in this region. Dibang Valley is witnessing a rise in the movement of uniformed men as the Government of India is heavily investing in military infrastructure here. A new settlement close to Anini now has army offices and quarters. There is limited interaction between the army and the local people, except during long-range patrols (LRPs).[25] Mishmi men are hired as guides and porters. Two to three trips, lasting 14–15 days, close to the international border are carried out every year during summer. Other than LRPs, staff of intelligence branch visit the border. They often work in close collaboration with the Mishmi men, who serve as porters and informers. Hunters and local villagers are also often approached by the Indian defence agencies for gathering intelligence. These activities are all welcomed by the local Mishmi, who make substantial amounts of money in a short period of time. Thus, they look forward to these activities every summer.

In the early nineteenth century, spies known as 'pundits' were sent by the British to these borders (Stewart 2006). In the 1880s, a famous pundit known as A. K., whose real name was Kishen Singh, visited Tibet and came in contact with the Mishmi. These frontier regions continue to be explored by modern spies (intelligence officers) who work for the Indian government. I met a Mishmi man in 2008 in Chaglagam (Anjaw district) who was hired by intelligence branch to plant hidden video cameras along the Sino-Indian border. I asked him, 'Don't you feel scared? It's a risky job. What if the Chinese find out and arrest you?' He proudly answered, 'The people on the other side are Mishmi

---

[23] Yaaku probably was not considered as a citizen at that time.

[24] One of India's paramilitary troops in India.

[25] Long Range Patrols (LRPs) are jointly undertaken by the security forces to check on the activities of China.

as well and they don't harm us because we too look Chinese.' He jok-
ingly pointed out, 'If you go, you will be shot,' and laughed. 'For that
matter, any educated-looking person will not be spared.'

Similar to Yaaku's story, these men who visit the border bring in
stories of better infrastructure and talk about how advanced Chinese
villages are. They talk of good roads, concrete houses, and vehicles
that are able to reach the border on the Chinese side. Such stories
sometimes create frustration among the Mishmi over their own living
conditions, where there is minimum infrastructure and a lack of proper
road or phone connectivity. At times, this anger is expressed towards
government officials, NGOs, and the army. In a meeting with the WWF
staff from Delhi, one of the village council members narrated the hardships of the Mishmi's earlier generations, and the discussion turned to
'salt'. To talk about salt was to highlight both the physical hardships of
their forefathers who undertook such difficult journeys to China just to
purchase salt and also to metaphorically talk about loyalty. 'Taking salt'
from someone bears the connotation of being loyal to them.[26] 'Salt'
from China is used as an intimidation tactic on government officials
or NGOs during the occasional face-off. People say, 'Humne China
ka namak khaya hai' (we have had salt from China). The Mishmi are
fiercely patriotic towards India but when they get mistreated or feel
discriminated by 'outsiders', they use the metaphor of salt to show that
they share deeper links with the Mishmi of Tibet and China than mainland Indians, who are new entrants to this region. According to one of
the Anini residents, 'In the beginning it was like this: we sold kasturi ka
gutti (musk pods) to China, there was no correspondence with India. ...
We Indians did not have correspondence with India at that time! Even
for salt, our grandfather bought it from Tibet. We were in touch with
that side, we sold animal skins to them and bought salt and clothes.'

The topics of China and salt are frequent during discussions in the
Mishmi Hills as the Chinese army is known to make a show of aggression every now and then at the Arunachal border. In 2013, Chinese
troops reportedly crossed the border and occupied territory 20 kms

[26] In the Mishmi Hills, people use the Sadiya-Rima route via Lohit district
to buy salt and other products. Mithuns are fed salt when they are born so that
they recognize the owner. Refer to the discussion on feeding salt to mithuns in
Chapter 3.

inside Anjaw district for nearly four days (*Times News Network*, 2013). The media in India highlighted this incident, which evoked the public's nationalist sentiments, but for the local people this is not new, as incursions have been known to happen frequently. Border problems in Arunachal continue to create friction between the two countries. During the recent trip of Prime Minister Narendra Modi to China, the state-owned Chinese Central Television (CCTV) station showed India's map without Jammu and Kashmir and Arunachal (Sharma 2015). This agitated social media users and the general public in India and started debates over India–China relations. This kind of 'cartographic aggression'[27] can be equated with military aggression, such as when troops from China entered Jammu and Kashmir during Chinese President Xi Jinping's visit to India in 2014. A year earlier, in 2013, during the earlier part of my fieldwork, two young archers were not allowed to go to the Youth World Archery Championship in Wuxi (China) because they were issued stapled visas, which is not the official visa (Dikshit 2013). China does not recognize Arunachal as part of India, so it did not issue these archers standard visas; instead, stapled visas were issued (Guyot-Rèchard 2017). One of the archers was Maselo Mihu, a girl from Kongo village—where I was based during my fieldwork. This incident was often brought up by the villagers to make the point that the Indian government was not treating people from Arunachal fairly and that they were caught up in the politics between India and China.

Biodiversity Conservation on the Border

In addition to road-building and militarization of the borders, there has been a tremendous increase in biodiversity-related activities that shape the border for wildlife conservation on the Indian side. Large protected areas have been created along the India–China border in the last couple of decades. In Tawang, the Tsangyang Gyatso World Peace Park was announced in 2004 to set aside 2,000 sq. kms for setting

---

[27] This expression is widely used by geographers. Cartographic expression is a term by which a country describes any act by a neighbouring country that shows part of its geographic area as its own territory. This is often used in the case of maps.

up a biosphere reserve on the recommendation of a conservation NGO (Mishra, Madhusudan, and Datta 2006). The creation of protected areas has often been in response to international concerns and because of influential NGOs in the region. The Government of India responds to such concerns and has turned over its borderlands for biodiversity conservation. Conservation is, arguably, one of the ways to keep the territory free of human occupation; at the same time taking such action wins India favour on the international stage. Through such initiatives, I would argue, India is trying to represent itself as environmentally concerned, in contrast to China, which often gets bad press for being reckless and destructive towards the environment.

The Dihang–Dibang Biosphere Reserve that spreads across an area of 5,112 sq. kms was created in 1998. In 2012, following the rescue of the tiger cubs, the Dibang Tiger Reserve was proposed, the northern boundary of which overlaps with the international border. Half of the Dibang Valley district (4,194 sq. kms) is already under state protection in the form of the Dibang Wildlife Sanctuary.[28] According to the Mishmi, this sanctuary was created without the people's consent, and this has been a point of contestation between the state's forest department and the local Mishmi. The sanctuary has a forest range office with just seven staff members[29] and two officers to manage it. Earlier, it was managed by a DFO who jointly handled the Mehao Wildlife Sanctuary and the Dibang Wildlife Sanctuary. From 2012 onwards, there has been a surge in activities in the name of tiger conservation in Dibang Valley (more about this in Chapter 6). Although the Mishmi showed mixed responses to the news of a proposed tiger reserve, they have common concerns about the environment. The anti-dam protests against the Dibang Multipurpose Project from 2007 till 2011 resulted in the political mobilization of the local Mishmi, while also raising their environmental consciousness. In 2008, the Mishmi blocked a road to prevent the National Hydro Power Corporation officials from entering the region and to resist dam-related activities. National and

[28] The sanctuary was created in 1998 vide no. CWL/D/42/92/744-844.

[29] This sanctuary was managed by the staff of the Mehao Wildlife Sanctuary. As such, there is no regular staff in the Dibang Wildlife Sanctuary, according to the managament plan. A full-time DFO was appointed in Dibang WLS, only in 2019.

global environmental NGOs and reporters covered this story (*Down to Earth*, 2008). Lately, the region is caught in the controversy surrounding the Etalin Hydropower Project, resulting in a national outcry to save Dibang through digital protests, social media agitations, and online petitions.

Similar to the early nineteenth-century explorers, contemporary scientific explorers visit these borderlands to survey, map, document, and describe the frontier landscape. These explorations have found meaning in the surging ecological studies carried out by both national and international scholars with the support of NGOs, research and conservation organizations. This has been driven in part by the inclusion of the region in the eastern Himalaya 'biodiversity hotspot' (Myers et al. 2000). A large number of public and civil-society organizations are currently engaged in supporting ecological and conservation activities in Arunachal. The Mishmi Hills are emerging as a new site for conservation with the efforts of NGOs to support conservation of wildlife but also to control traditional hunting practices and use of natural resources.

Geographic Information System (GIS), remote sensing technologies, and camera trap technology are being used by 'scientific experts' and 'state planners' to showcase the rich 'biodiversity', which often excludes the people but focuses on the dense vegetation cover and 'biological complexity' of the region (more on this in Chapter 6). These new actors from the scientific community seek help from the local Mishmi (who have the knowledge of the local wildlife and landscape) and use their services as porters and guides. Without the knowledge of the local Mishmi, NGOs and research groups would never be able to successfully carry out their research. Hunters are often sought after to record animal presence, bird sightings, and high-altitude lakes. Locally known hunters and young boys become key informants for researchers who look for potential sites to fix camera traps, identify animal footprints, and seek guidance to hike up mountains.

Hunters as 'Border Protectors'?

The India–China international border and the northern border of the Dibang Wildlife Sanctuary overlap, making this space ecologically and geopolitically crucial. Intelligence agents, military patrollers, wildlife biologists, and hunters are the only people to visit these borders.

Due to the difficult terrain, the absence of human habitation, and the weather conditions, these areas are rich in wildlife. Areas on this international border, such as Dibang, resemble the de-militarized zone (DMZ) between North and South Korea that hosts rich fauna and flora (Thomas 2009). The overlapping of militarized zones in areas of rich biodiversity makes these regions, what I call, 'value-added zones' that gain attention from the military, conservationists, and corporations alike. These frontier zones are recognized for their geopolitical signifi-cance, trans-boundary biodiversity richness, and cultural complexities, whose significance increases with the visits by powerful actors (the military, corporations, government establishments, conservation NGOs, and tour operators.). Unlike the DMZ, which has a concentration of soldiers in a small area and is patrolled heavily, Dibang borders are not mined and are, therefore, not dangerous. It is the climatic conditions and its rugged terrain that make this region inaccessible and impen-etrable for 'outsiders' and has, therefore, allowed the preservation of rich biodiversity.

As the state perceives these areas as 'wild', both the government and the NGOs have shown a growing interest in them. The Department of Environment and Forests submitted a proposal to the Government of India for converting this area into a tiger reserve.[30] This initiative is suspected by the local Mishmi to be a mechanism to prevent their access to the hunting grounds. Here, it may be recalled that the local hunters justify their hunting trips as also having a nationalistic purpose. Hunting trips, according to Mishmi hunters such as Apiya, are also a way to keep a check on Chinese intrusions into the Indian territory. I often heard him say, 'If we don't go to hunt, the Chinese will end up at our doorstep. Our going to the borders is also a way to check the Chinese intruders.' Mishmi hunters claim that they are protect-ing not only the nation's boundary but also the wildlife from Chinese hunters. 'The Chinese[31] hunt everything. They come with AK-47s and advanced weapons. They don't spare any animal or bird,' Apiya asserted, citing examples of how the Mishmi follow taboos, unlike the Chinese, so they do not hunt every animal that comes their way.

---

[30] F. no 15-12/2014-NTCA, dated 28 May 2014.

[31] When the Mishmi speak of the Chinese, it could be a local Chinese, Tibetan hunters, or the Chinese Army.

The absence of any permanent military presence at the international border allows the Mishmi to make these claims about both nation and nature. The proposal of a tiger reserve challenges both these claims of the Mishmi. It has added to the local people's concerns because it would curb their hunting practices and the possibility of a greater military presence would make their movement to the border more difficult. Increased surveillance and control of the local people is what the local Mishmi are concerned about. Under such a situation, a villager in Dambeun, the last village on the border, complained, 'Now the ITBP asks us to sign before going beyond the last check post at Dambeun to the wildlife sanctuary. If this place becomes a tiger reserve, the forest department will stop us from hunting. In addition to ITBP, the forest department too will impose such restrictions.'

During my fieldwork, I caught glimpses of the tussle for control over the area between the Mishmi and the government. In November 2013, a group of hikers from Mumbai visited the high-altitude lakes beyond Dambeun, which happens to be inside the sanctuary and technically requires a permission from the Range Forest Officer (RFO), which the group had not sought. The group had hired a Mishmi guide. While the group was up in the mountains hiking, the RFO issued a letter to the village council members, district authorities, and the ITBP.

The letter (Memo no: ASFR/estt/04/08/163-169 dated 13 Nov 2013) mentioned that anyone entering the sanctuary should get permission from the RFO (a Miju Mishmi from the neighbouring Lohit district; this was his first posting). This letter annoyed a number of villagers who questioned the authority of the RFO. The villagers feel that these mountains belong to them and that no permission should be required from anyone to hike up there. They also saw this move as a strategy of the forest department to gain control over their hunting practices. While the Mishmi had this concern, they were not bothered that the letter actually had authority in practice. The RFO was a new officer and a young man in his 20s. More importantly, he was from outside Dibang; all this made him vulnerable. After reading this letter, a villager reacted in a threatening tone, 'The RFO is just trying to show his power. What does he think of himself? *Dao dikhana padega*' (We need to show him a machete). The RFO left for Tezu (his hometown) the very next day after issuing this letter, suspecting some kind of backlash from the local Mishmi. One of the villagers told me, 'If we are earning some cash by working as tourist guides, why is the forest department setting hurdles. In fact, the forest department should encourage people to work as tour guides.' Ultimately no official action was taken by the forest department against the tourists. They completed their trek, but left earlier than they had planned to avoid any hassle. Such incidents irk the Mishmi and contribute to worsening their already strained relations with the forest department.

The Mishmi know that the Indian Army and the ITBP cannot do without their help and knowledge. A general sense prevails among these people that all activities inside the sanctuary will soon be monitored. The letters and signboards in Roing all indicate the forest department's eagerness to curb hunting. It is very likely that if the tiger reserve is set up, there will be a systematic disciplining of the hunters.

What the state considers illegitimate (illicit), the people could see as legitimate (licit). In the case of hunting, what the Mishmi hunters are doing is illegal because they defy the norms and rules of the forest department. But hunting is seen as a socially acceptable, and cultur-ally justified practice among the Mishmi. They consider this as 'licit', especially those who live in remote villages near the border, who go for musk-deer hunting or hunt to protect their crops and cattle. One wing of the state (the forest department) sees this as illegal, while the other wing (the army, ITBP, intelligence branches, and research teams) appropriates the very act of hunting to obtain intelligence about the Chinese as well as to gather information about wildlife.

India's Wildlife Protection Act, which prohibits the hunting of all wildlife animals, was passed in 1972 without any consideration regard-ing the people who live and depend on forest resources for their subsis-tence, especially those in rural areas. The government's lack of cultural sensitivity towards the 'tribals' of Northeast India made 'criminals' and 'poachers' overnight out of all those local people who hunted wildlife for subsistence, for trade, or for cultural reasons. People who appear as criminals in the official discourse may hold a different view of them-selves. What the state officials view as illegal may be considered well within the bounds of acceptable behaviour by the local communities (Van Schendel and Abraham 2005: 25). The distinction between legal and illegal revolves around opposed cultural meanings attributed to the activities in question (Van Schendel and Abraham 2005: 19).

The Mishmi become partners, collaborators, victims, beneficiaries, or even 'unlawful citizens' sometimes, depending on whether they aid or impede the activities of an agency at a given time. The state both condones and approves of hunting; the latter as a way to gain information regarding Chinese activity at the border. The Mishmi's knowledge of the area, their facial features, and their language make it more feasible for them to do this job than the staff of the army or the intelligence bureau, who are often from outside the state and do not look like the natives. They have only partial knowledge of the terrain. The risk is much higher for the state actors undertaking this job themselves than for the Mishmi, whose 'mongoloid' facial features help them with information gathering. Kiren Rijiju (minister of state for home, 2014–19), who is from Arunachal himself, suggested that the villagers near the Indo-Tibetan border could be trained to become informers: '[T]he government would like to train villagers along the 3,500 km Indo-Tibetan border to provide information about the suspicious activity' (Kiren Rijiju in Kaul 2014).

The Mishmi's trading trips to China in the past and their ethnic identity create some anxiety among the military agencies. The state is suspicious of not only the indigenous people but also the researchers who visit these regions. Even a lone researcher from outside Arunachal, like myself, is monitored. When I met a security official during one of my visits, he had already read some of my papers and was aware of my research. An ornithologist, now a faculty in the WII, studied birds along the borders of Arunachal. He was tracked back to Mysore, where he worked for a NGO in 2005–6, by government officials to verify his identity. An Indian PhD student registered in University College London, faced difficulties when the ITBP authorities questioned him about his work on camera traps, which he used to study tigers. He was viewed with deep suspicion, but the officials showed keen interest in his cameras, how they worked, their costs, how to procure them, and, more importantly, the location of the cameras. A security official posted in Anini was keen on these cameras for the purpose of surveillance and asked me about the nature of this equipment.

Commentary

The Mishmi take pride in their dual purpose in visiting the borders: for hunting and for patrolling. The former is an illegal activity according to the state, while the latter is seen as very much legal and is preferred by the local people as a livelihood option. After the 1962 war, the Government of India was very concerned about the loyalty of the people residing on the border as an 'uncertain factor' in the state–people relations (Singh 2010: 68). It was felt then that since the hill people shared ethnic and racial ties with the people across the border, there was every possibility that they might side with their 'neighbours' (Singh 2010), a concern that the British had in the early nineteenth century. Since the war, the region has entered a new 'development discourse' as a priority of the state agenda aimed at making Arunachal Pradesh a part of India's national space, as argued by the political thinker Sanjib Baruah (2003: 197–8). For the local people within and across the border, the agents of the state are both welcome and unwelcome, depending on who they are. Although the borders are politically constructed and are drawn arbitrarily on the maps, the situation on the ground for the local people on either side of the border is different from the perception of borders as lines of separation and territorial control. Local people see the presence of state actors as an opportunity—economic benefits to be gained through patrolling—and as a means of control, such as when the forest department bars tourists from entering the sanctuary without a written permission. During such tensions, the Mishmi stress that they are *Bharatwasi* (residents of India), but also remind the state authorities about their linkages with China by evoking the metaphor of salt; as potentially being 'loyal' to China as well. Such encounters may occur more frequently as the border regions, such as Dibang Valley, become 'cosmetically nationalized', to use Baruah's term, through roads, dam construction, and the establishment of protected areas. The border people often find different ways to engage with state actors. Similarly, authorities in each administrative office use the legal and political apparatus to find ways to engage with and control the local people for more effective administration.

5

MITHUN OUT AND TAKIN IN
Shifting Ecological Identities

'In most parts of India, it is the slaughtering of cows and consumption of pork that is known to create communal clashes but, strangely, here it is the sambar',[1] I was told by a forest officer in Roing soon after a riot broke out as a result of the killing of a sambar. In the winter of 2011, a group of Adi men, another indigenous group living in Roing, hunted a sambar, resulting in a riot. Though the hunting of wild animals is a widespread practice in Arunachal (Aiyadurai, Singh, and Milner-Gulland 2010), this was an exceptional case. These Adi men were caught red-handed hunting in the forests that were claimed by the Mishmi. This seemingly minor hunting incident exploded into an 'ethnic' riot among the locals (*Deccan Herald*, 2011). It is reported that members of the Adi students' union along with some villagers set fire to two villages (Ithili and Idili) inhabited by the Mishmi. Shops were destroyed, villages were ransacked, and the inhabitants were beaten up. It all began with an economic blockade imposed by the Adi students' union, which stated that their community's sentiments were hurt when a group of Adi men were apprehended during hunting in the community forests of the Mishmi. The stand-off between the Adi and the Mishmi over the hunting incident led to such a serious law-and-order

---

[1] Sambar (*Cercus unicolor*) is a deer species protected under the Indian Wildlife Protection Act. The sambar is hunted for meat, its skin is used for mats, and the skulls are mounted on the wall as sacred trophies.

problem that paramilitary and army personnel had to be called in to aid the police (*Deccan Herald*, 2011). The local administration issued a 'shoot-at-sight' order to the paramilitary forces to bring the situation under control.

The Mishmi and the Adi are both indigenous people of Arunachal and there have been tensions between the two for decades over forests, wildlife, and government jobs. The Adi are known to be politically and numerically stronger than the Mishmi in the Lower Dibang Valley district, which causes the Mishmi to feel that the Adi have been encroaching upon their lands and even their jobs.

Using this case of conflict between the Mishmi and the Adi over wildlife hunting, I will highlight the growing sense of awareness of wildlife protection in the region. I claim that there is a construction of a new 'ecological identity' among the Mishmi, which matches the conservationists' idea of nature conservation. I examine this identity within the context of this conflict as well as the increasing presence of conservation NGOs in the region. The construction of an 'ecological identity' among the Mishmi, I argue, is twofold. First, it is due to the growing influence of the global environmental discourse of biodiversity conservation in the region. Second, this ecological identity is also a result of the recurring local conflict and competition with the neighbouring Adi over forest resources. I contend that this new identity is biased towards 'wild' animals, which is clear from the way the urban Mishmi have redesigned the logo of their Literary and Cultural Society. The image of a domesticated animal that it carried before was replaced by that of a wild animal. This form of identity construction overlaps with the interests of biologists and conservationists who privilege the 'wild' form of natural heritage over its 'domesticated' or 'cultivated' version, which has always formed an important part of the way that the Mishmi imagined themselves.

Nature as an Object of Identity

Ecological identity, according to Thomashaw Mitchell, refers to all the different ways in which people construe themselves in relation to the Earth, as manifested in personality, values, actions, and a sense of self. This form of identity is peculiar in that a person's connection to the Earth and nature forms part of the individual's or a community's identity. Nature becomes an object of identification (1995: 3). This includes personal connections to the Earth, perceptions of ecosystems, and direct experiences of nature. Thomashaw argues that an ecological identity can re-frame a person's point of view, which in turn restructures values, reorganizes perceptions, and alters the individual's actions. For Thomashaw, identification is a core element within the process of developing an ecological identity. In this respect, when nature becomes an 'object' of our identification, we develop a feeling of affiliation or kinship with it. Clayton proposes an 'environmental identity', a similar concept, as a way in which people form their self-concept—a sense of connection to some part of the non-human natural environment (historical, emotional, or a belief that the environment is important to us and forms an important part of who we are) (2003: 46). This form of identity, like all other forms of identities, is strongly influenced by social factors. Individuals or groups view themselves as situated within social categories where there is an interplay of politics, activism, and social conflicts (Clayton and Opotow 2003: 10). Hall (1996) states that any question of identity involves the complex tasks of integrating subjective experiences, cultural assumptions, and ideological orientation. Different forms of identities are adopted from different positions (Hall 1991). Thomashaw, however, ignores the multiplicity of identities that people possess where different forms of identity take prominence at different times (Pomeroy 1995). Therefore, developing an ecological identity is a political activity because it changes the way we think, feel, and act with regard to our participation in society and in nature (Clayton and Opotow 2003).

One's cultural assumptions not only construct one's own identity but also the identity of the 'other' simultaneously. The construction of the other is a central concept in contemporary discourses on identity (Hall 1991). In this chapter I will show how the Mishmi construct themselves as the 'saviours' of wildlife, citing that their indigenous conservation taboos are better than those of their neighbours, who are 'not so strict' in their recognition of cultural taboos. In this way, the Mishmi paint their neighbours as the 'destroyers' of wildlife and identify them as the 'other'.[2] This form of identity construction helps

[2] A wildlife researcher who did his field work in Siang district, said that the Adi feel the same way about the Mishmi.

them gain popularity and credibility among the visiting NGO officials who work for wildlife conservation. Therefore, having an 'ecological identity' is political as it determines who is and who is not included in the formation of these identities and under what situations a particular identity is established. For example, particular environmental groups can influence or facilitate the development of an ecological identity. The influence of NGOs, in the case of the Mishmi, I argue, impacts the way they think of themselves with regard to wildlife conservation.

Conflicts over scarce resources such as land, water, and forests could generate certain identities linked to particular elements of nature. Environmental conflicts are essentially inter-group conflicts arising out of limited natural resources (Brosius, Tsing, and Zerner 2005; Baviskar 2008). During conflicts, identities are constructed and reconstructed (Coy and Woehrle 2000). For example, struggles over natural resources, according to Cederlof and Sivaramakrishnan (2007), sometimes take the shape of sub-national movements that work through regional pride, cultural affiliation, and tribal assertion. These movements link the cultural and political aspirations of the community using the rhetoric of nature worship, forest stewardship, and respect for forest and mountain landscapes, which Cederlof and Sivaramakrishnan call 'ecological nationalisms'. Features of such conflicts evoke the notions of 'authenticity' and physical attachment to a place, to nature, and to its historical memories. Communities symbolically and materially appropriate nature to increase their own political and economic control over others and over natural resources. I will discuss how the Mishmi living in the town of Roing use specific elements/symbols of nature in constructing an ecological identity.

The Mishmi living in remote villages, however, have different concerns, such as mithuns being killed by tigers and crop depredation by wild animals. The importance that the elite Mishmi attach to the 'wild and rare' form of nature is interesting and I will show why one particular wild animal was chosen as their icon, that is reflected in the new logo. First, I will examine the social and political factors through which the Mishmi are shaping their ecological identity and their use of animal symbolism in doing this. Second, I will reflect on how ideas of global conservation are influential at the local level, for a community which prioritizes the 'wild' over a 'domesticated' form of nature. Finally, I will show how the politics of animal symbolism shifts between 'wild to domesticated' and 'domesticated to wild' forms of nature.

Relations of the Mishmi with Their Neighbours

J. F. Needham, assistant political officer of the British administration, wrote in 1896, '[R]elations are now much strained between certain *Chulikattas*[3] and the *Bor Abor*s,[4] and I doubt if they will ever make real friends with one another again' (Needham 1896: 3). Mitchell (1883) reported that the Mishmi are always feuding with the 'Bor Abor'. Very scarce literature exists on Adi–Mishmi relations, but during my interviews with the Mishmi, the Adi were always spoken of with some contempt. A forest official who held the dual responsibility[5] of the Dibang Wildlife Sanctuary and the Mehao Wildlife Sanctuary till 2018 was an Adi and was reported to rarely visit Anini. While talking about wildlife conservation and the forest department, people would always, without fail, mention, 'He is an Adi, why would he bother about us?' The Adi are known to hold higher official positions in Roing and are far greater in number than the Mishmi. The Adi are also more educated and are known to have political clout. Most mid- and senior-level government job positions in Roing are occupied by the Adi. Thus, the Mishmi sometimes say that they feel threatened in their own land. Under these circumstances, land rights and hunting has become contentious issues in the region. Given this context of local conflicts with the neighbouring Adi, how do the Mishmi build their identity as ecological caretakers, specifically as the protectors of 'wild animals'?

[3] The Idus living in Dibang Valley were also known as *chulikattas*, which means cropped hair. The term comes from the characteristic haircut of the Idu Mishmi. This term is considered derogatory by the Idus and is not used these days. According to Hindu myth, Rukmini, wife of Lord Krishna, belonged to the community of Idus. Rukmini was carried away by Lord Krishna, which was followed by a conflict in which the Idus were defeated. They had to part with their hair, which earned them the name *chulikatta*.

[4] Bor Abor is another name for the Adi.

[5] A full-time divisional forest officer was appointed for the first time in 2019.

Caring for the 'Wild and Rare'?

The shift from hunting and gathering to agriculture is seen by archae-
ologists and anthropologists as a major change in human societies,
affecting not only livelihoods but also social relations and cosmological
ideas. The domestication of animals and plants is an important paradigm
shift in human history (Wilson 2007). The origin of farming is a 'neo-
lithic revolution', a term coined by Gordon Childe (1952), to represent
this radical shift from food collection to food production, which made
agriculturists and pastoralists different from hunter-gatherers or forag-
ers. This 'advent of agriculture' was seen as a sign of 'progress' as it was
thought to be the foundation for complex societies and a revolution for
the benefit of humanity (Childe 1952: 189). Thus, the domestication
of plants and animals has long been seen as a major human achieve-
ment (Cassidy and Mullin 2007) and a step closer to 'civilization'. A
marked difference between agriculturalists and hunter-gatherers is the
presence of domesticated animals and their use in economic and social
systems as objects of exchange and consumption (Bulliet 2005). Cows
and bulls were significant to ancient societies and were symbolically
important (Sharpes 2006). For example, for the Harappan civilization
of the Indus Valley back in the Bronze Age, the Zebu cattle was an
important enough cultural symbol to be represented in their impres-
sive seals.

While in the past, the ideas of domestication of animals and control
over nature was a paradigm shift that represented the rise of civilization, I argue that a new paradigm shift at present is the notion of
conserving 'wild and rare' animals. To care for rare animals such as
tigers, elephants, and pandas is seen as more 'progressive' than to care
for animals that can be farmed and domesticated, such as cattle and
horses. This seems to be the case in the field of biodiversity conservation where wild animals get more attention than domesticated animals.
In fact, overgrazing by domesticated animals in national parks is seen
as a 'cancerous disease' that can slowly deplete the forest resources
(Spillet 1966: 519).

Conservationists see domestication as interfering with nature
(Manning and Serpell 1994). Hence, domesticated animals are to be
exploited, whereas wild animals are to be studied and not exploited. In
this regard, being domesticated is to be second class, claims Clutton-
Brock (1994). Disregard for domesticated animals in 'wild' spaces

such as national parks leads park managers to actively eradicate these 'vermin' and 'pests'. This ambiguity of caring for the rare and eliminating undesired species is considered as 'violent-care of conservation' where, for example, critically endangered Hawaiian crows are cared for at the cost of trapping and killing feral pigs as part of conservation management (Dooren 2015: 9). Similarly, Franklin (2006) calls this 'species cleansing', where some groups of animals are eliminated to make space for some other preferred animals. In Australia, he shows that animals such as cats, brumbies, and rabbits are eliminated through a process of 'ritual purification' to make space for 'native' species such as kangaroos, wallabies, and koalas. In India, domesticated dogs and cattle are seen as a threat to wild animals and, therefore, seem fit for removal from the national parks. At a global and regional scale, there is a greater concern for animals that are likely to become extinct, which is showcased in wildlife campaigns. Is caring for endangered animals a new form of cultural practice that people are embracing? Moral duties towards wild and endangered species seem to provide a new way of thinking about life: that is, respect for rare life (Jamieson 2001). According to Jamieson, there is something about the rarity of an endangered species that heightens the element of respect for it. These species are believed to carry an important value, almost like a religious value (2001: 413). Highlighting the notion of rarity and respecting rare life is the philosophy of nature conservation movements and wildlife campaigns. Therefore, nature as 'dying' and nature as 'endangered' forms the popular narrative in science and in policymaking (Luke 1999). This form of nature, I claim, becomes a source of ecological identity among some groups, especially NGOs and activists, and such ideas are transferred on to the local indigenous people through awareness campaigns and conservation projects. In the case of the Mishmi, the story I want to relate here is how the motif of the IMCLS was changed from a mithun head, a domesticated cattle (Figure 5.1), to a takin head, a type of wild ungulate.

Among domesticated animals, mithun, 'the ceremonial ox', is the most prized and culturally valued animal among many indigenous people in Northeast India and Southeast Asia (Simoons and Simoons 1968). As discussed in Chapter 3, displays of mithun skulls can be found in Mishmi houses, especially those living in villages

Figure 5.1   IMCLS logo (top) and mithun (bottom)
Source: Author.

(Figure 5.2). Mithuns are considered 'living banks',[6] a form of social security required during medical or financial emergencies. In the region of Northeast India, mithun is a popular cultural symbol among many indigenous groups. Among the Nyishi, the Adi, the Naga, and many other groups, mithuns play an important role in sociocultural life (Simoons and Simoons 1968). The symbol of the mithun appears in the state emblem of Arunachal as well.

The 'Mishmi takin', on the other hand, is a wild animal found in Dibang Valley and in other parts of Arunachal. According to the International Union for Conservation of Nature and Natural Resources

[6] Described to me by a villager in Papum Pare (2013 survey of the Itanagar Wildlife Sanctuary).

Figure 5.2   Display of mithun skulls
Source: Author.

(IUCN),[7] it is categorized as 'vulnerable', indicating that their population is decreasing. The Indian Wildlife Protection Act (1972) places takin as a Schedule I species, at par with the tiger.[8] Locally called ākrū, takins are hunted regularly for meat and skin (Figure 5.3). Takin horns are mounted on the wall and their skins are used as mats. Takins appear in the mythological stories of the Mishmi but not as prominently as mithuns. I was curious about why mithun, a revered animal of the Mishmi, was replaced by a 'wild' ungulate called takin in the IMCLS logo.

[7] International Union for Conservation of Nature and Natural Resources (IUCN) is the world's oldest and largest global environmental organization, with almost 1,300 government and NGO members in 185 countries.

[8] The Act has a list of schedules of protected plant and animal species. Hunting or harvesting these species is outlawed. Species under Schedule I and II have absolute protection, and severe penalties are imposed on those who hunt them if convicted. Schedule III and IV species are also protected, but the penalties are much lower. Schedule V species may be hunted if declared as pest and dangerous by the officials.

Figure 5.3   Takin (left), a Mishmi hunter with takin (right)
Source: Sahil Nijhawan (left); illustrated by Gnana Selvam (right).

Mithun out and Takin in: Why?

'He may have been your teacher, but how can he write this in a national magazine?' Dr Roha replied agitatedly after I told him that the author of the article he was reading had been my teacher at WII. It was clear that he did not like the author's suggestion that takin might be renamed from Mishmi takin to Arunachal takin (Johnsingh 2013). The author of this article made this suggestion based on the geographic distribution of takin in others parts of Arunachal (Siang, Dibang Valley, Anjaw, Upper Subansiri); therefore, renaming this animal based on its geographical distribution seemed logical. The suggestion of renaming, however, irked some of the Mishmi.

In November 2013, I was invited to a dinner to celebrate the constitution of the new IMCLS committee in Roing. The IMCLS was set up in 1987 and is an apex body of the Idus whose objective is to preserve the indigenous art, language, and culture of the Idu Mishmi. Dr Roha was one of the new members. A medical doctor by profession, he is well read, with a great sense of wit and humour. He sat comfortably on the large bamboo sofa in a corner, quietly reading the article. Once he finishing reading, he commented, 'I don't agree with this.'[9] I leaned over the magazine to see what he was talking about. It was I who had shared Johnsingh's article (2013) with the society members. I thought it would interest them, especially since it was about their district and also carried names of some well-known Mishmi based in Roing.

---

[9] The discussion was in both Hindi and English.

Dr A. J. T. Johnsingh, a well-respected wildlife biologist in India, had visited Roing that year and the article was about that particular visit. He is often referred to as the 'father of Indian wildlife biology' and is also known to be the first Indian to have a PhD degree in wildlife biology (Johnsingh 1982). The article talks about the well-wooded Mishmi Hills, the takin habitat in Arunachal, and the poaching issues in Dibang Valley.

Dr Roha turned the discussion to takin as he expressed his disagreement with the article. 'What is that you do not agree with?' someone asked. He was quiet for some time and then started to read the article aloud for the others, slowly and clearly, word by word: 'Existing information indicates that outside the Mishmi Hills, takins are found in the districts of Tawang, East Kameng, Upper Subansiri, Siang Valley, and Changlang. In the light of this information on the animal's wide distribution in the region, it may even be called the Arunachal takin instead of the Mishmi takin' (Johnsingh 2013).

There was a lot of curiosity about who the writer was, but the last sentence in the article became the main point of discussion: 'it may even be called the Arunachal takin instead of the Mishmi takin.' What surprised me was that Dr Roha did not object to the fact that the article also talked about local poaching as a reason for the decrease in the takin population; rather it was the suggestion of renaming the animal that became the highlight of that evening's discussion.

I had almost forgotten about this discussion until I met Kati, another new member of the IMCLS in January 2014. Kati is a journalist, a young, smart, and active man who once was the face of the anti-dam movement in Dibang Valley. It was during my interview with Kati that I came to know that the new logo of IMCLS had takin instead of mithun in it, making me curious about this shift. Kati explained to me why takin was more important than mithun. According to Kati, 'Mithun is a ceremonial sacrificial animal and the logo makes us seem like carnivorous people and makes us look barbaric.' He added, '*Jo cheez ko hum khate hai, usko hum log* glorify *kar rahe hai?*' (Are we glorifying that what we eat?) He continued, 'Why not do the reverse? Why not put up something that reflects our good practice, conservation practice?' Kati has travelled widely within as well as outside India, attending conferences on indigenous peoples and environmental movements. He has acquaintances with NGOs, bird watchers, and conservationists. His reflections on takin, I assume, come from his associations with

NGOs and wildlife biologists. Kati and other IMCLS members were actively engaged in the designing of the logo during the months of November and December in 2013. The logo initially proposed had the images of the Mishmi wren-babbler (a bird), the Mishmi takin, and the Mishmi teeta (a plant). Note that all these species have Mishmi as a prefix (Table 5.1). Kati believes that highlighting these species reflects the Mishmi's care for wildlife. He said, 'By representing these species, we are trying to show the world that we have our high standard of civilization, it means we respect all living beings, especially wildlife.'

The Mishmi wren-babbler is a small rare bird, first reported in 1947 by Salim Ali and Dillon Ripley, and is known to be found only in the Mishmi Hills (Ali and Ripley 1948). The bird is famous among ornithologists because it was rediscovered in 2004 along the Mayodia Pass, around 56 kms from Roing (King and Donahue 2006).

A rough sketch of the proposed logo was uploaded by Kati on Facebook[10] to get feedback from others. The logo had the Mishmi takin, the Mishmi wren-babbler (bird), and two twigs of the Mishmi teeta on the sides, making the logo resemble the United Nations logo with the olive branches replaced by the Mishmi teeta leaves. One thing that Kati told me came as a revelation: species with the term 'Mishmi' attached to their name were selected to be part of the logo. He said, 'Highlighting these species will help highlight the name "Mishmi" as well.' That is when I noticed that a selective approach had been followed in choosing the species, and there appeared to be an attempt to highlight the name of their 'tribe'. He believes that these species gave an 'identity' to the Mishmi. A Mishmi student, Phidi Pulu, who studied design in IIT Bombay[11] created the new logo. The new logo has a takin head against snow-covered mountains (the Mishmi Hills) in the background. Two branches of the Mishmi teeta frame the logo. The Mishmi wren-babbler does not appear in the final version of the new logo.

[10] The Mishmi are very active on online forums. Facebook users are very active and vocal about local, national, and international issues. There is a Facebook page called 'Voice of Mishmi', where news reports and articles of common interest to the Mishmi community are posted. One of the posts was of my article on hunting and conservation which was commented on by Mishmi Facebook users.

[11] Indian Institute of Technology (IITs) are premier public engineering institutes located across India.

Table 5.1 Birds, mammals, and plants with the 'Mishmi' prefix

Mishmi names	Description	IUCN status	Remarks
Mishmi wren-babbler (*Spelaeornis badeigularis*)	Bird (also called rusty-throated wren-babbler)	Vulnerable	Known to be found only in the Mishmi Hills
Mishmi takin (*Budorcas taxicolor taxicolor*)	Mammal	Vulnerable	Found in the south-east of Tibet and in parts of Arunachal
Mishmi teeta (*Coptis teeta*)	Plant	Endangered	In India, it has only been recorded from the state of Arunachal (Mayodia Forest, Dibang Valley districts, Upper Siang, and Lohit district), also found in China
Mishmi Hills	Location	—	—
Mishmi	Language	Endangered	A language in the Tibeto-Burman family; it does not have a script

Source: Author.

Other considerations were kept in mind while designing the logo. Members of the IMCLS did not want the logo to resemble other logos, which appear, according to Kati, very intimidating, masculine, and militaristic. For example, the Adi Baane Kebang[12] logo has a headgear with a hornbill beak and two spears. Therefore, Kati said, 'For the Mishmi logo, we wanted to be humble and soft. We tried to be all encompassing.' I was curious to know why no people were represented in the logo. Kati replied, 'Our culture symbolizes wisdom, knowledge ... but where does the knowledge and wisdom come from? They come from the land, the rivers, and the nature.' Unlike the previous IMCLS committees that focused on assimilating Mishmi culture within mainstream Hinduism, the new committee is playing a revivalist role of bringing back 'pride' to the Mishmi society, focusing more on Mishmi culture, and developing the Mishmi society with a focus on nature conservation. Recently, a new beetle called the Mishmi beetle (*Lucanus mishmi*) has been discovered, and a picture of it was posted on a Mishmi person's Facebook page (see Appendix 5). Kati commented on the post: 'Another new name for Mishmi community—our identity connects us with our land, nature, forests, and rivers. So preserve our Mishmi identity.' Hence, the Mishmi keep highlighting that their identity is closely associated with nature and their land. Therefore, one reason for them changing the IMCLS logo is that the Mishmi takin symbolizes conservation and presumably has a higher value, while the mithun symbolizes slaughter, a certain kind of barbarism, and connection with bodily functions and has a lower value.

I wanted to know why the Hoolock gibbon[13] or the tiger was not chosen for the logo, as both are culturally very important. The Mishmi consider the Hoolock gibbon and the tiger sacred and there is a prohibition on the hunting of these animals. Kati was funny but strategic in his response, 'We are also suggesting that it should be called the "Mishmi Gibbon". We want the scientific community to write this as "Mishmi Gibbon".'

[12] Adi Baane Kebang is an organization that focuses on culture, tradition, and welfare of the Adi people. It is located in Pasighat, capital town of east Siang district, Arunachal Pradesh.

[13] Hoolock gibbon is the only ape found in India and an endangered animal. The Mishmi observe a strict taboo on hunting gibbons and this is evident in the number of gibbon calls one can hear around the Mishmi villages.

He laughed. That's when I realized that the word 'Mishmi' was attached to all the animals and birds chosen for the new logo. There was no mention of tigers, which they consider as their elder brothers (see Chapter 6). Despite an apparent concern with conservation values, the Mishmi had carefully selected the animals and birds with whose names they attached the term 'Mishmi', leaving out Hoolock gibbons, tigers, and bears which are also threatened, charismatic, and rare. Kati emphasized, 'Highlighting these species will also help highlight the word "Mishmi".' He reiterated this claim by asking rhetorically, 'Why do these animals have the name "Mishmi" attached to them, tell me? This has something to do with our people. Someone has given the credit of wildlife preservation to our community. Because of our Mishmi community, these species are surviving. If takins are also found elsewhere, why then is it called "Mishmi takin"?' This type of a selective approach is found not just among the Mishmi but also at the state level when the 'state animal' or the 'state bird' is chosen. Some animals and birds are nominated as state animals and birds, highlighting the politics behind animal symbolism.

'Racism' in Wildlife Conservation

A Range Forest Officer[14] in Roing had some advice for me when I told him that I plan to work with the Mishmi people for my research. He said, 'Try to work on a wildlife species, it will be beneficial for your career. If you say you are studying tigers, you will be taken seriously. If you work on smaller animals, nobody will take interest in your work. You see, there is "racism" in conservation!' He chuckled. This point about 'racism' lingered in my mind for quite some time. I could not forget what he had told me about this discrimination in wildlife conservation. The officer was concerned about how some animals got preferential treatment because of their status of rarity and endangerment. Even the protected areas were subject to discrimination, he said:

> Some protected areas are low profile so they don't get any attention from NGOs and the government. Mehao Wildlife Sanctuary's habitat ranges from 500 m to up to 4,000 m, covering pine forests. It is known more for birds. If Mehao had been a tiger reserve, this place would get

[14] The officer of Mehao Wildlife Sanctuary and stationed in Roing.

close to 2 crore rupees, and a range forest officer like me would be on his toes all the time. You would have to wait for at least a month to get an appointment with me. More money means more projects and more work. Even NGOs and conservation groups take interest in protected areas that are tiger reserves. Tigers get all the attention. There is some kind of racism and discrimination here. Other animals like gibbons and takins do not get funds, attraction, or publicity like the tigers. And what about the animals outside protected areas, are they not important? Are the animals inside protected areas more important than others? (Interview with the author, 9 January 2013)

The officer questioned the rationale behind discriminatory approaches in wildlife conservation. Except for the research of the PhD student from NERIST[15] and the work of the Wildlife Trust of India, no serious research has been conducted in the Mehao Wildlife Sanctuary,[16] even though it is more accessible than the Dibang Wildlife Sanctuary. Mehao mainly receives birdwatchers, photographers, and short-term visits by researchers, whereas the Dibang Wildlife Sanctuary has recently been a key site for NGOs, both national and international, and has received much attention from the government of India, despite its remoteness, precisely because tigers have been reported there.

When a student chooses to do research in wildlife ecology, it is very likely that she or he chooses to work inside a protected area, even though a substantial number of wildlife, especially large felids,[17] are found outside the protected areas (Ghosal et al. 2013). Protected areas are given more priority than areas that are not legally protected. Similarly, species listed in the Scheduled List of the Wildlife Protection Act or those in IUCN's protected area management list are the preferred animals for research. Rare and endangered animals receive the highest levels of funding, protection, and visibility for research, compared to those at the bottom of the list.

[15] North Eastern Regional Institute of Science and Technology, based in Itanagar.

[16] A new long-term project was launched by WII in Mehao Wildlife Sanctuary, in 2019. Currently there is a team stationed here for mammal surveys, mapping, and socio-economic surveys.

[17] Felidae is the family of cats. A member of this family is called a felid.

If researchers and scientists are selective in their choice of research 'animal' and topic, why shouldn't the Mishmi be selective in choosing what they want to project as their symbol of cultural and natural heritage? The Mishmi's logo can be compared with the national animals and birds that are chosen by countries and states to represent the identity of their area.

Nationalizing and Federalizing Wildlife

The ecological fantasy is part of the nationalist fantasy and vice versa.

—Hage (1998: 13)

The National Board for Wildlife in India declared the Asiatic lion as the national animal and the peacock as the national bird of India in the 1960s. In 1972, the tiger replaced the lion because of the wide distribution of tigers as opposed to lions, which are restricted only to the state of Gujarat. The board suggested that every state should identify a state animal, bird, tree, and flower to highlight the importance of that species and take conservation initiatives. Only the states with charismatic animals and animals of global importance took this directive seriously. Small unglamorous animals were considered 'plebeian' species by wildlife biologists and were not considered worthy of attention (Rehmani 2011).

This policy was part of the larger agenda to create awareness about wildlife. The latest to join the 'honour' of being a state species is the Blue Mormon (*Papilio polymnestor*), which was declared as Maharashtra's state butterfly in June 2015. This was the first instance of a state of India identifying a state butterfly (Rashid 2015). This is reportedly the second largest butterfly in India, which is probably the reason for declaring it as a state butterfly. The role of researchers, activists, and nature lovers in choosing state symbols also needs to be acknowledged. As we can see from the Table 5.2, only glamorous species become symbols and unglamorous animals do not get much attention. This points to the issue of 'racism' in wildlife conservation that the officer discussed. Assam is a good example to bring up, where the one-horned rhino was the focus of attention of the conservation actors. The state animal of Assam—the great one-horned rhino—received a lot of attention, funds, love, and care. This included the ambitious programme 'Indian Rhino Vision 2020',

Table 5.2   Status awarded to India's biodiversity

Status	Species
National animal	Tiger
National bird	Indian peacock
National flower	Lotus
National fruit	Mango
National river	Ganga
National tree	Indian banyan
National aquatic animal	River dolphin

Source: Author.

aimed at increasing the rhino population by the year 2020, to coun-
ter its decline because of poaching. The key initiatives of the rhino
programme include anti-poaching activities and the reintroduction
of rescued animals into the wild. While the focus has been on rhinos,
few know about the white-winged wood duck, the state bird of Assam.
The bird has not been as fortunate as the rhinoceros. However, it is
also endangered, and biologists believe that 'whatever small isolated
numbers are surviving are only by chance, not design' (Rehmani 2011:
155). This highlights the fact that offering a 'national' status to a species
is just another act of, what Rehmani (2014: 159) calls, 'symbolism *par
excellence*' indicating that these gestures need to be followed by concrete
actions on the ground.

The role of ecology in building nationalism and the importance of
the elements of nature in this regard is evident. Campaigns to 'save' the
planet choose to capitalize terms such as 'earth', 'biodiversity', 'nature',
and 'environment' in their promotional materials, similar to the nomi-
nation of animals to national and international status. These attempts,
Abram (1997) says, are overly facile because they lead us to imagine
that we are respecting this planet but we accord appropriate honour
only by capitalizing its name. The appointment of these animals as mute
ambassadors reflects eco-nationalism or eco-regionalism, a theme that
Adrian Franklin explored in detail with respect to Australia. According
to him, eco-nationalism is a specific blend of environmentalist and
patriotic sentiments (2006: 19). The attention on animals, especially
native animals, and the places to which they belong, helps inculcate
in people feelings of belonging to the land, their connection to their

motherland, their origins, and their histories. Therefore, preserving nature also becomes a particular form of nationalism. Rangarajan articulates the idea of 'ecological patriotism' providing the example of tigers in India (Rangarajan 2009). Around 1972, he writes, the Bengal tiger began to be referred to as the Indian tiger to link nationalistic emotions to the animal. Heritage is not only natural but also national and preserving it becomes a 'nationalistic enterprise' (2009: 303).

State Animal of Arunachal: Gibbon Replaces Mithun

In 2011, the state of Arunachal decided to replace the mithun with the Hoolock gibbon as the state animal. This created a controversy; the All Arunachal Pradesh Students' Union was upset and requested to review the decision of choosing the Hoolock gibbon as the state animal and to give the 'honour' back to the mithun. Hoolock gibbons are not culturally significant to all Arunachalis as gibbons are largely found only in the Mishmi Hills and adjacent regions. It has a limited presence, making it more culturally important for the Mishmi than for other indigenous groups. However, according to the Wildlife Protection Act of 1972, only an animal which is 'purely wild' or 'undomesticated' can be tagged as a state animal. For this reason the mithun could technically not be a state animal.

The change in the definition is due to the rising concern for biological conservation. Originally, however, the mithun was made the state animal because of its cultural significance. Unlike the Mishmi's decision to reject the mithun in the IMCLS logo, the students' union in Itanagar demanded the return of the mithun as the state animal. The Hoolock gibbon qualifies to be a state animal because it is listed under Schedule I, it is endangered and is protected by law, while the mithun is a domesticated animal and is not qualified to be a state animal anymore. In fact, a few years back, the state zoo in Itanagar removed mithuns from its premises.[18] At that time the Central Zoo Authority[19] had objected to the placing of domesticated animals in the zoo for public viewing. According to the Central Zoo Authority: Every zoo shall refrain from housing domestic animals and pets within the zoo premises and

[18] This is the same zoo to which the tiger cubs from Dibang were shifted.

[19] All zoos in India are regulated by an autonomous statutory body constituted by the Wildlife Protection Act, called the Central Zoo Authority.

adequate safeguards shall also be put in place to prevent the entry of domestic livestock, stray animals, and pets into the premises of the zoo (Central Zoo Authority 2009: 29).

Thus, the mithun was voted out, both at the state level and in the Mishmi Hills. Interestingly, the students' union (mostly Nyishi) had argued in favour of the mithun because of the cultural distinction attached to the animal in the region, whereas the Mishmi argued against the mithun precisely because of the cultural reasons (sacrificial rituals) that make them look 'barbaric'. While the mithun is culturally significant and economically valuable to the Mishmi, the takin, a wild ungulate, gains more prominence ecologically. In both the cases, what is interesting is that the local communities are playing an important role in negotiating how they wish to be represented.

Which animal gets to be protected and who decides, when, and how is a sociopolitical process. I have shown how the Mishmi decided to bring in the takin as a symbol of their cultural and ecological heritage. The Mishmi have also been skilful in choosing an animal that has 'Mishmi' attached to its name. The prefix gives them a claim over these animals, birds, and the landscape. People in Dibang Valley use the symbols of animals, birds, and other elements of nature, particularly the 'wild', to define their identity. Local communities align such views to the 'global ecological imagery' of the pure and the wild (Conklin and Graham 1995). The international ideology of wildlife conservation, the availability of funds, and the state of research on wildlife species decide which species get prioritized. In Dibang Valley, both global and local factors influenced the change in their ecological identity. But the reasons that motivated the Mishmi to choose the takin over the mithun would not be complete without giving some consideration to the local politics of resource use and hunting, especially with the neighbouring tribe, the Adi. Conflict with the Adi over issues of hunting in 2011 may have been a key event that prompted the Mishmi to seriously think about their identity in relation to conservation.

Local Conflict Over Hunting

According to the Adi people, it is their tradition to hunt, and they were hurt when they were apprehended for hunting a sambar (FIR dated 11 March 2011). Even fishing had triggered tensions in the region in the past. A Mishmi man shot two Adi men dead for fishing in their territory in 2007. The Adi men had been warned earlier not to fish in the Mishmi area, but repeated attempts by them to fish led to heated arguments, eventually resulting in open fire. It was a long legal case and the victims' families were finally compensated. There was another incident a few years ago when Adi men from Kakung village were seen hunting in Koronu, a Mishmi village. Their hunting came to light when one of them shot his partner, mistaking him for an animal. The Adi men reportedly threatened Mishmi villagers not to file a police report. Another incident occurred when a high-level government official from the neighbouring Siang district was seen hunting in Koronu village. He was apprehended by the Mishmi and was handed over to the police. However, despite hunting being illegal, the case was not registered, angering the Mishmi. These cases point to the helplessness of the Mishmi in opposing the Adi, who seem to dominate the local bureaucracy. This helplessness is also expressed in the popular opinion that the Adi hunt all kinds of birds and animals, while the Mishmi exercise some restraint in hunting due to their taboos. The frequently heard comment about the Adi forests is: '*Wahan to ek chidiya bhi nahi milega*' (You won't find even a single bird in their forests).

> Look at their forests, animals are very rare, they all have been hunted down. Here in the Mishmi Hills, there are several animals. The proof is that there are even tigers here. ... Lots of NGOs are interested because there are many endangered species in the Mishmi Hills. We don't kill Hoolock gibbons, we don't even touch them, but look at the Adi, they hunt Hoolocks for skins and also eat them. According to the Mishmi belief, if you live by hunting, then you have to pay back with your life.[20] (Interview with a Mishmi residing in Roing)

According to the Mishmi, therefore, wildlife is still preserved in their forests because of the taboos they observe. Under such circumstances, the Mishmi display their pride by showcasing the biodiversity in their forests. The Mishmi use their cultural knowledge to gain recognition

[20] Hunting of Hoolock gibbons is a grave sin according to the Mishmi. Unlike the ritual (*tamamma*) that one can perform after killing the tiger, no such ritual exists to repent for the killing of the Hoolock gibbon. The Mishmi believe that one who kills a Hoolock gibbon is destined to die an unnatural death and, therefore, has to pay back with their life.

for their rich biodiversity and are building this image to also symbolically compete with the Adi. By 'othering' the Adi people, the Mishmi
project themselves as the caretakers of the 'wild'. The Mishmi also
want to show that they are not a 'barbaric' community who slaughter
cattle during rituals and want to break away from the stereotype that
their 'tribe' is 'primitive' and 'violent'.

Studies have shown the importance of a community's educated
elites in competing for state resources and political power through
which they gain advantages and draw benefits (Phadnis 1989; Hornborg
and Kurkiala 1998). The construction of this new ecological identity
focused primarily on conservation is largely the work of the Mishmi
in the town of Roing. In the remote Mishmi villages of Anini, people
do not care much about whether the animals are endangered or not.
The Mishmi living in towns are more savvy and capable of articulating
their ecology-based identity by establishing linkages with international
researchers, NGOs, and wildlife researchers. The use of online social
media has contributed to the construction and sharing of this identity. The Mishmi in Roing, at large, have better access to the internet
than the people in Anini and other remote Mishmi villages. The rise of
Hinduism in the region also contributes to the way the Mishmi perceive the animal sacrificial rites.

Influence of 'Hinduism'

The increasing presence of mainstream Hindu religious groups in
the region and their influence on the local cultural beliefs cannot be
ignored. Roing now has numerous Hindu temples built by people who
have come from mainland India. The mainlanders, largely Hindu caste
groups, look down on the Mishmi and other 'tribal' groups. There is a
subtle undercurrent of their influence on the Mishmi, some of whom
are abandoning rituals involving slaughter. This has even resulted in a
few becoming vegetarians. Some Mishmi members who now follow
the Brahma Kumaris[21] have given up meat, fish, and even eggs.

---

[21] The Brahma Kumaris are a new social movement that teaches a form of
meditation that focuses on the soul. Their activities promote respect for all faiths
and meditation through social service activities. This movement has its headquarters in Rajasthan and have offices and members present in Roing and Anini.

During my fieldwork, I met a lady from Bangalore, a member of Art of Living (AoL),[22] who had come to Roing to teach yoga and spirituality to the local Mishmi students. Members of the AoL and the Brahma Kumaris carry out programmes with school children, and I have heard them preaching their views on food habits. Such groups often promote vegetarianism, indicating that beef eating is a crime and a sin. The lady from AoL told the Mishmi teachers and students who came to learn yoga to give up onion, garlic, tea/coffee, alcohol, and, of course, meat! These initiatives gel well with the aims of some sections of the Mishmi society who are attempting to merge the animistic Mishmi beliefs with Hinduism.

There is a temple in Roing which has images of both Hindu and Mishmi deities, named 'Adiju-Shiv Mandir' (Figure 5.4). 'Mandir' is a Hindi word for temple. 'Adiju' is the name of a spirit in Mishmi

Figure 5.4   A Shiv temple in Roing with both Hindu and Mishmi deities painted on the walls
Source: Author.

[22] Art of Living is a volunteer-based educational NGO. Its programmes claim to combine the mystical and the modern to help create a life of purpose, joy, and confidence. It has its headquarters in Bangalore.

mythology. Similarly, there is a temple in Hayuliong (Anjaw) called 'Mishmi-Ram Mandir'. Such hybridization may lead to a gradual fusion of animism and Hinduism, marginalizing or undermining the Mishmi way of life. Socio-spiritual groups have increasingly been seen preaching in the remote areas of Arunachal, reproducing the perception of the Mishmi's cultural practices as primitive, uncivilized, wild, and *junglee*,[23] and insisting on the need to reform such practices. Hinduism, therefore, may also have influenced their decision to give up the mithun as a symbol of their cultural and ecological identity, in addition to the influence of global conservation. While the Mishmi take pride in 'being tribal' and in their indigenous conservation taboos, they also resist having their culture labelled as 'barbaric'. In this resistance, therefore, some of them are abandoning eating animal meat and inculcating dominant Hindu practices.

Community-based organizations are also working as part of development initiatives to promote Mishmi cultural heritage. One such group is the Research Institute of the World's Ancient Traditions and Cultures (RIWATCH) in Khinjili. It is a non-profit, non-governmental, community-based research organization in Lower Dibang Valley. Its aim is to empower ethnic communities and strengthen their value systems. The key person behind establishing RIWATCH was earlier affiliated with the Vivekananda Kendra and is a mainlander who was allied with a national cultural outfit. The museum set up by RIWATCH displays drawings of Hindu gods and goddesses along with the artefacts of the Idu Mishmi and shamans. There seems to be an an attempt here to showcase indigenous peoples as integrated into the nation as 'global Hindu subject[s]' (Choksi 2019). This is not unique to this region. Elsewhere in the state, the project of 'Hinduization' by Hindu cultural outfits such as RSS has been highlighted (see Sethi 2014).

While the role of cultural groups affiliated with Hinduism is recent, there has been an active presence of Christian missionaries in Roing for at least three decades now. There are close to five–six churches (Catholic, Protestant, Little Folks, and so on). The formal institutional way of Christianity is different from the informal influence of Hinduism. The common saying here is 'Christian *darwaja se aata hai aur Hindu khidki*

---

[23] *Junglee* is a Hindi word derived from *jangal* (woods, forest), also applied in a derogatory way to 'tribals' or 'forest-dwelling' people.

se aata hai hamare ghar mein', meaning 'The Christian enters through the door, while the Hindu uses the window to enter our homes'. There is a concern about both the groups among the Idu Mishmi. While both the religious forces could be seen as problematic, Christians do not seem to preach to the Mishmi about their eating habits or about their animal sacrificing rituals. Both continue to spread beyond the towns. Not much has been researched on this matter.

Commentary

In Roing, both global and local factors help in shaping the ecological identity of the Mishmi. I go back to where I started in this chapter. The local politics surrounding resource use and hunting cannot be ignored, especially with the neighbouring Adi. The conflict with the Adi in 2011 over issues of hunting was a crucial incident that, along with other factors such as the influence of Hindu belief groups, is contributing to the construction of an ecological identity of the Mishmi. The Mishmi often claim that their indigenous taboos on hunting are better and more strict than the Adi's, and therefore, the Mishmi contribute more to the preservation of local wildlife. Under such circumstances, natural and cultural heritage serves as soft power for partnering with conservation NGOs and for distinguishing themselves from the Adi group. The Mishmi's claims on local wildlife and their indigenous taboos relating to its conservation become a sort of 'cultural capital' (Bourdieu 1986). Conklin and Graham (1995) state that indigenous groups value their role as environmental stewards, providing a common transnational currency of meanings to link with NGOs.

Establishing the identity of a community is key to the articulation of its claims. Karlsson (2000) argues that it is only when a community creates an identity, when it can be named and recognized, can it engage in political activities such as exercising claims to their ancestral lands. Using the elements of nature, these claims take the form of 'ecological nationalism', especially when the claims are over natural resources associated with regional pride, cultural affiliation, and tribal assertion (Cederlof and Sivaramakrishnan 2007). Tribal assertion, in places where middle-class activism is lacking, takes the form of minority identity politics (Baviskar 2003). The Mishmi's identity politics uses the notions of cultural value, physical attachment to the place, and historical memories.

Karlsson maintains that a community's self-reflexivity is the focal point that shapes and reshapes the identity of a population. Identity is fluid, not a monolithic construct. Identities change based on different circumstances and get constructed, reconstructed, and articulated (Li 2000). The level of consciousness is central to the processes of construction. From his study among the Rabhas, Karlsson claims 'cultural identity as partly a conscious construct, thus not inborn or primordial' (2000: 239), which is also reflected in the case of the Mishmi. Choosing to include or exclude symbols of nature was a deliberate attempt to project the 'wild' as preferable, especially in the case of a 'wild' animal that has regional and international support. It is ironic that the Mishmi reject 'wild' when it is used to refer to them but prefer it in the context of animals, birds, and landscape. The IMCLS's logo therefore reflects a 'Western understanding' of nature that excludes people and cultural elements.

Through the images of wild and endangered species, the Mishmi challenge the way they are perceived by mainlanders (as 'primitive', 'barbaric', and 'wild'). The aim is also to project themselves as a responsible community that cares about animals, such as the takin, and as compassionate, loving, and not dangerous or warrior-like, in contrast to the other tribes. These self-reflexive ways of thinking about and projecting themselves is also a conscious effort to reach out to national and global environmental NGOs in the region and benefit from the opportunities and resources that they might bring in.

Local communities often mobilize or adopt the elements of transnational environmental discourse, which helps them become 'highly visible players' (Brosius 1999: 279). Local people use the ideas of Western conservation to strengthen their own views on the subject and to form alliances with NGOs. As politically savvy actors, local people make use of all opportunities and natural resources being available to them through these partnerships. This is similar to the views of the Amazonian Indians regarding nature and the ways of using natural resources are consistent with the principles of Western conservationists (Conklin and Graham 1995).

The Mishmi claim a cultural and ecological superiority over their neighbouring tribes who are politically and numerically stronger. While movements in general are associated with gaining political power (as conventionally defined), environmentalism and other new movements are also engaged in cultural politics (Melucci 1980). Brosius emphasizes that such groups, while asserting local concerns, constantly make references to global discourses and are increasingly brought into contact with transnational funding agencies and networks (1999: 281). Such strategies could be one of the multiple routes to transformation and empowerment (Baviskar 1995: 45). In order to be heard, Stuart Hall argues, people on the margins find 'some ground, some place, some position on which to stand' (Hall 1991: 52). In the case of the Mishmi, the position they take is to be heard as the supporters of wildlife conservation. This position may or may not be stable and can change with issues, depending on the global environmental discourse. In another incidence, the Mishmi highlighted the importance of tigers in their mythology and the credit they claimed for tiger conservation as a tool to question the government's plans for the proposed Dibang Tiger Reserve (Chapter 6). Identity, thus, is not static but evolves constantly to suit new opportunities. These environmental imperatives, one should bear in mind, are deployed with respect to claims about local authenticity, national sovereignty, or global significance (Brosius 1999). For the Mishmi, the focus on wild animals is a form of cultural capital which they use to construct their 'ecological identity', to make claims on resources, and also to network with NGOs. Through discussions and local meetings, the Mishmi are trying to popularize the word 'Mishmi' and bring it into the spotlight. A dual identity is being constructed: one is the 'ecological' image, that is, projecting themselves as the caretakers of wild animals, while the other is their ethnic identity, which they wish to promote in the region by endorsing the local natural elements with the term 'Mishmi'. There is a multipurpose advantage for the Mishmi in using 'nature conservation' and a specific form of 'nature' to gain political, ecological, and social recognition in times of a global environmental crisis.

In 2019, I met a member of the Idu society who could potentially become the next president of the IMCLS. He read the draft of this chapter and commented, 'All this is fine but we plan to change the motif back to mithun.'

6

TIGER CONSERVATION AND ITS PREDICAMENTS

We and the beasts are kin.

—Seton (1966: 12)

Apiya Angeche was very vocal about the forest department's role in Dibang Valley, especially with regard to the issues of tigers and the wildlife sanctuary. His question was straight: 'Why have a tiger reserve here? We don't hunt tigers, they are our brothers! Tigers and humans were born to the same mother. We kill tigers only as a last option, when they become a threat or when they are killed in traps accidentally. We are protecting them anyway.'

Anyone visiting the Mishmi Hills and interested in wildlife and conservation cannot fail to come across the mythological story of the Mishmi and tigers as brothers. Such narratives of tigers as siblings are popular in other parts of Arunachal Pradesh as well (Aisher 2005; Aiyadurai 2007). For the Mishmi, the tiger (āmrā) is their elder brother. The tiger is the most revered and feared animal, and killing it is prohibited. In fact, it is viewed as 'homicide'.

This chapter highlights the kinship relation of the Mishmi with tigers and how this relation contests the claims of the state and science on the landscape and wildlife of this region. I aim to examine how the Mishmi react when the state demands more land for tiger protection or when NGOs meet the villagers to discuss their plans for a survey on tigers; how do such interactions play out? Through these narratives

I explain how the Mishmi relate to tigers and the role of the state and of science in tiger conservation and how the Mishmi's conception of 'nature' stands in contrast with the way the state and science perceive tigers and their conservation. The focus of this chapter is on the Mishmi's indigenous ideas about tigers and the way they utilize their cultural knowledge during meetings with conservationists to question the activities of tiger researchers. When conservationists and the local villagers meet, how do these actors negotiate their positions in making claims over nature?

As related in Chapter 1, social attitudes towards and the relationships shared with animals are complex, diverse, and multifaceted (Morris 1998). Among several indigenous communities, there is no radical distinction between humans and animals, and people have feelings of friendship and empathy towards animals. Animals are believed to be under the control of the guardian spirits of the forest. The relationship of these communities with nature changed drastically with the shift in their socio-economic situation and nature came to be seen as a commodity. Scientific conservation, Ingold (1994: 11) argues, is rooted in the assumption that humans control the natural world. Conservation's primary mode of function is to set aside areas of wilderness and to restrict or ban all human intervention in those areas.

In 2004, the extinction of tigers in the Sariska Tiger Reserve (Rajasthan, India) shocked the nation and the conservation community. It came as a wake-up call for the Government of India. In response, the National Tiger Conservation Authority (NTCA)[1] and the Wildlife Crime Control Bureau were set up (MoEF n.d.), who initiated a country-level tiger population estimation that would take place every four years. Young researchers and biologists from across India were recruited and trained by the prestigious WII to survey tiger habitats and estimate the population of the tigers and assess their prey. According to the latest census (2018), there are 2,967 tigers in India, a 30 per cent increase from the previous censuses of 2010 and 2006 when the count was

---

[1] NTCA is a statutory authority under the Ministry of Environment and Forests and Climate Change, Government of India. One of the objectives of NTCA is to conduct research and monitoring of tigers, co-predators, and their prey and habitats.

at 1,706 and 1,411 respectively (Jhala, Qureshi, and Gopal 2019). In Dibang Valley, no census of the wildlife was undertaken till 2018, but surveys on tigers had begun there from 2013 onwards, following the tiger cubs' rescue. Surveys included preliminary camera trap exercises, scat collection, examination of tiger habitats, and the status of their prey (Gopi, Qureshi, and Jhala 2014). The enthusiasm over the rescue of the two tiger cubs in Dibang Valley and subsequent plans to reconstitute the Dibang Wildlife Sanctuary as the Dibang Tiger Reserve have to be seen in this light.

When the tiger cubs were rescued in December 2012, much attention began to be paid to the Dibang Wildlife Sanctuary. In January 2014, there was a camera trapping of an adult tiger, which set in motion the idea of converting the sanctuary into a tiger reserve. Given its limited budget and field staff, its not feasible for the existing Dibang Wildlife Sanctuary to protect tigers and their habitat. Creating a tiger reserve would mean more funding, setting up of a tiger task force,[2] and the employment of local youth as field guards.

In 2013, the government of Arunachal Pradesh issued a circular (Memo no. ASFD/DWLS/ESZ/167-196, dated 19 February 2013) to the village councils of Dibang Valley to initiate the constitution of an ESZ[3] around the Dibang Wildlife Sanctuary, which meant that some areas surrounding the sanctuary would be acquired for wildlife conservation. Other than this circular, no other formal communication took place between the forest officials and the local residents of Dibang Valley, triggering concerns especially among those living close to the border of the sanctuary. Whilst there is no habitation inside the sanctuary, it is surrounded by hunting and fishing grounds and ancestral and

---

[2] To review the management of the tiger reserves in India, the Ministry of Environment and Forests set up the task force vide notification no. 6(4)/2005-PT in 2005. Also, following the loss of tigers from the protected reserve of Sariska in Rajasthan, the NTCA has sanctioned special tiger protection forces in tiger reserves, with the provision of 112 posts (9 forest guards and 18 foresters, with the requirement that around 30 per cent of the forest guards should be recruited from the local youth).

[3] Eco-sensitive zones (ESZs) are delineated areas around the existing protected areas declared as 'buffers and corridors' to check the impact of industrialization and unplanned development in and around the protected areas.

'sacred' lands[4] of the Mishmi. While information at the local level was far from clear, online newspapers and NGO websites carried the news of the tiger cubs' rescue, highlighting the importance of this region as a potential tiger reserve. Newspapers carried pictures and stories of the successful rescue of the cubs (*The Indian Express*, 13 October 2013). All the while, the villagers continued to face economic loss from wild animals' attacks on their cattle with no relief or support from the forest department. As researchers and NGOs continued to arrive for research on tigers, the villagers grew perplexed by this sudden interest in the tigers of the region. The news of the proposed tiger reserve had not reached the people yet, but the possibility of changing the nomenclature from 'Dibang Wildlife Sanctuary' to 'Dibang Tiger Reserve' was all over the internet and the newspapers, marking this as an important site for conservation. However, the much needed discussion with the people on the ground was yet to occur.

When the state asks for more land for tiger conservation and when NGOs meet the villagers to tell them about their plans to map tiger habitats, how do the Mishmi react? Such encounters have the 'messy and surprising feature' of global interactions that result in awkward, unequal, and unstable interconnections across difference, thereby producing 'friction' (Tsing 2005: 4). The tense, contradictory claims and counterclaims over tigers create spaces of 'discomfort' and, in some contexts, 'resistance to green development' (McAfee 1999a: 148). This valley has seen people's movements against dams, but the current discussions and debates revolve around the issues of tigers and the establishment of the proposed tiger reserve.

[4] One such area is Athu-Popu, which is considered as a sacred site by the Idu Mishmi. It is believed that this is one of the places that the departed souls take rest on their journey to the 'other' world, towards eternity. The site is attached to a story of the Igu Sinerwu, who grieved on receiving the news of his mother's death. It is believed that his tears left a mark on a huge rock, which still stands at the site. The Idu Mishmi have held expeditions to this site. Those who have visited the site speak of a wild paddy field near Athu-Popu, believed to be cultivated by the departed souls. Athu-Popu is at an altitude of about 3,500 metres above sea level, is situated at Kayala Pass, close to the Indo-China border, and is approximately 120 kms from Malinye, one of the administrative circles of Dibang Valley.

Tigers Are Our Brothers

Indigenous responsibilities to and for the natural world are based on an understanding of the relatedness or affiliation, of the human and non-human worlds.

—Jamieson (2001: 4)

The story of tigers as brothers can be heard commonly from the people of the Mishmi Hills. According to Mishmi mythology, the Mishmi and tigers were born to the same mother and were siblings; the tiger was the elder brother, and the human, the Mishmi, the younger brother. This myth and the taboo against hunting tigers was told to me by an *īgù* :

One day, a younger brother hunted a deer and left it with his elder brother before going into the jungle to collect firewood. On his return, he was terrified to see his brother eating the meat raw. He told his mother that his elder brother was a tiger. 'If he can eat the raw meat, then one day he will eat me too,' he said. This became a serious concern.

A plan was made by their mother to have a competition between the two brothers. The one who crossed the river and reached the other side of the bank first would kill the other. The tiger decided to swim across the river, whereas the Mishmi took the bridge. The tiger was the first to reach the bank. When the tiger was about to come out of the river, however, the mother threw an ant's nest at the tiger's body to prevent him from winning. To get rid of the ants, the tiger went back into the river and scratched itself against a rock. The Mishmi, meanwhile, reached the bank and shot the tiger with an arrow. Thus, the tiger died and its body floated in the river. It was swept away to a far off place. After several years, a bird saw the bones of the tiger scattered on the riverside. The bones were white and bright under the sunlight. The bird thought them to be eggs and sat on them to incubate. It is believed that the large bones transformed back into a tiger. From the tiny bones emerged a leopard, a leopard cat, a clouded leopard, and civet cats. This is the story of the tiger being born again. Therefore, tigers cannot be killed.

According to the Mishmi, tigers can only be killed or trapped when there is a loss of property or for personal safety. If a tiger is killed, an elaborate ritual (*tamamma*) is conducted over five days, with restrictions on both the family members of the one who killed the tiger, as well as on the villagers as a whole. There are five clans (Meme, Umpo,

Mena, Misichi, and Misiwu) of the Idu Mishmi who are exempted from performing this ritual.

According to Morris (2004), treating animals as persons sets up a relational epistemology towards the animal kingdom and other 'natural' beings. In the case of the Mishmi, there is a kinship relation that the Mishmi share with tigers. Morris also argues that we need to distinguish carefully between social practices and cultural representations. If a tiger is killed or trapped accidentally, a senior īgù is invited to carry out the required ritual (*tamamma*), which involves a huge expenditure because it is equivalent to the funerary ritual conducted for humans. During this elaborate ritual carried out over five days, strict taboos (*èná*) are observed not only by the person who killed the tiger but also by the entire village. Every *igu* owns a belt (*āmrā la*) made of linearly arranged tiger canines, through which he receives power (Figure 6.1). This belt is a necessary ritual item for īgù while performing a funeral or any other important ritual, such

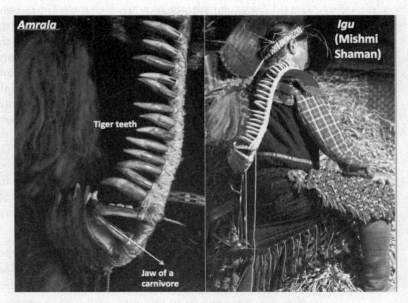

Figure 6.1   A shaman (*īgù*) and the tiger-teeth belt (*āmrā la*)
Source: Author.

as *amrase*[5] or Reh.[6] To prevent attacks by spirits (*khēnyū*) and to awaken the spirit of the tiger, the *īgù* wears these tiger-tooth belts. The teeth are collected by an *īgù* when he is invited to perform the ritual. The belts are transfered to junior *īgù*. It is difficult to gauge the age of these belts.

Like tigers, Eastern hoolock gibbons (*Hoolock leuconedys*; or *àmē pá* in the local language) also enjoy the status of religious protection among the Mishmi.[7] Due to a sibling relationship with them (Sarma, Krishna, and Kumar 2014), the Mishmi are careful not to harm these animals in any way. While killing animals such as tigers and gibbons is perceived to be equivalent to homicide, other animals such as takin (*Budorcas taxicolor*), musk deer (*Moschus chrysogaster*), Asiatic black bear (*Ursus thibetanus*), wild pig (*Sus scrofa*), Serow (*Capricornis sumatraensis*), Malayan giant squirrel (*Ratufa bicolor*), Temminck's tragopan (*Tragopan temminckii*), Kalij pheasant (*Lophura leucomelanos*), and Blyth's tragopan (*Tragopan blythii*) are frequently hunted. The use of these animals is diverse and widespread: their meat is used as food and their skins as bags and mats. Animal skulls are used as sacred objects to be mounted on skull boards. However, as Morris suggests across his works, human relationships with animals are never monolithic. In the case of the Mishmi, attitudes towards animals are complex, ranging from complete protection (for example, of tigers and Hoolock gibbons) to restricted hunting (of ungulates and bears). Morris's discussion (1998, 2000) of the types of 'person' is useful here. Different kinds of animals are treated differently depending on the degree of their personhood. Some animals are completely protected as other human beings, while others are seen as non-human animals with moral agency and consciousness. Along the same lines, Tsing argues for a 'more-than-human sociality', through which she advises scholars to explore 'multispecies landscapes' and the dynamic relations between

---

[5] A healing ritual, usually carried out for a day.

[6] Reh is one of the most important festivals of the Mishmi for the propitiation of the supreme creator, the Nanyi Inyitaya. Many believe that Nanyi Inyitaya is part of the new form of institutionalized religion among the Idu Mishmi.

[7] The Adi community, who also inhabit the lower Dibang Valley, do not observe any taboos against hunting Hoolock gibbons.

different species—webs of relations that extend well beyond 'individual enrollment for human tools' (2013: 36).

There is a sense of responsibility attached to the animals, and the taboos (*èná*) observed during hunting and trapping make hunting (*ìrhùnyì*) a serious activity. Rituals are part of the journey and follow a complex set of taboos. The 'moral code' observed by hunters during these trips, such as getting angry, abusing or cursing someone, and cracking jokes is to respect the fact that they are in someone's territory and that it is important to watch one's behaviour. One such rule is to use unique code words for animals during hunting. For example, *ālā* (musk deer) is called *tambe aaroku-chi*, which means 'meat of the high mountains'. These code names for animals also reflect the hunter's rich knowledge of the habitat and the types of forest in which animals are found.

Uttering the incorrect names is believed to have a negative effect on hunters, which could manifest in the form of a sudden illness, an accident, or even by losing one's way back to the village. Therefore, these names are important for hunters to remember. Hunters have the obligation to make a 'symbolic payment' in the form of meat and metal[8] to *ngōlō*, the most feared and respected spirit of the mountains. Therefore, when a hunt is successful, an offering has to be made. A small chunk from the ear of the dead animal is cut with a machete, followed by a prayer. Among all the other spirits, *ngōlō* is the most important, especially, for those who venture into high mountains. Mishaps in Mishmi's lives, especially, of hunters are directly attributed to *ngōlō*.

Several spirits (*khēnyū*) are also believed to reside in the farms, houses, rivers and forests, to help in providing enough farm yield, safety, good health, and wealth to the Mishmi. People follow proper conduct and behaviour to have continuous support of these spirits and achieve success in farming and hunting. If they are unable to satisfy these spirits, they believe that their harvests and hunts may fail. In some societies, forests are seen as ancestors (parents) who unconditionally provide food in a 'giving environment' (Bird-David 1990). For example, among the Nayaka of southern India, Bird-David (1990) describes, forests are viewed as parents, in relation to whom the Nayaka themselves are the

---

[8] Hunters always carry a piece of metal, usually brass, or even the bottom of a cartridge to perform this ritual.

children. The spirits that inhabit the hills, rivers, and forests are referred to as *dod appa* (big father) and *dod awa* (big mother). This 'giving environment' contrasts with the 'reciprocating environment' where provision of food is conditional upon proper conduct. Morris, however, feels that it is misleading to interpret the forest only as a parent or constituting a 'giving environment' (2014: 227), reducing the complexity of human–environment relations to a single metaphor. Among the Mishmi, a reciprocal relation with the spirits exists, specially during hunting, farming, or slaughtering of domestic cattle. The relationship, especially between humans and the natural world is acknowledged through rules and regulations, often underpinned by feelings of fear and respect, and through exchanges permeated by feelings of gratitude and regret (Morris 2000: 21). While hunting is viewed as a serious activity, it is also an important empirical and pragmatic activity for subsistence, trade, and the protection of humans and their property (crops and cattle).

According to the Mishmi, hunting is not just a violent act of harming, injuring, and killing animals but is also an exchange between the villagers and the spirits. The presence of skull boards in Mishmi houses is evidence of the relationship of respect and fear that exists between the Mishmi and *ngōlō*, the mountain spirit (Figure 6.2). As I mentioned in Chapter 3, the Mishmi feel that over-hunting or hunting more than necessary is similar to stealing. If animals are over-hunted, they believe that the hunters will be punished with illness or even sudden death due to unnatural reasons. Due to the fear of *ngōlō*, hunting activities among the Mishmi are regulated, which is seen as an inbuilt mechanism that results in the conservation of wildlife. These restrictions, according to the Mishmi, indirectly lead to fewer hunting trips and, therefore, limited hunting of wild animals.

When I talk about conservation, the Mishmi rebut, 'We are also conservationists!' The taboos associated with hunting force the Mishmi hunters to space out their hunting trips. In addition to this, the Mishmi point to their small population, the rugged terrain, the immense knowledge of the landscape and the extraordinary skills that a hunter needs to navigate, and progressively fewer hunting attempts and the fact that only a few hunters are active in the region to show how their culture is directly or indirectly helping in the conserving wildlife, especially in comparison to the Adi, as mentioned in Chapter 5.

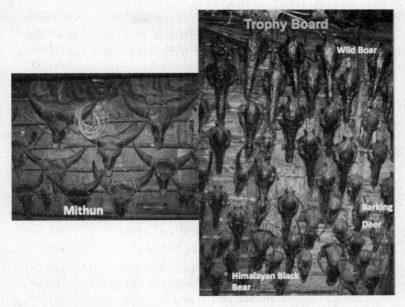

Figure 6.2   Display of domesticated and wild animal skulls
Source: Author.

Among the Adi, the taboos are not strictly followed, claim the Mishmi. They argue that the Dibang forests still have wild animals because of their cultural taboos and practices.

These claims are expressed by the Mishmi during their meetings with scientists and NGOs to show that their knowledge about the natural world is superior to that of conservationists or forest officials. In January 2014, a tiger survey team from WII was not permitted by the Mishmi to enter the forests, an incident that I will explain in a following section of this chapter. The WWF team from Delhi arrived in the same month to map the Dibang Wildlife Sanctuary. They were permitted to visit the sanctuary, but only after an interrogation by the village council members. Incidents such as these are rare, but the sudden surge in the state's interest in tigers, without an official consultation with the local people, is leading to sticky situations. People fear that the government will take more of their land if a tiger reserve is set up. Athuko, a resident of Anini, told me, 'We are not opposing them [the forest department].

We have already given 4,194 sq. kms to wildlife.[9] Where will we sit? Where will we have developmental activities, if we give all to wildlife? If there is no human existence, what is the meaning of wildlife? We have to focus on people.'

Using the tiger kinship story and their hunting rituals, the Mishmi express their stewardship of the forests and project themselves as the guardians of local wildlife. This is also reflected in the way the villagers and hunters narrate their concerns about wildlife. To evoke the story of tigers as siblings is 'to recite a genealogy, to recall affiliational ties and to affirm a reciprocal bonding' (Jamieson 2001: 5). The Mishmi's view of tigers is different from that of the state, which looks at the tiger as a national animal and has invested heavily in protecting the species.

Tiger as a National Animal

The 1970s in India was an important period with respect to tiger conservation, a time when the the Government of India created a number of tiger reserves across the country, a practice that continues still. The tiger was made the national animal of India in 1973, the same year that Project Tiger was implemented. The Dibang Tiger Reserve could be the latest to join the list. Starting from 9 tiger reserves in 1973, the number went up to 50 in 2019 (Mathur, Nayak, and Ansari 2019). Once considered a 'devilish brute' and then a 'large-hearted gentleman' during the colonial era (Rangarajan 2012), the rise of the tiger's status to become the national animal of India is remarkable. This makeover of the tiger's image points to a transition in the relationship of humans with nature in India, especially with large carnivores.

In the early 1970s, European biologists affirmed that wild tigers existed in sufficient numbers only in the forests of India and Bangladesh, and highlighted the need to save them (Greenough 2003). This caused India to focus on its tigers as a national project and boost its national prestige by formulating conservation laws, evident in the passing of the Wildlife (Protection) Act in 1972. The passage of the Act was made possible by former Prime Minister Indira Gandhi, who took a personal

---

[9] 'Wildlife' is a term that the Mishmi use to in relation to the forest department and the wildlife sanctuary. Sometimes, the term is also used for NGOs and wildlife biologists, who are identified as wildlife-*wale* (wildlife-people).

interest in wildlife conservation (Rangarajan 2009; Wright 2010). This project also served as an opportunity to exhibit India's scientific expertise and ecological responsibility to save tigers from extinction. Gandhi believed that nationalistic politics and environmental concerns strengthen each other, generating an attachment to terrain and, therefore, an 'attachment to the nation' (Greenough 2003: 222). India's fast-degrading environment and its concerns overlapped with the concerns of global institutions that saw India as a suitable 'receptor site'[10] (Frank, Hironaka, and Schofer 2000). These sites were 'symbolic markers' (Schwartz 2006: 116) that reflected India's self-determination and commitment. Since then, there has been a global rise in the number of protected areas and a proliferation of treaties that have led India to commit to the cause of global wildlife conservation. In 1969, an IUCN conference was held in New Delhi that raised global awareness of the plight of the Indian tiger and helped establish an Indian chapter of the WWF (Lewis 2003).

Lewis (2003) has argued that wildlife conservation is a US export which 'reinvented' itself and was replicated in India's ecosystems. Indeed, from an ecological point of view, creating tiger teserves was seen as a solution. The national park[11] model was replicated in various habitats and ecosystems across the country. The ecological rationale behind this was that saving tigers would maintain the ecological balance. When the top predator is conserved, the argument went, the resources within the entire ecosystem will be secured. From this point of view, the tiger is viewed as an umbrella species.[12] As a keystone species,[13] tigers are

[10] Social structures such as scientific institutions act as receptor sites, which can receive, decode, and transmit signals from international organizations to national or regional actors. These sites also act as implementers of global blueprints for environmental protection.

[11] Yellowstone National Park in the USA, the first national park that became a prototype and model, was replicated all over the world.

[12] Umbrella species are those selected for making conservation-related decisions. Protection of these species indirectly protects other species that are part of the habitat and gives refuge to a whole range of other smaller species dependent on each other in the food chain.

[13] Keystone species have a disproportionately large effect on their environment and play a critical role in maintaining the structure of an ecological community.

crucial because their removal can trigger the collapse of the entire ecosystem. Similar views were echoed by pioneering ecologists[14] who supported the idea of protecting 'wilderness' in the form of biodiversity preserves and argued for the need to develop an 'ecological sensibility' to respect other life forms (Morris 2014: 97). Their idea of wilderness did not mean pristine landscapes but landscapes inhabited and altered by humans, 'humanised or cultural' landscapes (Morris 2014: 100) with embedded meanings and significance. Walter and Hamilton (2014) suggest that the idea of such cultural landscapes should be adopted as the ethical and foundational philosophy of all conservation programmes, where indigenous perceptions of landscapes and cultural and spiritual meanings are infused into the model of conservation. These views depart from the ideas of untouched wild landscapes promoted by the scientific conservation dogma.

Dibang Tigers: Indian or Chinese?

The researchers who had visited Dibang Valley before 2012 blatantly discarded the Mishmi's reports on tigers, asserting that the animal was unlikely to survive in this terrain with such a low prey population. The sudden focus on tigers by the state, scientists, and NGOs caused the local people to be bewildered and question this unprecedented excitement. Concrete evidence of the existence of tigers (live animals and blood samples) from the tiger rescue operation in 2012 changed everything. 'Scientific' evidence with camera traps, scats, and pugmarks was needed to start formal research. In addition to tigers, scientists were motivated to visit Dibang Valley to see what other species existed there.

The geopolitical location of the Dibang Wildlife Sanctuary makes it crucial and fascinating for wildlife science and conservation. After rescuing the tiger cubs, one of the concerns of the scientific community was to confirm their identity. The question was whether they belonged to the classification of *Panthera tigris tigris* (Bengal tiger found in the Indian subcontinent) or *Panthera tigris corbetti* (Indo-Chinese tiger found in continental Southeast Asia). Were these Chinese tigers or Indian tigers? Tigers are free ranging and this is a trans-national

[14] Lewis Mumford, Renè Dubos, and Murray Bookchin.

landscape, therefore the probability of 'Chinese' tigers crossing over to the Indian side was fairly high. One of the visiting scientists in Anini said, 'Hypothetically, if these cubs were a Chinese subspecies, it indicates the biological wealth of the area; and the overlapping of the two subspecies is an indication of biological uniqueness.' The DNA testing of their blood samples confirmed that they were indeed Indian tigers (*Panthera tigris tigris*).

From the perspectives of the Indian state actors and scientists, formed out of their own disciplinary professions (Pimbert and Pretty 1997), relations between the Mishmi and nature appear complex and multifaceted. The disciplinary specializations underpinning wildlife conservation often lead them to focus on the particular elements of the ecosystem in which they specialize, such as tigers, gibbons, or hornbills. As a result, the relationship of a species with other entities (villages, farms, and roads) often gets ignored. The concept of nature is unitary in science (Greenough 2003), where every organism is governed by DNA and the same evolutionary concepts. DNA studies are increasingly becoming crucial in defining 'species'. The state adopts this approach as well and provides logistical support and official protection to save certain species. Classification of the natural world is inherently both a practical activity and a social process (Morris 2004).

Different 'Avatars' of Tigers

During the tiger cubs' rescue operation in 2012, the situation was tense. The Mishmi were curious to know why these cubs were being taken away and where to. The cubs were temporarily kept in Roing zoo, where visitors flocked to get a glimpse of them. When the decision to take the cubs to the Itanagar Zoological Park was made, the Mishmi students' union raised objections. 'These are our tigers, why take them to Itanagar? If they are here, our people will see them,' said the president of the union. Despite these protests, the cubs were shifted to the Itanagar Zoological Park in September 2013.

For the government to take a decision on a proposed protected area, such as the possibility of forming a tiger reserve, with no engagement with the public is not new in Dibang. In 1998, the Dibang Wildlife Sanctuary was declared without any public consultation, which has made it a sensitive issue among the Mishmi, so much so that words such as 'tigers', 'wildlife', 'forest department', or even 'NGOs' spark instant arguments and debates. The discussion of a proposed tiger reserve has only added to the already existing discontent among the Mishmi. People fear that the government will seize more of their land without asking, as was the case when the Dibang Wildlife Sanctuary was created. However, not all are against the tiger reserve.

In Anini (where the administrative headquarters of Dibang Valley district is situated), people often raised the question, 'Why are these tigers called "Royal Bengal Tigers"?' 'Were they brought from Bengal? No. You call them Arunachal tigers, I don't like to hear the name "Bengal tiger". These are not from Bengal. These are ours.' Even though the name 'Royal Bengal tigers' has been changed to 'Indian tigers', the former is popular and used not only by people but also by the media. A school teacher in Anini was forthright in his concerns, 'Wildlife belongs to those who conserve it. We have preserved it. It should belong to us.' Due to the lack of effective law enforcement, local people ridicule the forest department and the Mishmi's assertion of their right over wildlife becomes stronger, effective, and impactful.

Through the lens of their kinship with tigers, the Mishmi question the logic of the state having to protect the tigers. The Mishmi make claims on their ancestral lands and forests through notions of 'relatedness' in the form of kinship with tigers and sentiments of 'fear-cum-respect' in relation to the forest guardian, ngōlō. 'There are many taboos. ... Social taboos are there. We are preserving wildlife because of these taboos. If we had hunted without restrictions, wildlife would have been finished by now,' said Athuko, the village council member. These claims were expressed during meetings with scientists and NGOs to demonstrate the locals' knowledge about the natural world.

This cultural and ecological knowledge of the Mishmi is articulated while engaging with the state's intervention to protect tigers. The Mishmi version of caring for tigers is different from state-cum-science's vision of tigers as state property, as a national animal, as an endangered species, or as a keystone species. These different 'avatars' of the tiger—as a brother to the indigenous people, as a national animal for the nation state and its citizens, and as an endangered species for biologists—lead to different understandings of 'nature'. While these groups articulate their own ways to protect tigers, their approaches differ enormously. Taboos and law enforcement protect tigers in vastly different ways, and this is at the heart of the conflict between the local people and the forest department.

'Friction'?[15] When Researchers Met the Mishmi

If ever there was a rich site of cultural production, it is the domain of contemporary environmentalism.

—Brosius (1999: 277)

In January 2014, a group of young researchers (Kumar, Rahul, and Philip) from the WII arrived in Anini, which was a base from where the surveys were carried out in different parts of the district. Their supervisor, who had originally accompanied them, left Anini after a successful camera trap of a tiger, leaving behind the researchers to continue the survey. This was their first trip to Arunachal. These men, in their 20s, were not as lucky as their supervisor in getting a photographic image of a tiger. They had formed two teams: I joined Kumar, one of the researchers, whose plan was to survey the forests beyond Malinye, a village towards the eastern part of the district which is around 5–6 kms from the sanctuary. To reach Malinye, one has to come to Etalin, a junction point to either reach Anini or Malinye. Etalin is approximately 52 kms from Anini and about 42 km from Malinye. The other team consisted of Rahul and Philip who planned to survey the adjoining areas. After dropping Rahul and Philip at Etalin, Kumar and I went to Malinye and stayed with Naba Tipu, the *gaon burrah*, the night before we were to start a 4-day trek. Naba Tipu was very cooperative, and we quickly prepared a plan for the next four days[16] with his help. He complained about tigers killing mithuns in the village. Three mithuns had been killed that year, but no compensation was given by the forest department.

The following morning was chilly with a bright sun and a clear sky; perfect weather to trek up the mountains. Kumar took some pictures of the mountain peaks and was happy with how they turned out. We waited eagerly at Naba Tipu's house for a Mishmi assistant to join us

---

[15] I borrow this term from Anna Tsing (2005).

[16] 11 January: Awali; 12 January: Emupani; 13 January: back to Awali; and 14 January: back to Malinye.

so that we could start our trek on time, but Haro, a village council member of Malinye, arrived and with this our plans were turned upside down. What I witnessed that morning is a reflection of the ground reality of wildlife conservation interventions. This was not the first time I was meeting Haro. I had met him in Angrim Valley a couple of months ago when he had been very friendly and had flirted with me with offers of mithun (meaning a marriage proposal). Haro was a different person here, though; very stern and authoritative. He was surprised to see me and asked, '*Arey* madam, *aap yahaan?*' (Madam, you're here?) I introduced him to Kumar. Haro started to speak to Naba Tipu about tigers in the Mishmi language and his tone got harsh. That's when I sensed that there was something wrong. Though he spoke in Mishmi, I understood the context of the conversation. Without any further exchange of greetings, Haro looked straight at Kumar and asked, '*Aapka yahaan aane ka maksad kya hai?*' (What is the purpose of your visit?) The conversation was in Hindi, which Kumar, Haro, and I understood and spoke fluently. As Kumar began to explain, more villagers started to collect and a small crowd gathered around the hearth.

Kumar answered that he was from an institute. 'Which institute?' Haro asked abruptly. Kumar spoke about the WII in Dehradun and that this trip was to be a rapid assessment of tigers. Kumar explained slowly and provided the details of his project. He was the only 'outsider' there besides me. Local villagers listened keenly to every word uttered by Kumar. All eyes and ears were fixed on him. Kumar said, 'We wanted to know if there are tigers here and ...' Haro interrupted before Kumar could complete his sentence, 'Yes, there are tigers here.' Haro waited to see Kumar's response. This discussion had assumed the form of an interrogation and Haro seemed to be enjoying it. He turned cynical and a bit nasty later. The other villagers remained quiet and watched. Here is how the discussion went:

Kumar: Yes, there are tigers, but we have to see the footprints.
Haro: What will you do with the footprints, you will write it in the report, no? If you write in your report that there are tigers here, the area will be declared a tiger reserve, our village will be taken away, and we will be asked to leave.
Kumar: No no no. It is not that easy. Things don't happen that fast. I am just a student, very low in the hierarchy. A tiger reserve will be the forest department's duty. They will take time, at least 5–7 years to declare this

a tiger reserve. It is not so easy, that I simply write it in a report and they make the declaration the next day.

Haro: But when you write it, people will read it. It is not that you have come here only to see tiger footprints. You will obviously write about it in your report, right? Seeing is one thing and writing it in a report quite another. See, it is like this, if you hit me and I hit you back, that's okay. But if you write that I hit you, it is another thing, you understand?

This analogy disturbed Kumar as well as me. I saw that Kumar had started to get uncomfortable. Kumar stopped talking about wildlife and sat quietly for a while. Feeling helpless, he said, 'We have come all this way from Dehradun, we've planned for the next several days, and have even bought rations for our survey.' Haro replied adamantly, 'You should have come here first to discuss this with us and then plan everything.' Placing things in perspective, Haro began to explain:

See, what has happened in the past is that the government has taken so much land from us without our consent. *Hum ko dhokha hua hai* [We have been cheated]. Our elders did not know that and no procedures were followed during the declaration of the Dibang Wildlife Sanctuary. The government has already taken some 4,000 sq. kms from us for wildlife. If they make it a tiger reserve, these villages will fall inside the protected area as well. Where will we go? We are also *bharatwasi* [Indian citizens].

The ideas of India and nationhood are often evoked during such discussions. The Mishmi and other people in Northeast India feel that they have been marginalized for decades and, consequently, the government officials' attitude towards the locals is discriminatory. The question of belongingness comes into play during such encounters. The Mishmi often raise questions about who belongs where, indicating to the officials that the latter are the 'outsiders', while they themselves are the real or original owners of the land. This form of 'ecological nationalism' is practised by people in these frontier regions through their affiliation to the mountains and lands, and the cultural pride in their customs and taboos (Cederlof and Sivaramakrishnan 2007).

Kumar clarified, 'Villagers can continue to use the land inside the tiger reserve, even if it is declared. The core zone is where there will be no villages. In the buffer zones, you can do activities. Some activities are allowed and some are not.' He looked around to see the people's reaction. The villagers were not convinced with the logic of his explanation. Kumar looked on cluelessly as the villagers started to discuss amongst themselves in the Mishmi language. Haro was now ready with his final judgement: 'You cannot go into our forests, we will not allow you.' Kumar now turned to Naba Tipu with whom we had dinner, *yū*, and had chatted all night, and asked, 'Naba, *aap kya kehte hai?*' (Naba, what do you say?) Expressing his helplessness, Naba Tipu said, 'What can I say? Whatever is decided is decided.' Haro's verdict were final and he said authoritatively, 'If I say yes, then it is yes. No means no, nothing more than that.'

'What will I tell my supervisor? I am on probation,' Kumar pleaded again. Kumar was a new recruit and fresh from training. This was his first project. He desperately needed data and felt that this trip would have an impact on his performance. He placed his palms on his head, shaking it slowly. Haro repeated that Kumar should have paid a visit to the village before making his plans. Kumar nodded his head and said, 'Ya ya, I have learnt a lot of lessons today.' We left Malinye disappointed and returned to Etalin, where the other two researchers, Rahul and Phillip, were waiting to start their survey.

Upon hearing Kumar's story, Philip, another team member, was agitated. 'What, man! What are you saying? What exactly are these Mishmi guys saying, why? What did you tell them? I seriously can't believe this, man. We can't go back, we have come all this way.' Philip felt that a conspiracy was being hatched against them and suspected that someone was spreading rumours about the tiger reserve. Philip got very impatient. He turned to Kumar to find out if he had managed to collect any 'data'. 'Did you use the questionnaire or not? Did you get any data?' Philip asked in desperation. Kumar's jaw dropped in utter disbelief over Philip's obsession with data. Kumar politely answered, 'I tried to ask some questions, but the situation was not conducive.' In fact, Kumar had tried to ask some questions related to the socio-economic situation of the region, but it ended up being a mini entertainment show for the Mishmi. The conversation went something like this:

Kumar to Haro: How old are you? [This was on the questionnaire.]
Someone in the crowd (shouting): Write 17! [Haro looked no less than 30. There was laughter from the crowd.]

Kumar: Do you think the population of tigers has increased or decreased? *Haro*: How do we know? You are the researcher. If I answer this, you will write it in your report, so I won't say. [This was followed by more laughter.]

While we were at Etalin, a jeep with five Mishmi men arrived. I had a sense of déjà vu as the same episode from earlier in the day in Malinye played out in front of me again in a matter of only a few hours. These men from Etalin had many queries, such as: Where have you come from? What is the purpose of your visit? Where are the research permits and inner line permits? At the end of the discussion, they refused to allow the researchers to do the survey. One of the men said, 'Don't feel bad, but we have been cheated in the past, that's why.' They narrated the same issues that Haro had told us earlier. This kind of mistrust shown towards researchers, who are seen as the staff or representatives of the forest department and NGOs, is not a stray incident in Dibang. Satya, a PhD student from the United Kingdom, who also did field work in Dibang Valley, shared a similar experience. Here is an excerpt of what he wrote in his report:

There appears to be widespread dislike for the forest department and any entity they represent (for instance, wildlife conservation). The District Forest Officer (DFO), the senior most forest official in Dibang Valley, has been unresponsive to people's complaints about mithun dep- redation by wild animals. However, recently he sent around a notice to the villages within a certain radius of the protected areas' boundary declaring that their land was going to be included in an eco-sensitive zone with restrictions on hunting and farming. This has created further mistrust between the people and the department. Though the land is described as 'useless and unproductive' by some local people, the idea that the forest department can take it or control access to it by simply issuing a notice, is unacceptable. (SN 2014)

Unlike the WII team, Satya never had serious issues with the Mishmi until 2018.[17] This is partly because of his liaising with a

---

[17] A major controversy erupted in Dibang Valley when a resident got hold of a letter written by Satya to the Environment Appraisal Committee in 2018 regarding a hydroelectric project, which the Mishmi believed was not in their favour.

Mishmi entrepreneur in Roing for logistical support. The WII's team
is a representative of the forest department, and their lack of communication with the local people may have made their work more
difficult. Finally, the following week, the Mishmi guide in Anini who
had helped organize this entire trip, made arrangements for the team
to survey the forests beyond Dambeun and inside the wildlife sanctuary, the same area where their supervisor had been. There were
no issues in this trip, because one of the forest guards, a resident of
Dambeun village, facilitated all visits by the forest department or any
of its associates (NGOs, researchers). Such support was available neither in Malinye or Etalin. The team consisted of seven people (three
researchers: Kumar, Philip and Rahul; three Mishmi porters: Naba Pitu,
Jikru, Hata; and me) and the survey was carried out for four days inside
the Dibang Wildlife Sanctuary. We saw plenty of tiger pug marks and
tiger scats, and a camera trap caught a clouded image of a leopard. We
walked for 9–10 kms a day, leaving very early in the morning so that
we could cover the distance before it got hot and humid, and return
to the camp before sundown. One of the porters, Naba Pitu, carried a
gun, an essential item when walking through the forests. The porters
walked in the front and the researchers followed them. The researchers
wore dull olive-green uniforms, military-style camouflage pants, and
waist pouches that held their notebooks, pens, a knife, and a torch.
They carried their personal belongings in backpacks with the WII logo,
apart from GPS units and binoculars hanging from their necks. Camera
trap units and rations were carried by porters in large bamboo baskets.
Rahul walked close to Naba Pitu in the front, jotting down the local
names of trees and rivers, and recording the GPS location of key features such as streams and different habitats. Kumar and Philip walked
slowly behind, carefully searching for signs of wildlife (footprints, scats,
and so on). Every time they came across a sign, they stopped to record
the GPS location, take photographs, and collect samples, which they
recorded with a specific number and date (Figures 6.3). This was a
scientific ritual that the porters originally found very funny but later,
quite irritating. 'They just collected that *tatti* [excreta in Hindi], why
are they collecting again?' asked Hata, restlessly. Stopping multiple
times on the way and having to wait for the researchers extended the
trip and irked the porters, who intended to reach the camp site as early
as possible to collect firewood, set up tents, and cook for the team.

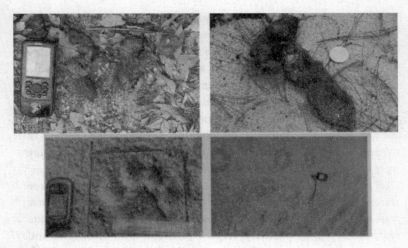

Figure 6.3 Tiger pug marks and scats
Source: G. V. Gopi.

Figure 6.4 Wildlife researchers fixing a camera trap unit a camera trap unit
Source: Author.

The porters walked swiftly and effortlessly, despite the heavy basket, in an environment familiar to them. They had been on this trail many times on patrolling duties with the army and the ITBP, as well as on hunting trips. This was in contrast to the team members who walked slowly and silently, careful not to make a noise and drive the animals away, as they looked for signs of wildlife. The Mishmi porters looked at the tiger team with amusement, especially over the team's enthusiasm for tiger scats. 'What will you do with tiger *ka tatti*?' asked Hata. Rahul explained that this sample would be analysed in a lab to know what the tiger had eaten. The porters laughed at this.

A little while later, Naba Pitu spotted an animal footprint and waited for the team to come and see it. The team had a look and walked ahead. Naba Pitu was taken aback. Philip identified it as a bear's footprint and continued walking. Naba Pitu did not understand why the team did not show interest in bear footprints in the way that they stopped and examined tiger scats. This is something that I noticed all through the survey too. Their focus was mainly on tigers; other forms of animal evidence were not given the same amount of attention as the tigers. The youngest of the porters, Jikru, about 20 years old, was a jolly-natured youth who sang Mishmi songs and whistled Bollywood tunes as we trekked along. He focused on the foliage and imitated birdcalls. At one point, he pointed his gun at the canopy to shoot, but the bird flew away.

Once we reached the camp, Naba Pitu and Jikru went to collect firewood and to look for animals; they returned with fish to cook for dinner. The researchers followed the rules of visiting a sanctuary like disciplined scholars, whereas the Mishmi porters did not care about these rules, or perhaps were not even aware of them. Fire, wildlife hunting, fishing, smoking, and playing music are banned inside wild-life sanctuaries according to the forest department's rules. For the Mishmi, to hunt, fish, and collect firewood are practical things to do, at times necessary for their survival in the forests. The region experiences sub-zero temperatures during winters and one cannot help but have a fire for cooking and for heat. Every act of the Mishmi during the survey could be deemed unlawful. While the researchers followed the protocol, the Mishmi saw these forests as resources that they have been using as their right. There was an obvious mismatch between the two groups. The peak of disconnect between these two groups of actors was reached when Naba pulled out a packet of smoked meat from his backpack and offered takin meat to everyone. This shocked the researchers, as having takin meat is illegal according to the law.

What the research team thought of the sanctuary was very different from how the Mishmi porters saw this space. For the team, it was a space for wildlife protection and a natural laboratory, and their role was to collect samples and 'scientific' data in order to test hypotheses, experiment, survey, and ultimately manage and conserve wildlife and forests. As a trained wildlife biologist myself, I could understand the responsibilities that came with being a researcher. 'Leave nothing but footprints', 'shoot with your camera', 'focus on observing and writing about the forests and wildlife' are the rules that were taught during my field training. The team did what they were supposed to do. For the porters, however, the sanctuary is where they hunt, collect firewood and bamboo, and fish; it was business as usual.

This meeting space between biologists and villagers produces cross-cultural encounters, sometimes leading to confusion, amusement, frustration, and potential conflict. Because of the nature of this particular exchange, the confusion and frustration was even more evident. These spaces of collaboration often become spaces of contestation because of the profound disconnect between the expectations and goals of each group, which leads to disappointment for both (West 2006). The presence of mediating institutions and individuals can play an important role in bridging the gap between researchers and the Mishmi, but they may not always reduce this friction.

Mediating Voices

The Mishmi living in Roing act as the mediating voices between conservation groups and the local Mishmi community. Mishmi elites make frequent trips outside Arunachal and have developed networks with influential government officials, businessmen, and NGOs. One such Mishmi elite is a highly influential Mishmi man who is a member of the Arunachal State Wildlife Board and is the key contact for all the NGOs and biologists visiting the region. He played a major role in the tiger cubs' rescue, and one of the tiger cubs was even named after him. Cultural mediators, Conklin and Graham suggest, often act as spokespersons for the entire community, as if it is a 'homogenous community' (1995: 704). Sometimes, these mediators are blamed for not voicing the diversity of opinions within a community. While this Mishmi elite member is well known among the scientific and NGO communities, some local people in Anini show great contempt towards him. One of the reasons for this is that he does not take up local issues, such as the depredation of mithuns by tigers, with the forest department. The villagers expect him to help them in getting compensation from the forest department for cattle deaths by carnivores. Therefore, his role is ambiguous. Although he belongs to the Mishmi community and enjoys close associations with the forest department and NGOs, he is heavily criticized and accused of not being of any help to his own 'Mishmi brothers'. Such mediators have the ability to participate with all three groups (local communities, the forest department, and conservation groups) but sometimes have 'no or little legitimacy at the local level' (Brown 1998: 312).

Conservation actors lack certain resources and must depend on others, such as the Mishmi, for their research and conservation activities. The local forest department was dependent on Delhi- or Assam-based NGOs for technical and scientific expertise in activities such as animal handling/capturing, wildlife rescue operations, and wildlife monitoring and surveys. NGOs are often dependent on the forest department for logistical support and for procuring research permits. NGOs, in turn, offer their scientific expertise (in mapping, estimating tiger population, and habitat assessment) to the forest department. These NGOs from mainland India do not have the cultural knowledge of the local practices or the landscape and, therefore, often seek help from the local people.

Dibang is continuously being constructed as a space of rich biodiversity and is socially being produced by both global and local ideas of nature. This complicates the situation further. On the one hand, the Mishmi are trying to retain their land and prevent further acquisition by the state, while on the other hand global forces are shaping and reshaping the space as valuable for biodiversity conservation. Due to a deficit of trust and respect, negotiation may not always take place on friendly terms when such actors meet.

At the official level, a public interest litigation (PIL)[18] and a right to information (RTI)[19] request has been filed by local residents to uncover the basis for declaring 4,194 sq. kms as a sanctuary. Using their belief of sharing kinship relations with tigers, the Mishmi question the logic of the state having to protect the tigers in the area. Angeche said,

> See, this jungle is my clan's. We save the animals here. We can go when-ever we want, without permission, but for hunting, one has to take per-mission from the clan member. If, as a clan member, I do not permit, then one cannot hunt. If this becomes the government's property, then anyone can hunt, it will become a matter of free will.

These anxieties get manifested as disagreements during encounters between Dibang residents and the visiting research teams, NGOs, and the forest department. Attacks on Mishmi cattle by tigers, the rescue of the tiger cubs, the indifference of the forest department to the villagers' complaints, and the arrival of the letter from the Government of India regarding the creation of an eco-sensitive zone have all accumulated to amplify their grievances. Any individual or group visiting Dibang Valley for research on tigers or forests, thus, becomes an easy target to project their frustrations on. While there is no organized local campaign or movement against the state with regard to tiger conservation, there have been incidents of intimidation and acts of 'non-cooperation' with the visiting research teams.

The discussions invariably come to centre on local taboos and how the Mishmi care about tigers. Through their claims on the local wild-life, their indigenous taboos relating to the conservation of wildlife are framed as a sort of 'cultural capital' (Bourdieu 1986). In addition to Morris, scholars across the domain of social sciences have found human-relatedness to be central to many notions of 'nature' (Descola 2013; Ingold 1996; Mullin 1999; Kohn 2013). Relatedness through

---

[18] Public interest litigation (PIL) is a legal instrument given to the public by courts. Any person can file a petition in the court in the interest of the general public. A Mishmi man filed this PIL in 2013.

[19] A young graduate from the Dibang Valley filed an RTI application in November 2012. The Right to Information Act is meant to empower the citi-zens of the country and promote transparency and accountability in the work-ing of the government.

kinship varies—for example, in parent–child relations, sexual relatedness, procreation, or simply 'name-sake' relatedness (Bird-David 1990;
Ingold 1996). Kinship with other life forms is part of the identity
of many indigenous groups. Such genealogical ties and a sense of
belonging bind individuals to groups, to places, and to their own past
(Jamieson 2001). People in Bangladesh and Nepal have similar kinship ties with tigers. In Nepal, tigers, humans, and bamboo are seen
as brothers. A story about the conception and birth of the first man
also marks the birth of several other species, underlining their brotherhood (kinship) and relatedness (Hardman 2000). The forest-dwellers
of Sundarbans conceive of themselves as tied in a web of relatedness
with tigers (Jalais 2010: 10). In Malawi, relations between people and
animals evoke 'kinship' (Morris 2000: 167). Killing an animal is like
killing a kin-person and, therefore, may have consequences, a risk ame-
liorated through precautionary rituals.

Species that are valuable to communities often have an ecological
keystone value and contribute as such to the integrity of local ecosystems. Close similarities between ecologically valuable (keystone)
species and socially valuable species often trigger people's participation
(Ramakrishnan 1998).

Commentary

I have outlined some critical threads that connect how the Mishmi of
Arunachal Pradesh relate to tigers, how their relations with animals
range from protecting some animals (tigers and the Hoolock gibbons),
utilizing some animals for meat (takin, serow, barking deer), trading
some animals' parts (pods of musk deer and gall bladders of bears),
and, if required, killing carnivores that attack their cattle (wild dogs,
tigers) or raid their crops (bears, ungulates, wild pigs). These multifaceted meanings are in conflict with the state's view of 'wild' animals
as 'scheduled animals'[20] (GoI 1994) or species catalogued as 'endangered', 'critically endangered', 'vulnerable', or of the 'least concern'
(IUCN 2014). State institutions view animals through the lens of
population numbers and the levels of threat they face. Tigers and their

---

[20] See p. 115n8 of this book.

conservation evoke emotions at the local level (as kin), for the state (as a national symbol), and for science (as a species under the threat of becoming extinct).

In the context of management, Gissibl, Hohler, and Kupper (2012) argue that the notion of keystone species can sometimes marginalize alternative readings of the landscape. National and scientific avatars of tigers are similar to 'cosmopolitan tigers', an imagery created by the urban class that has the capacity to erase the local meanings attached to tigers (Jalais 2010). Here in the eastern Himalayas, we see how the hegemonic Western and scientific narratives of tigers marginalize alternative ways of understanding them and other animals. Further, these views have been naturalized and absorbed into an ecological nationalist frame and have acquired considerable power in state agencies and among experts and key conservation lobbies; it is a sort of statist takeover that assumes new forms in other key regions, such as South Africa (Bonner 1994).

If there is a definitive Mishmi approach, it tends to be pragmatism. When a tiger becomes dangerous, as a last resort, they kill or trap their 'problematic' brother. Killing tigers (a Schedule I species) is illegal according to the wildlife protection laws of India (GoI 1994). This brings the Mishmi into direct conflict with the law. As the national animal, the tiger's image has been built up since the 1970s. This has boosted nationalistic feelings towards this species, has helped the government make sovereign claims over tigers, and has led to the tiger becoming the icon of wildlife conservation in India. This way of placing nature at the centre of a project for the nation state has been identified as 'ecological patriotism' (Rangarajan 2009: 304). But this can also be a way of disempowering some, as with the Mishmi, while empowering others, such as the foresters and exclusivist conservationists. Ironically, this runs opposite to the approach outlined in the Tiger Task Force report (2005). The state pushes its agenda at the local level to gain global partnerships on the international platform for its commitment to tiger conservation. Using the tiger story and their hunting rituals and taboos, the Mishmi project themselves as the guardians of wildlife and stewards of the forests. Such new forms of 'political performatives' (Cederlof and Sivaramakrishnan 2007) include two very different versions of nature: cosmopolitan/metropolitan and native/indigenous. The Mishmi view is grounded in notions of cultural value, physical attachment to place, and oral history. From the state's point of view, some places have more conservation value than others. In some sense, the Mishmi's and other stakeholders' claims to the place and species are aligned, but their understandings of nature are not.

Nature conservation projects that engage local communities produce different outcomes. The story of the Mishmi Hills is not over. What I witnessed during my fieldwork was just the beginning of a long struggle of contested claims on wildlife, which is likely to become more complex in the future. The geopolitical location and the resource-rich forests of Dibang Valley make this landscape, like others across this internationally contested state, extremely crucial. It experiences the contesting forces of national security, nature conservation, and development, where the military, the scientific community, and corporations play an active role. They promise opportunities of employment and 'development' to the local communities. In this cacophony, the Mishmi views could get drowned out, or perhaps they may get stronger. Within the Mishmi community, there are groups who feel that a tiger reserve will bring jobs for the local youth. The promise of employment as forest guards and tour guides is creating interest among the local public. There are young men in Anini who are skilled[21] entrepreneurs and work as guides for tourists, trekkers, and naturalists who visit in small numbers. According to them, a tiger reserve is a good initiative that will mark Dibang Valley as an important tourist location on the global map. It is understandable for the Mishmi to have mixed feelings, but to see them as naïve would be a mistake. I began this book by describing a meeting with the residents of Dibang, an NGO official explained the importance of tigers as top predators and how they keep the prey population under control.

Why is the story of the Mishmi relevant to 'nature' conservation in the present day? The intersecting aims and mutual misunderstandings of the Mishmi, the biologists, and the forest department tell us a lot about the idea and practice of nature conservation in the present day, and reinforce the value of a continuing shift towards community- and

[21] A resident of Kongo village in Anini registered an NGO in 2018. This was the first NGO to be set up in the district by an Idu Mishmi. Another young Idu man who lives in Itanagar has also set up an eco-tourism venture in partnership with the mainlanders.

place-based approaches to conservation. This case itself shows how dominant narratives of nature conservation, including those which uphold tiger protection practices, can erase or devalue cultural, historical, and symbolic meanings (Walter and Hamilton 2014), even those which uphold tiger conservation practices. The place-based views that the Mishmi have of their environment, and the complex multispecies realities associated with them, highlight precisely why place-based perceptions must be acknowledged by the state and wildlife biologists in order to make way for new forms of conservation research and practice (Adger et al. 2011; Williams, Stewart, and Kruger 2013).

We must be careful not to romanticize indigenous groups such as the Mishmi as protectors of nature or 'ecologically noble savages' (Redford 1991; Baviskar 2003; Li 2000). The Mishmi's bio-cultural knowledge is articulated in response to the state's intervention to protect tigers and the forest department's indifference to the local people's needs. State and NGO officials need to be sensitized towards the local ways of perceiving wildlife and nature. This might trigger a breakthrough in the conservation of tigers in Dibang. Without consultations with the local people, it is likely that this conservation effort will lead to either coercion and/or marginalization of local communities, making long-term conservation difficult; something which has already occurred in places such as the Sariska Tiger Reserve. Dibang provides a good opportunity for us to rethink conservation and make a fresh start by involving people in positive and innovative ways. Morris (1998) reminds us that relations between humans and animals are often complex, intimate, reciprocal, personal, and, crucially, ambivalent. In Dibang valley we find the multiple views of the local communities standing against the 'monolithic' view of the modern state. Here, as elsewhere, the Mishmi's ways of relating to nature cannot be reduced to a singular metaphor.

7

CONCLUSION

> If 'the environment' only includes everything, which is not human, not social, then the concept is sociologically empty. If the concept includes human action and society, then it is scientifically mistaken and politically suicidal.
>
> —Beck (2010: 254)

I began this book with stories of conservation interventions and conflicts surrounding the tiger cubs' rescue in Dibang Valley. These stories, and others that I have related throughout the book, have exposed layers of clashing ideas about nature and the complex issue of wildlife conservation. In telling these stories, I aim to highlight the tensions and challenges of conservation projects, why the local people participate in them, and why some resist cooperating with the research projects. Dibang valley is a 'resource frontier' where nature conservation, nationalism, and capitalism overlap with each other, bringing together different actors with varying agendas. I use human–animal relations as an anchor to highlight the tensions between conservation actors and the Mishmi, and how the views of local communities are in disagreement with the state, NGOs, and science's view of nature. Nature conservation continues to be a sensitive issue on the ground, especially when multiple actors are involved in conservation projects. This book highlights contrasting views of what constitutes nature in Dibang Valley through discussions on human–animal relations. It attempts to tease out some threads that connect these different views.

In Chapter 1, I offered a broad review of the existing academic material on what constitutes nature and why it is a contested domain. I drew upon literature from anthropological and sociological perspectives to examine nature conservation, which is too often regarded as a strictly biological and environmental matter. I used my background in biology and wildlife conservation in India to great advantage, by positioning myself simultaneously as a wildlife researcher and as an anthropologist to represent the interest of the Mishmi people in the national and international conversation on conservation. This position enabled me to discern subtle 'frictions' that other parties involved in Dibang Valley overlook, such as the indifference of conservation science to local beliefs and values, and conservation policy's orientation towards elite and cosmopolitan symbols rather than local forms of (human and non-human) life. In this book, I aim to problematize the simple conception of 'nature' as the 'human' world's discrete and autonomous other. I demonstrated that there are multiple, simultaneous, and contradictory relations connecting different entities—mithun, takin, and tiger on the 'nature' side, and the Mishmi locals, government officials, and wildlife researchers on the 'human' side. I show that these relations form a complex network that does not fall into the human/nature binary.

I discuss my ethnographic approach in narrating stories from the borderlands of India through my interviews with the Mishmi and my interactions with forest department officials and wildlife researchers. My training as a wildlife biologist and my consequent shift to anthropology have majorly influenced my adoption of research methods for this book. I explore the Mishmi's relations with animals and how their social world is part of a complex human–animal–spirit cosmology. The chapter shows how cultural, economic, and political tensions run along these networked connections among particular humans and non-humans. For example, wildlife researchers who do not know that tiger hunting is a taboo for the Mishmi and are unable to distinguish between Mishmi and Adi hunting ethics thus offending the Mishmi people's sense of cultural dignity when they brusquely assert that tigers need protection.

Cultural taboos reflect the Mishmi's world view where animals and spirits are seen as part of their world. It is necessary for the Mishmi to engage in exchange processes with the spirits through reciprocal

relations for the well-being of their society. In Chapter 3, I focused on
their hunting rituals and taboos, and how these practices are in conflict
with the nation's laws. The geopolitical location of Dibang Valley brings
the ideas of nature conservation, nationalism, and its colonial linkages
together with the 'frontier' or 'border' region that it is today, which are
examined in Chapter 4. I used archival literature to explore how the visits
by British colonial administrators shaped the anthropology of the
Mishmi Hills. Present ideas of both the landscape and the people of the
Mishmi Hills are influenced by the writings left behind by the British.
The relation of the border communities and the state continues to be
complex as the Mishmi living on the Sino-Indian border negotiate with
a range of actors—including the Indian Army, conservation actors, and
local administrators—who see these borders very differently from how
the Mishmi do. While the Mishmi are sought out for their knowledge
of the landscape, they are also looked upon with suspicion at times
because of their kinship with the 'Chinese Mishmi' (Deng). Notions of
nationalism are mirrored in all the actors in these borderlands since the
biodiversity-rich Dibang Wildlife Sanctuary and India's boundary overlap and meet at the international border with China. These frontier
regions are crucial zones where the sentiments of saving endangered
tigers, protecting India's territory, and exploiting resources for the
'development' of the 'tribes' come together in the form of conservation and nationalism. The local Mishmi hunters not only operate in
these borderlands but also claim that their trips to the border serve to
keep a check on Chinese incursions into the Indian territory. Thereby,
they lay claim to a dual role as both 'hunters' and 'border patrollers'.
The Mishmi's claims of protecting both wildlife and India's borderlands resonate with the state's interest in nation building and wildlife
conservation, but the Mishmi's practice of hunting, an illegal activity,
combined with border patrolling emphasizes their ambiguous relations
with the state.

The idea and practice of nature conservation should not be seen
as apolitical. Even within the Mishmi community, as I investigated
in Chapter 5, the Mishmi elites in Roing are fostering and shaping a
Mishmi identity using symbols of nature, in response to local and global
environmental concerns. This chapter highlighted how the Mishmi
identity shifts in response to both their conflicts with other groups in
the area and the spread of conservation activity in the region. The idea

of an ecological identity is not innate or timeless but something more strategic and dialogic, arising from deeply held values and familiar practices as well as from a growing awareness of new stresses and opportunities with regard to livelihoods. As the takin replaces the mithun to signify group identity in the very modern sphere of the IMCLS, it is clear that leaders in this effort are concerned with projecting the civilized aspect of Mishmi culture in modern terms. They are equally concerned with appealing to conservation ideologies that have been so influential in shaping landscape-level outcomes since the middle of the twentieth century.

The Mishmi elite claim an 'ecological identity' for their community by using elements of nature as objects of identification, often favouring the 'wild' over the 'domesticated' forms of nature. I argue that the Mishmi elite make a conscious effort to redefine their identity through the wildlife conservation ethos brought in by wildlife conservation NGOs from mainland India. The Mishmi's redesigning of their cultural society's logo—by replacing mithun, a cattle used for ceremonial slaughter, with takin, a wild and endangered species—reflects the fact that these indigenous people are constantly engaging with ideas from the global conservation discourse and using them for their own benefit. Mishmi take pride in the different animals found in their region, which seems to be undergirded by various aspirations of the elite urban Mishmi. The Mishmi attempt to negotiate the best possible ways to deal with these various actors, and are not always friendly and cordial. The situation gets messy and chaotic on the ground, as I demonstrated in Chapter 6. Meetings between the Mishmi and researchers are fraught with misunderstanding, which ultimately lead to the abandoning of research plans, as happened in Malinye. I also tried to show that the national government's conservation agenda proceeds in connection with global discourses, while a highly local politics of knowledge and power asymmetries percolate to the ground here. For example, Mishmi locals and junior wildlife researchers negotiate with one another over access and ownership, while government officials remain unaware of how national conservation policies are failing to touch the ground.

Using tiger conservation in Dibang Valley as a central theme, my book focuses on the diverse, multifaceted, and often contradictory relations of humans with nature, and especially their relationships with animals. The Mishmi claim that tigers are their brothers and take credit for tiger conservation, as they have taboos against hunting tigers. Using their notion of a sibling relation with tigers, the Mishmi question the state's idea of converting the Dibang Wildlife Sanctuary into Dibang Tiger Reserve, as well as the scientific surveys of tigers and habitat mapping undertaken for this purpose. In the final chapter, I highlighted how the Mishmi relate to tigers and how these relations contradict the versions of human–animal relations laid out by the state and science. The state considers tigers as its national property, while biologists view tigers as an endangered species. Both these understandings stand in opposition to the local interpretations of tigers and, more generally, nature itself.

Tigers evoke fear and compassion. I was fortunate that my fieldwork overlapped with the visits of some wildlife research teams and NGOs. I had the opportunity to meet people with diverse opinions and feelings about tigers, forests, mithuns, and takins. This allowed me to understand the varied, complementary, and contradictory views of different people on nature. I also realized how sensitive the issue is on the ground for the Mishmi, which is often not understood by the visiting state authorities and researchers. The visiting researchers carried back data on the tigers, their habitats, and their prey, but not adequate information was gathered on the loss that people incurred because of tiger attacks on their domesticated mithuns. Though their reports carried some information about the local Mishmi, overall they appear in the reports in an cosmetic sense that lacks the complex sociocultural and political understanding of their lives and the issues they face. As a researcher, I wanted to approach the central subject of my study from multiple points of view. What does the story of the Mishmi, wildlife biologists, and the forest department tell us about the practice and ideology of biodiversity conservation? I would like to highlight the deficit of the 'social' in nature conservation and the need for an interdisciplinary understanding of the subject.

Sociological Emptiness

I borrow the term 'sociological emptiness' from a paper by Ulrich Beck (2010), entitled 'Climate for Change, or How to Create a Green Modernity'. Beck asks why the issue of environmental destruction that is threatening humankind has not yet been met with the same enthusiasm as issues of war or poverty. One of the explanations he provides is that the discourse on environmental politics is an 'expert and elitist discourse' and common people's views on it are not counted (2010: 254). In wildlife conservation, the views of wildlife enthusiasts and wildlife experts are often heard more 'loud[ly] and clear[ly]' than the views of the local people, such as the Mishmi, who live in the borderlands where wildlife projects are increasingly being implemented. Very often, stories from the ground are subdued by the hegemonic discourse of science, activism, and technocratic management. Wildlife conservation will continue to be a story of science and the state, and will continue to be, what Baviskar (2002) calls, 'Bourgeois environmentalism', a form of environmentalism that represents the narrow but powerful voice of the urban elites. For example, the focus of biodiversity conservation in Dibang Valley has largely been on tigers. During my fieldwork, the Mishmi's concerns around receiving compensation for their cattle killed by tigers were not addressed during my fieldwork, either by the forest department or by the visiting research teams. This disconnection with local concerns has been a bone of contention on the ground.

There are valid reasons why the 'social' is often not included in conservation projects. Researchers of wildlife conservation are often not trained to carry out social surveys and, sometimes, lack the societal connection. They rarely consider issues outside the purview of wildlife research, particularly when they are fixated on one particular species. This is, according to West (2010), a kind of eco-fetishism.

Nature conservation continues to speak the language of protectionism, endorsing the model of a protected area, even after decades of criticism. The proposed Dibang Tiger Reserve is an example of this continuing legacy of 'fortress conservation', as delineated by Brockington (2001). If Dibang Wildlife Sanctuary becomes a tiger reserve, it will be the fourth such in Arunachal, followed by Namdapha, Pakke and Kamlang Tiger Reserve. Dibang Tiger Reserve, if established, will probably bring employment to the local youth, but many believe this may bring the local peoples' farming, fishing, and hunting activities, the mainstay of their subsistence, under surveillance. At this point, it's difficult to say to what extent a tiger reserve will be effective in preserving the tiger population. What is evident is that the visiting ecologists and wildlife researchers lack a 'social' understanding of wildlife conservation. Science-based conservation practice does not acknowledge social issues, such as local needs, social inequality, and power relations.

The absence of social sciences and humanities in conservation biology or wildlife management is not new, but a continuation of this absence is a matter of concern. Scientists trained in wildlife sciences are the ones who implement conservation projects, and hence these projects are dominated by aspects of biological sciences. For example, conservation activities are often focused on quantifying the forest cover, counting animal populations, and measuring threats to the health of an ecosystem (Aiyadurai 2011). Anthropological inputs in understanding human–animal conflict or wildlife management are scarce.

Wildlife managers have many challenging responsibilities, the carrying out of which depends, in part, on their training. Ironically, these professionals are trained only in animal studies, while a deeper understanding of the human dimension tends to be a weak link. The fault lies with the pedagogical training that focuses more on the technologies of wildlife biology and not on sociology, anthropology, economics, history, psychology, or political science.

Wildlife conservation projects in India are shaped by scientific knowledge, with little or no insights from the social history of the landscape. Saberwal and Kothari (1996) show that social sciences and humanities are absent from most conservation biology or wildlife management courses in the developing world. Therefore, when biological scientists design projects, not adequate attention or priority is given to the perspectives and needs of the local people. Anthropologists and social scientists could address this deficit when the local cultures and conservation practitioners are too far apart, and could also bridge the gap between biologists and social scientists. One way of doing this is to ethnographically document local perspectives on conservation and to provide a cultural context in which locally sensitive and acceptable conservation practices can be aimed for. There is a clear need for interdisciplinary approaches to nature conservation; to make real progress in conservation, communication between different academic ways of understanding the world has to be taken seriously (Adams 2007: 276). Official ways of protecting biodiversity should consider the tacit knowledge of indigenous groups, as Sillitoe (2009) suggests.

Does Being a 'Brother' Help the Tiger?

Does being a brother to the Mishmi help the tiger as a species? By having a deeper understanding of the sociopolitical and cultural aspects of the landscape, will the Mishmi be able to help their 'brother' better? An answer comes from the mythological story itself. According to the Mishmi practice, 'We can kill a tiger under two circumstances: (1) when it becomes a threat to humans; and (2) when it becomes a threat to humans' property—cattle and livestock.' So, when a tiger becomes a nuisance, one is allowed to kill it, provided that *tamamma* is performed afterwards. However, if the tiger becomes part of a lucrative trade, will the local people continue to revere the tiger as their brother?

While I am critical of the nationalistic or technocratic views of nature conservation, I do not glorify the locally rooted conservancy as a more promising way of conservation. Studies have shown that community-owned conservation regimes are sustainable only under controlled situations. One should not look at cultural beliefs and tradition as unchanging and frozen in time. Will the Mishmi continue to follow these rules, for example, if a trade route opens up for tiger parts? Some say that such wildlife trade already exists in this region. With market penetration, culture and tradition may become less of a priority. The economics of a tiger's market value may supersede cultural beliefs. For example, a local resident who runs a clothes shop in Roing is known to trade in tiger parts. During my stay, a tiger was killed in a nearby village. One does not know what happened to its body parts, or whether this tiger was killed because it had become a threat to humans or to human property, or if there were some other motives. As social taboos get eroded, I claim, it is likely that the belief of tigers as brothers will not protect the animals in the long run. The narrative of kinship with tigers makes a compelling case for the Mishmi to resist the tiger reserve and the forest department's activities. Therefore, people use this mythological narrative as a tool to ascertain their identity and pride. The idea of tigers as brothers would continue under some circumstances, but when this 'brother' becomes problematic or provides a high market price, it could be eliminated for material gains.

However, a tiger's cultural value may not help it in the long run. As socio-economic situations change, more roads, sophisticated weapons, and changes in landscapes and infrastructure come up, local hunting would stop being sustainable and the species may not survive for long.

Legal protection does help in conserving a landscape. I believe that there is a need to have new and better ways of seeing nature where it can be protected without antagonizing the local people.

Why the Story of Dibang Valley Needs to Be Read

On 5 December 2018, an article published in The Indian Express, titled 'Tiger in the Snow: The Big Cat Now Roars in the High Altitudes of Arunachal Pradesh' (The Indian Express, 2018), and a research article in the *Journal of Threatened Taxa* (Adhikarimayum and Gopi 2018) created a stir among scientists and the conservation community. These articles demonstrate how wildlife conservation and research in India tell only a partial story. The story of a charismatic species, the 'new discovery' of a species, news about undocumented landscapes, and the use of high technology in studying wildlife make for a happy story of wildlife conservation. News about large carnivores receives a lot of media attention, especially the ones that claim to be the 'first' documented tiger presence, which are very hard to ignore. The 'human story' in wildlife research and conservation is now emerging but the voices of the local communities affected by wildlife conservation are often not heard.

The lack of proper communication between researchers and villagers or between the forest department and villagers creates confusion and suspicion about the presence of these scientists and surveyors in the area. One of the residents was candid in saying, 'If they write in their report that there are tigers here, our forests will fall under the tiger reserve and the forest department may take away our land.' Another resident, however, was convinced that if they reported to the authorities about the tigers and a tiger reserve were to come up, it would lead to 'development'. Some even feared that if the villagers did not cooperate with the researchers, their village might be excluded from the list of beneficiary villages, and they might miss out on development. In spite of the lack of clear responses from the state, local residents largely feel that they would welcome a tiger reserve and that some land should be preserved for wildlife, but the important question that they ask is: Why is such a large area (4194 sq. kms) reserved? In a *gram sabha* (village meeting) organized on 20 August 2018, two demands were put forward by the local residents: (1) to de-notify the

Dibang Wildlife Sanctuary, to re-assess and re-survey the sanctuary, and to restrict the new proposed sanctuary to 1,500 sq. kms; (2) the proposed area should be obtained after following the due acquisition process, and the government should compensate the affected families. This meeting was the result of a PIL (15/2015) filed by Ngasi Mena (a member of the Idu Mishmi) and six other residents of Dibang Valley against the State of Arunachal Pradesh, pleading for the de-notification of the present Dibang Wildlife Sanctuary. These voices of resistance or anxiety from among the Idu Mishmi have not been addressed by wildlife biologists and conservation NGOs during their research and in their reports.

Conservation narratives always seem to be about the wildlife census, discoveries of new species, recognition by global conservation communities, funding agencies, and receiving 'green' awards, but the ground reality reveals an alarming picture of how conservation impacts the lives of the local communities who live in and near these wildlife habitats. There are many reasons why wildlife conservation does not address the social issues that are important for effective conservation and to make it a socially just practice.

The reluctance of wildlife biologists to address social issues in their work is a reflection of their own shortcomings. Any open discussion with the local residents may bring up uncomfortable questions about conservation and may possibly destabilize the long-held views of the conservation philosophy of 'protectionism'. When the researchers were not permitted to carry out their work, not being able to collect 'data' was a bigger concern for them than the social backlash. One of the researchers lamented, 'How can we go back without data, we have come all the way to Dibang.' Most researchers that I came across were interns, fresh out of training, and eager to use camera traps, a state-of-the-art technology, to capture images of tigers and other rare species.

Often wildlife studies are focused on one particular species, which separates the species from its anthropological and social meanings. Researchers also are reluctant to consider issues outside the preview of wildlife research, especially social sciences, which seen as a discipline which is lower in hierarchy, than the natural sciences. This blinds the researchers to the social implications and creates, what Ulrich Beck calls, 'sociological emptiness' (2010: 255). In the case of Dibang,

I would call it 'sociological tokenism' because of their reluctance in engaging in the human dimensions of wildlife conservation. For a long time, local people's views, opinions, and claims were often disregarded or treated as anecdote. Wildlife reports from Dibang do carry some basic information about the Idu Mishmi, but not their views or inputs. In my opinion, a complete silence from wildlife researchers about the socio-political issues of the protected areas or about conservation practice is unjust.

There are many reasons for this reluctance. One of them is the pedagogical challenge. Wildlife researchers are often not trained to carry out social surveys and therefore, may not take interest in the local social issues. This reflects in conservation projects, which are shaped by scientific knowledge, with little or no insight from the social history of the landscape. Therefore, when wildlife scientists design projects, they often lack the local people's perspectives and little priority is given to their needs. A senior wildlife biologist confessed that for a long time, the word 'communities' for him meant 'bird communities' and 'forest communities', and he realized only much later that the word also included humans.

The Idu Mishmi's Voices from the Ground

What is heartening is that the Idu Mishmi are not against the idea of a wildlife sanctuary but only question the need for dedicating such a large section of land to it (half of the district of Dibang Valley). and demand a reduction of the area reserved. This issue was raised by a resident in the *gram sabha*: 'We are not against the wildlife sanctuary but our rights must also be protected.' These sentiments have the potential to usher in a new era of community-centric conservation. This may provide a new direction and a great opportunity to truly integrate the local community in the conservation of tigers.

Finally, the credit for the presence of tigers in the region (as known from the mega claims of wildlife biologists) must partially go to the local Idu Mishmi's sociocultural ethos and to the formidable landscape of these sparsely populated borderlands, which are largely uninhabitable and unfit for agriculture. Such landscapes are de facto natural reserves. Because of their remoteness, high altitude, and the Idu Mishmi's system of indigenous conservation beliefs and practices, places such as Dibang Valley are a safe haven for wildlife and forests. It would be a mistake to assume that new scientific knowledge and the local people's conservation ethos alone can save wildlife. Large dams cleared by the Ministry of Environment and Forests and the increasing road and market connectivity to the borderlands could prove more damaging. Meanwhile, varied voices from the ground need to be heard. Local communities must be given due credibility instead of letting their voices drown amidst the loud celebratory claims made by wildlife scientists about tigers.

EPILOGUE

Kongo village at Anini is my second home now, which I continue to visit once a year. In 2017, after I completed by PhD thesis and joined IIT Gandhinagar as a faculty member, I returned to Kongo to offer my gratitude to the village's residents. It was a festive occasion abuzz with murmurs of a letter having been submitted by a researcher to the Ministry of Environment, Forests & Climate Change (MoEF&CC). A new factor had further complicated the claims of the Idu people and their anxieties over the government's proposal of a tiger reserve: a letter by Satya, dated 26 January 2017, written to the chairperson, Expert Appraisal Committee (EAC) on River Valley and Hydroelectric Projects, MoEF&CC, regarding the 3,097 MW Etalin hydroelectric project in Dibang Valley. The purpose of the letter was to request the EAC to re-examine at the EIA report submitted earlier by another organization. It demanded that the government develop a thorough understanding of the impacts of such a project on the district's wildlife, especially the highly endangered tiger, and people before granting it clearance. Using nearly 283 camera traps, Satya's study of almost two years captured a total of 12 individual tigers and 8 individual clouded leopards at various locations in Dibang Valley. The letter did rounds in the region through WhatsApp.

To see the name of this researcher whom the Idu Mishmi had helped, provided logistical support, offered hospitality, and gave interviews to during his fieldwork came as a shock to them. One of them said, '*Haamare peeth mein khanjar mara hai*' (He stabbed us in the back). At that time, the researcher has returned to the UK for writing his thesis. Some angry residents felt that his research privileged the cause of tiger conservation over the welfare of the local Idus. They could not contact him despite several attempts. One of the residents ended up calling his father in Delhi and threatened him. This long silence from Satya created intense tensions and, by the following year, had led to major friction between the two parties. The impact has been felt by all other researchers visiting the valley since then, all of whom would be questioned and sometimes interrogated about the nature of their research. An MPhil student from Sikkim University who arrived in Anini in 2017 for a four-month long research project was seen with suspicion, raising curiosity about whether he was using camera traps and who was funding his research. Similarly, a WII research team that arrived here for the wildlife census also faced difficulties and, in fact, was not permitted to conduct research. This resonated with the events I had witnessed in 2014, which arised due to the mistrust the locals had towards the forest department, but now the source of the mistrust had shifted to wildlife researchers.

Researchers often become the scapegoat or bait when terms are negotiated with the state. In 2018, the Mishmi Elite Society, a community-based organization in Anini decided not to allow researchers to enter the sanctuary until the dispute about its boundaries was resolved. It took a high-level meeting of the Idu Mishmi with the forest department and the NTCA at Anini to resolve the issue. Some members of the community have been fighting a lawsuit to get the government to provide clarity on the rationale behind the size of the sanctuary, apart from questioning the very need for a tiger reserve. Visiting research scholars have faced the scrutiny of residents, and researchers undertaking the camera trap style of tiger research over the years have been accused of extracting data from the forests without sharing it with the community. Some Idu Mishmi feel that ecological studies from the region could delay or even prevent development. They often ask, 'What is the benefit of this wildlife research to our community? If you are not able to give us benefits, at least do not prevent us from reaping the economic benefits from dams and projects.' Some locals believe that the results of wildlife research stand in conflict with developmental agendas (such as the construction of the Etalin hydroelectric project) or even with wildlife conservation (such as the creation of the Dibang Tiger Reserve).

While the local residents have been concerned about the tiger reserve proposal and have been demanding a re-demarcation and rationalization of the sanctuary (minutes of a meeting organized by the IMCLS in Anini on 4 March 2019), the district faced a new controversy that captured national headlines following the COVID-19 crisis. The names of Etalin, Dibang Valley, and Idu Mishmi flashed on social media campaigns on Facebook and Twitter (Dibang Resistance@TheRiseofDibang, #LetIndBreath). Multiple online petitions were circulated, appealing to the public to save Dibang Valley from the damage that would be caused by the Etalin project. The most viewed YouTube videos on this topic were by Faye D'Souza, a famous journalist and television anchor, and by Abhineet Mishra, a well-known satirist, who did a show on Dibang Valley. This helped bring the issue to the attention of a larger audience, resulting in heated debates and a huge outcry against the project.

This reminded me of the Idu Mishmi protesting in 2007 against the National Hydroelectric Power Corporation (NHPC) and the Dibang Multipurpose Dam project in Lower Dibang Valley (2,880 MW), another issue that was given due attention in the mainstream media. The image was spectacular, a large banner held by the Idu Mishmi declared: 'No dams. No compromise upon the construction of dams on our soil. No displacement: Go back NHPC.' This image played an important role in bringing attention to this issue, which would have been ignored otherwise, in Delhi. The project was later approved, and the movement fizzled out soon after, but it gained momentum again with a fresh demand to release compensation for those who were affected by the project.

Given that Dibang Valley is one of the most remote parts of India and lacks infrastructural development, any promise of dams or roads is a sign of the arrival of good times for the local community. Responses to the Etalin project were deeply divided and continue to be so. While the Idu fear that these mega projects threaten their culture and could dispossess them from their lands and livelihoods, some sections of this community also offer support to these projects. It is important to highlight here that young Idu people from Roing and Anini have been reaching out to the media voluntarily and are expressing their views on the matter on social media platforms. This 2020 episode was different, not only because of the intense digital protest campaigns but also because it highlighted the deep fissures that exist between conservationists and communities, and developers and researchers. In fact, it even created a rift among the researchers working in Dibang Valley.

On 23 April 2020, a group of 24 scientists from 14 institutions wrote to the director general of forests, Forest Appraisal Committee (FAC, MoEF&CC), raising concerns about the Etalin hydroelectric project. Their letter specifically protested against the diversion of forest land for the project, something that the FAC subcommittee report recommended on the condition that the developer should donate for wildlife conservation in the area. The project will require diversion of 1,150.08 hectares of forest land and felling of 2.7 lakh trees. The research carried out by the WII was pointed out to be inaccurate, biased, and incomplete in the 58-paged peer review of the Wildlife Conservation Plan for the impact zone of Etalin hydroelectric power (HEP). In a bizarre turn of events, the WII was reported to have asked for INR 4 crores to be granted for tiger conservation from the developer despite having ruled out the presence of tigers in the area based on a single season's study.

Within the Dibang Valley, the nearly 14,000 strong Idu Mishmi community is deeply divided over the hydroelectric project and wildlife conservation. While the people living close to the proposed Etalin site seem to be in favour of the project, many living in towns across Arunachal Pradesh and in other metropolitan centres have been resisting the project. The dams will no doubt cause lasting ecological devastation, apart from concerns that the region lies in an active seismic zone. The Idu people, of course, are aware of this. I organized a two-day seminar at Anini in 2019 titled 'Dibang Research Seminar: Initiating a Dialogue between the Idu Mishmi and Research Scholars', in which 12 researchers from 6 national institutes/organizations and NGOs, including 2 independent Idu Mishmi researchers and shamans from Dibang Valley, presented their research. Presentations ranged from tiger ecology, frog diversity, and the discovery of new butterflies to ecotourism and the belief systems of the Idu Mishmi. The general public from Dibang Valley and Etalin enthusiastically participated in the seminar. Thus, it is not that the local people are unaware of how ecologically diverse and biologically rich Dibang Valley is; they fear that the research on wildlife, especially on tigers, may hamper their opportunity to develop and progress.

Dibang Valley is considered to be the last frontier of biodiversity even within Arunachal Pradesh. Since 2012, in particular, this region has become a hotbed for wildlife biologists. One among 36 such global biodiversity hotspots across the world, the Dibang Valley is part of the eastern Himalayan global biodiversity hotspot and harbours rare, endemic, and endangered species. While the tigers get the prime focus, the region is home to more than 75 species of mammals, including clouded leopard, Asiatic golden cat, Asiatic wild dog, red panda, Mishmi takin, red goral, and gongshan muntjac. Bird surveys reveal the presence of Blyth's tragopan, Sclater's monal, rufous-necked hornbill, Ward's trogon, Hodgson's frogmouth, beautiful nuthatch, wedge-billed babbler, and the recently discovered Mishmi wren-babbler. There are reports of new species of amphibians, moths, and butterflies being discovered in the region.

In addition to research scholars, the local Idu Mishmi and their sociocultural ethos deserve the credit for conserving this ecological wealth, as does the landscape of these sparsely populated borderlands. Such landscapes are de facto natural reserves because of their remoteness. More importantly, the Idu's belief system encompasses indigenous conservation practices that allow places such as Dibang Valley to remain havens for wildlife and forests. For example, the belief that tigers (*amra*) are their brothers which forms the basis of the Idu's kinship or brotherhood relations with tigers, has definitely prevented harm to the tiger population. This unique relationship between tigers and the Idu Mishmi is part of a more extensive social–ecological–cosmological network regulated by a complex taboo system. The Idus have followed and preserved the sociologically inbuilt conservation strategies, which is a conservation model that is worth acknowledging and adopting.

Members of the Mishmi community have been critical of the letters and online petitions of scientists and activists and have questioned their credibility. The latter are seen as 'outsiders' and are accused of being unfamiliar with the issues of Dibang Valley. This is not true, as many of them have been visiting Dibang for various surveys and have interacted with the local people at length. Some of those who work in Dibang Valley are young PhD scholars or interns at the beginning of their careers. Due to institutional restrictions, they are often not permitted to have an independent voice in this politically hyper-sensitive issue. Satya does not receive much of a welcome in Dibang Valley anymore because of his discreet letter to the MoEF&CC. During the seminar, an Idu Mishmi posed this question to all researchers, 'We give you all the support— food, accommodation, hospitality—show you our forests and mountains, and share our knowledge. How can you stab us in the back?' While some Idu Mishmi expect researchers to not interfere with the development projects in the region, other locals regularly reach out to researchers requesting support for their anti-dam and pro-conservation efforts. As evident from this, there are often mixed responses to these issues by the Idu Mishmi, therefore I do not wish to paint the entire community as speaking in one voice.

While the friction between the local Idus and the researchers is evident, there are disagreements of varying degrees among the wildlife researchers in Dibang themselves over the presence of tigers in the region. As mentioned earlier, a four-month survey by the WII reported no tiger presence in the Etalin project area. In contrast, Satya found evidence of tigers living in the submergence zone and using the landscape extensively (though this information remains unpublished). The scientific opinion on the impact of the project on the region's biodiversity is divided into two camps. The WII believes that the effect will be minimal and can be mitigated through compensatory afforestation and regulation of hunting. On the other hand, those who have conducted surveys in Dibang and other similar habitats in Arunachal believe that the biodiversity value of these forests is irreplaceable. When I forwarded the response of wildlife scientists to FAC's proposal to an influential Idu Mishmi member whom I have known for several years and is known for his pro-dam stand, he responded:

Their concerns are manufactured by some researchers, and it will give a wrong message. Idu Mishmi will take a tough stand against the proposed tiger reserve if the FAC turns down the development of the 3,097 MW Etalin hydro project. The MoEF&CC directed the developer to pay money for the conservation of wildlife. This is a step we appreciate. We will stop every conservation and research work in Dibang Valley district in retaliation to this 'letter of concern' to the chairperson of the FAC by those who are unfamiliar with the Dibang Valley.

While the rift among the various interest groups continues to grow, voices from the ground are growing fainter. Moreover, during the lockdown in response to COVID-19, the standing committee of the National Board for Wildlife cleared 16 linear projects that pass through protected areas in other parts of the country. Like the rest of us, the Idus were also under lockdown, many without phones or even access to the internet. While there is news globally that nature is recuperating during this extended lockdown period, the clearance of these projects, in contrast, makes way for more ecological destruction. In fact, the lockdown period was used cleverly by the Indian government to promote infrastructure building, that is, a capitalist capture of nature and its resources. Issues as sensitive and important as the Etalin hydro project deserve more attention and, most importantly, the voices of the Idu Mishmi need to be heard in this matter. The government's haste in pushing this project during the COVID-19 lockdown indicates that the pandemic was instrumentalized by the state to avoid these difficult conversations.

Dibang Valley has witnessed massive developmental projects recently, as researchers and wildlife biologists continue to visit and study its ecology. One can only hope that the complex picture of the overlapping worlds of the ecological, the social, the national, and the political in these borderlands is acknowledged. More importantly, one must first learn to listen to the native residents of Dibang Valley and look at the issues of wildlife conservation and development through their eyes. Only such an approach can open the doors for new methods of conversation and enable a reconciliation between all interested parties.

APPENDICES

APPENDIX I: LIST OF KHĒNYŪ (SPIRITS)

ngōlō	resides in high mountains
bwēká	dwells in rivers and lakes
àsā	dwells in in tall and wide trees
āmrāji	causes landslides and creates
khəpā	dwells in deep forests, caves and deep gorges
athru	strangles women during childbirth
àsāsū	moves around the villages at night
mitu épā	guardian of mithuns
àmbū	responsible for blood dysentery
émō	responsible for epilepsy
Ìthrí	responsible for respiratory troubles
cidi	responsible for leprosy
wā	responsible for gangrene
āpōmō	responsible for bodily diseases
erhōsū	responsible for accidental fire in the house
àpu mīsù	spirit of land
andro-zinu	spirit of the house
mànū	spirit of agricultural land

Source: Linggi (2011).

APPENDIX 2: ANIMALS IN DIBANG VALLEY AND THEIR LOCAL NAMES

Common Name	Scientific Name	*Idu Name*
Eastern hoolock gibbon	*Hoolock leuconedys*	*àmē pá*
Rhesus macaque	*Macaca mulatta*	*àmē*
Alpine musk deer	*Moschus chrysogaster*	*ālā*
Indian muntjac	*Muntiacus muntjak*	*mānjō*
Gongshan muntjac	*Muntiacus gongshanensis*	*mānjō īmbù*
Sambar	*Cervus unicolor*	*màcō*
Mishmi takin	*Budorcas taxicolor taxicolor*	*ākrū*
Himalayan serow	*Capricornis sumatraensis*	*māą̀ y*
Red goral	*Naemorhedus baileyi*	*àmí*
Wild pig	*Sus scrofa*	*àmə*
Red panda	*Ailurus fulgens*	*àyimīnjīnī*
Asiatic black bear	*Ursus thibetanus*	*āhū*
Sun bear	*Helarctos malayanus*	*āhūlo*
Asiatic jackal	*Canis aureus*	*bāmbū*
Wild dog	*Cuon alpinus*	*āprūprú*
Tiger	*Panthera tigris*	*āmrā*
Common leopard	*Panthera pardus*	*āmrā kəcì*
Clouded leopard	*Neofelis nebulosa*	*kəcì mànū*
Leopard cat	*Prionailurus bengalensis*	*anchanggu*
Marbled cat	*Pardofelis marmorata*	*āmrā ārhūlī*

Asian small-clawed otter	*Amblonyx cinereus*	ārhō
Yellow-throated marten	*Martes flavigula*	ākōkŏ
Civet sp.	—	àpe
Chinese pangolin	*Manis pentadactyla*	àkùsōrō
Indian crested porcupine	*Hystrix indica*	āsō
Brush-tailed porcupine	*Hystrix brachyura*	àle
Orange-bellied Himalayan squirrel	*Dremomys lokriah*	àdànggò
Squirrel sp.	—	àdàkà
Flying squirrel sp.	—	kāme
Himalayan rat	*Rattus nitidus*	kācīnggō
Bat sp.	—	kàphū

Source: Author. Idu names are from Blench, R., Linggi, M., Meme, H., Lele Yona and A. Linggi (2018). A Dictionary of Idu:
Ango Ajopŏ. 2nd edition. Idu Language Development Committee. Mishmi Publishing House, Roing.
Scientific and common names are from IUCN Red List of Threatened Species (https://www.iucnredlist.org)

APPENDIX 3: ITEMS IN
A HUNTER'S KIT

Items	Idu Names and Remarks
Gun	*āgerē*
Cane backpack	*étō*
Tarpaulin	people stayed in caves earlier, but now use tarpaulin for making tents
Metal piece	*aanphoodi*
Match box	*āmī khrə*. In earlier days, flint stone *ālo ndro* was used to make fire
Machete	*è. ècè*
Bow-Arrow	*iḷiprá-īpūtà*
Poison	*mrà* (aconite)
Rice	*kebra*
Salt	*prā*
Chilli	*ìntsī*
Tea leaves	*phǎlā*
Rice beer	*yū*
Bag	*ākùcí*

Source: Author. Bow-arrow and poison arrows are not used for hunting anymore. These days kit includes torches, tents, sleeping bags, and mobile phones. There is no phone network in places where hunters go, but they use phones for taking photos.

APPENDIX 4: KEY VISITORS AND EVENTS IN THE MISHMI HILLS (1825–2017)

Year	Visitors/Events	Remarks
1825	Lt Burlton	The Mishmi were first mentioned by Lt Burlton (British officer). He explored the upper course of the Brahmaputra.
1826	Lt Richard Wilcox	Visited the Mishmi country and carried out a number of surveys in Assam.
1836	Dr William Griffith	A British botanist, he travelled up to the Lohit river to explore the natural history of the area.
1848	Permanund Acharya	Murdered in the Mishmi Hills when he travelled to Tibet from Assam.
1873	T. T. Cooper	A Britisher who explored routes for tea trade.
1854	Fathers Krick and Bourry	French missionaries murdered in the Mishmi Hills.
1885	J. F. Needham	Visited Mishmi Hills and nearly reached Rima.
1911–12	Mishmi Mission	Punitive mission by Major Dundas (British officer).
1945	B. H. Routledge	British Political Officer posted in the Mishmi Hills.
1950	Anini outpost	The first ever office to be set up by the Indian government in the region.

(Cont'd)

Year	Visitors/Events	Remarks
1980	Rajiv Gandhi	The first and only prime minister to visit Anini.
1980	Lohit to Dibang district	Dibang district was carved out of Lohit district, with Anini as its headquarters.
1983	Road construction	First metalled road constructed up to Anini.
1998	Dibang Wildlife Sanctuary	4194 sq kms of the district set aside for wildlife conservation.
2001	Dibang district	Dibang district was divided into two: Dibang Valley and Lower Dibang Valley.
2013–14	Wildlife conservation	Dibang Tiger Reserve (proposal stage)
2017	Dhola-Sadiya bridge, also called Bhupen Hazarika Bridge	Inaugurated by Prime Minister Narendra Modi.

Source: Author.

APPENDIX 5: *LUCANUS MISHMI* (A BEETLE SPECIES)

Source: Oxford DAM.

BIBLIOGRAPHY

Abram, D. 1997. *The Spell of the Sensuous: Perception and Language in a More-Than-Human World*. New York: Vintage Books.

Adams, W. M. 2004. *Against Extinction: The Story of Conservation*. London: EarthScan.

———. 2007. 'Thinking Like a Human: Social Science and the Two Cultures Problem'. *Oryx* 41, no. 3: 275–6.

Adger, W. N., J. Barnett, F. S. Chapin, and H. Ellemor. 2011. 'This Must Be the Place: Underrepresentation of Identity and Meaning in Climate Change Decision-Making'. *Global Environmental Politics* 11, no. 2: 1–25.

Adhikarimayum, A. S., and Gopi, G. V. 2018. 'First Photographic Record of Tiger Presence at Higher Elevations of the Mishmi Hills in the Eastern Himalayan Biodiversity Hotspot, Arunachal Pradesh, India'. *Journal of Threatened Taxa* 10, no. 13: 12,833–6.

Afiff, S., and C. Lowe. 2008. 'Collaboration, Conservation and Community: A Conversation between Suraya Afiff and Celia Lowe'. In *Biodiversity and Human Livelihoods in Protected Areas: Case Studies from the Malay Archipelago*, edited by N. S. Sodhi, G. Acciaioli, M. Erb, and A. K. Tan, 153–64. Cambridge: Cambridge University Press.

Agrawal, A., and C. Gibson. 1999. 'Enchantment and Disenchantment: The Role of Community in Natural Resource Conservation'. *World Development* 27, no. 4: 629–49.

Agrawal, A., and E. Ostrom. 2006. 'Political Science and Conservation Biology: A Dialog of the Deaf?' *Conservation Biology* 20, no. 3: 681–2.

Aiga, H. 2007. 'Bombarding People with Questions: A Reconsideration of Survey Ethics'. *Bulletin of World Health Oganisation* 85, no. 11: 823–4.

Aisher, A. 2005. *Through 'Spirits': Cosmology and Landscape Ecology among the Nyishi Tribe of Upland Arunachal Pradesh, Northeast India*. PhD Thesis, University College London, United Kingdom.

Aiyadurai, A. 2007. *Hunting in a Biodiversity Hotspot: A Survey on Hunting Practices by Indigenous Communities in Arunachal Pradesh, Northeast India*. Rufford Small Grants Foundation UK, Nature Conservation Foundation, Mysore.

———. 2011. 'Wildlife Hunting and Conservation in Northeast India: A Need for an Interdisciplinary Understanding'. *International Journal of Galliformes Conservation* 2: 61–73.

———. 2018. 'Hunting in Northeast India and the Challenges of Implementing Wildlife Protection Act'. In *Nature Conservation in the New Economy: People, Wildlife and the Law in India*, edited by G. Shahabuddin and K. Sivaramakrishnan, 31–54. New Dehi: Orient BlackSwan.

Aiyadurai, A., and S. Banerjee. 2019. 'Bird conservation from obscurity to popularity: a case study of two bird species from Northeast India'. *GeoJournal*. Available at https://doi.org/10.1007/s10708-019-09999-9. Last accessed on 4 June 2018.

Aiyadurai, A., N. J. Singh, and E. J. Milner-Gulland. 2010. 'Wildlife Hunting by Indigenous Tribes: A Case Study from Arunachal Pradesh, Northeast India'. *Oryx* 44, no. 4: 564–72.

Aiyadurai, A., and S. Varma. 2003. *Dog and Bull: An Investigation into Carnivore–Human Conflict in and around Itanagar Wildlife Sanctuary, Arunachal Pradesh*. Wildlife Trust of India, New Delhi.

Aiyadurai, A., and N. Velho. 2018. 'The Last Hunters of Arunachal Pradesh: The Past and the Present of Wildlife Hunting in Northeast India'. In *Conservation from the Margins*, edited by U. Srinivasan and N. Velho, 69–93. New Delhi: Orient BlackSwan.

Alcorn, J. B. 2005. 'Dances around the Fire: Conservation Organizations and Community-Based Natural Resource Management'. In *Communities and Conservation: Histories and Politics of Community-Based Natural Resource Management*, edited by J. P. Brosius, A. L. Tsing, and C. Zenner, 37–68. Walnut Creek, CA: AltaMira Press.

Ali, S., and D. Ripley. 1948. 'The Birds of the Mishmi Hills'. *Journal of the Bombay Natural History Society* 48, no. 1: 1–37.

Alvard, M. 2000. 'The Impact of Traditional Subsistence Hunting and Trapping on Prey Populations: Data from Wana Horticulturalists of Upland Central Sulawesi, Indonesia'. In *Hunting for Sustainability in Tropical Forests*, edited by J. G. Robinson and E. L. Bennett, 214–30. New York: Columbia University Press.

Anderson, B. 1982. *Imagined Communities: Reflections on the Origin and Spread of Nationalism*. London, New York: Verso.

Argyrou, V. 2005. *The Logic of Environmentalism: Anthropology, Ecology and Postcoloniality*. New York and Oxford: Berghahn.

———. 2009. 'Virtualism and the Logic of Environmentalism'. In *Virtualism, Governance and Practice: Vision and Execution in Environmental Conservation*, edited by J. G. Carrier and P. West, 24–44. New York: Berghahn.

Armerio, M., and G. Von Hardenberg. 2014. 'Editorial Introduction to Special Issue: Nature and Nation'. *Environment and History* 20, no. 1: 1–8.

Asiwaju, A. I. 1985. *Partitioned Africans: Ethnic Relations across Africa's International Boundaries 1884–1984*. New York: St. Martin's Press.

Bailey, F. M. 1912a. 'Journey through a Portion of South-Eastern Tibet and the Mishmi Hills'. *The Geographical Journal* 39, no. 4: 334–47.

———. 1912b. Report on the Work of the Dibang Column—Mishmi Mission (1911–1912), IOR/MSS/EUR F 157, 304 (d). London: British Library.

Banks, D., and B. Wright. 2006. *Skinning the Cat: Crime and Politics of the Big Cat Skin Trade*. Report by the Wildlife Protection Society of India (WPSI), Environment Investigation Agency (EIA), New Delhi.

Baral, K. C. 2009. 'Colonialism and Ethnography: In Search of an Alternative Mode of Representation'. *Man and Society: A Journal of North East Studies* 6, no. 84F: 83–94.

Baruah, S. 2003. 'Nationalising Space: Cosmetic Federalism and the Politics of Development in Northeast India'. *Development and Change* 34, no. 5: 915–39.

Baruah, T. K. 1988. *The Idu Mishmis*. Itanagar: Directorate of Research, Government of Arunachal Pradesh.

Basu, D. R., and V. Miroshnik. 2012. 'China–India Border Dispute and Tibet'. 東南アジア研究年報 (Annual Review of Southeast Asian Studies) 53: 43–51.

Baud, M., and W. Van Schendel. 1997. 'Toward a Comparative History of Borderlands'. *Journal of World History* 8, no. 2: 211–42.

Baviskar, A. 1995. *In the Belly of the River: Tribal Conflicts over Development in the Narmada Valley*. New Delhi: Oxford University Press.

———. 2002. 'The Politics of the City'. *Seminar* 516. Available at https://www.india-seminar.com/2002/516/516%20amita%20baviskar.htm. Last accessed on 25 June 2020.

———. 2003. 'Tribal Politics and Discourses of Indian Environmentalism'. In *Nature in the Global South: Environmental Projects in South and Southeast Asia*, edited by P. Greenough and A. Tsing, 289–318. Durhan & London: Duke University Press.

———. 2008. *Contested Grounds: Essays on Nature, Culture, and Power*. New Delhi: Oxford University Press.

Beck, U. 2010. 'Climate for Change, or How to Create a Green Modernity?' *Theory Culture and Society* 27, no. 2–3: 254–66.

Bennett, E. L., and M. Rao. 2002. *Wild Meat Consumption in Asian Tropical Forests Countries: Is This a Glimpse of the Future for Africa?* Switzerland and Cambridge, UK: International Union for Conservation of Nature and Natural Resources (IUCN), Gland.

Bennett, E. L., and J. G. Robinson. 2001. *Hunting of Wildlife in Tropical Forests: Implications for Biodiversity and Forest Peoples*. Washington, DC: World Bank Environment Department.

Bèteille, A. 1998. 'The Idea of Indigenous People'. *Current Anthropology* 39, no. 2: 187–92.

————. 2006. 'What Should We Mean by "Indigenous People?"' In *Indigeneity in India*, edited by B. G. Karlsson and T. B. Subba, 19–31. London: Kegan Paul.

Bhattacharjee, P. C. 2002. 'Cross-Country Trade of Arunachal Pradesh in Retrospect'. In *Cross-Border Trade of Northeast India*, edited by S. Dutta, 33–41. Kolkata: Greenwich Millennium Press Ltd.

Bhattacharjee, T. K. 1983. *Idus of Mathun and Dri Valley*. Shillong: Directorate of Research, Government of Arunachal Pradesh.

Bhaumik, S. 2009. *Troubled Periphery: Crisis of India's North East*. New Delhi: Sage Publications Ltd.

Bird-David, N. 1990. 'The Giving Environment: Another Perspective on the Economic System of Gatherer-Hunters'. *Current Anthropology* 31, no. 2: 189–96.

Blench, R. 2018 'Attempts to Write the Idu Mishmi Language and a Proposal for a Modern Orthography'. Available at http://www.rogerblench.info/Language/NEI/Mishmi/Idu/Idulang/igrms-mishmi-tarun_chp_10. Last accessed on 30 November 2019.

Bourdieu, P. 1986. 'The Forms of Capital'. In *Handbook of Theory and Research for the Sociology of Education*, edited by J. G. Richardson, 241–58. New York: Greenwood Press.

Bose, M. L. 1979. *History of Arunachal Pradesh*. New Delhi: Concept Publishing Company.

Bonner, R. 1994. *At the Hand of Man: Peril and Hope for African Wildlife*. New York: Vintage Books.

Bouissac, P. 2010. *Semiotics at the Circus*. New York: De Gruyer Mouton.

Brockington, D. 2001. *Fortress Conservation: The Preservation of the Mkomazi Game Reserve, Tanzania*. Suffolk, UK: James Curry Publishers.

Brosius, J. P. 1999. 'Analyses and Interventions: Anthropological Engagements with Environmentalism'. *Current Anthropology* 40, no. 3: 277–309.

————. 2006. 'Common Ground between Anthropology and Conservation Biology'. *Conservation Biology* 20, no. 3: 683–5.

Brosius, J. P., A. Tsing, and C. Zerner. 2005. *Communities and Conservation: Histories and Politics of Community-Based Natural Resource Management*. Walnut Creek, CA: AltaMira Press.

Brown, K. 1998. 'The Political Ecology of Biodiversity, Conservation and Development in Nepal's Terai: Confused Meanings, Means and Ends'. *Ecological Economics* 24, no. 1: 73–87.

Bryant, R., and Parnwell, M. 1996. *Environmental Change in Southeast Asia: People, Politics and Sustainable Development*. London and New York: Routledge.

Bulliet, R. 2005. *Hunters, Herders, and Hamburgers: The Past and Future of Human–Animal Relationships*. New York: Columbia University Press.

Carson, M. K. 2014. *Park Scientists: Gila Monsters, Geysers, and Grizzly Bears in America's Own Backyard*. New York: Houghton Mifflin Harcourt Publishing Company.

Cassidy, R., and M. Mullin. 2007. *Where the Wild Things Are Now: Domestication Reconsidered*. Oxford and New York: Berg.

Cederlof, G., and K. Sivaramakrishnan. 2007. *Ecological Nationalisms: Nature, Livelihoods and Identities in South Asia*. Seattle: University of Washington Press.

Central Zoo Authority. 2009. Notificaton, 10 November. Itanagar: Government of Arunachal Pradesh, Ministry of Environment and Forests.

Chandra, A. 2014. 'How Hindi Became the Language of Choice in Arunachal Pradesh'. *Scroll.in*, 22 August. Available at http://scroll.in/article/675419/How-Hindi-became-the-language-of-choice-in-Arunachal-Pradesh/. Last accessed on 4 September 2014.

Chaudhuri, S. 2008. 'Plight of the *Igus*: Notes on Shamanism among the Idu Mishmis of Arunachal Pradesh, India'. *European Bulletin of Himalayan Research* 32 (Spring): 84–108.

Childe, G. 1952. *New Light on the Most Ancient East*. London: Routledge & Kegan Paul Ltd.

Choksi, N. 2019. 'Heritage Regimes and the Question of Repatriation in India'. Paper presented at the American Anthropological Association (AAA)/Canadian Anthropology Society (CASCA) Annual Conference, Vancouver, Canada, 24 November.

Clayton, S. 2003. 'Environmental Identity: A Conceptual and an Operational Definition'. In *Identity and the Natural Environment: The Psychological Significance of Nature*, edited by S. Clayton and S. Opotow, 45–65. Cambridge, MA: MIT Press.

Clayton, L. M., M. Keeling, and E. J. Milner-Gulland. 1997. 'Bringing Home the Bacon: A Spatial Model of Wild Pig Harvesting in Sulawesi, Indonasia'. *Ecological Applications* 7, no. 2: 642–52.

Clayton, S., and S. Opotow. 2003. *Identity and the Natural Environment: The Psychological Significance of Nature*. Cambridge, MA: MIT Press.

Clutton-Brock, J. 1994. 'The Unnatural World: Behavioural Aspects of Humans and Animals in the Process of Domestication'. In *Animals and Human Society: Changing Perspectives*, edited by A. Manning and J. Serpell, 23–36. London: Routledge.

Conklin, B. A., and R. L. Graham. 1995. 'The Shifting Middle Ground: Amazonian Indians and Eco-Politics'. *American Anthropologist* 97, no. 4: 695–710.

Corlett, R. T. 2007. 'The Impact of Hunting on the Mammalian Fauna of Tropical Asian Forests'. *Biotropica* 39, no. 3: 292–303.

Cooper, T. T. 1873. *The Mishmee Hills: An Account of a Journey Made in an Attempt to Penetrate Thibet from Assam to Open New Routes for Commerce*. London: H. S. King & Co.

Coy, P. G., and L. M. Woehrle. 2000. *Social Conflicts and Collective Identities*. UK: Rowman & Littlefield Publishers, Inc.

Cronon, W. 1996. *Uncommon Ground: Rethinking the Human Place in Nature*. New York: W.W. Norton & Company.

Datta, A. 2002. '*Status of Hornbills and Hunting among Tribal Communities in Eastern Arunachal Pradesh*'. Unpublished report, Wildlife Conservation Society and WCS-India Program, Bangalore.

———. 2007. 'Protecting with People in Namdapha: Threatened Forests, Forgotten People'. In *Making Conservation Work: Securing Biodiversity in This New Century*, edited by G. Shahabuddin and M. Rangarajan, 165–209. New Delhi: Permanent Black.

Datta, A., M. O. Anand, and R. Naniwadekar. 2008. 'Empty Forests: Large Carnivore and Prey Abundance in Namdapha National Park, North-East India'. *Biological Conservation* 141, no. 5: 1429–35.

Deccan Herald. 2011. 'Shoot at Sight Order at Roing Area of Lower Dibang Valley'. 19 March. Available at http://www.deccanherald.com/content/147061/shoot-sight-order-roing-area.html. Last accessed on 24 December 2016.

Dele, R. 2017. *Idu Mishmi Shamanic Funeral Ritual Ya*. Delhi: Bookwell Publications.

Descola, P. 2013. *Beyond Nature and Culture*. Chicago: University of Chicago Press.

Dikshit, S. 2013. 'Arunachal Archers with Stapled Visas Prevented from Leaving for China'. *The Hindu*. Available at http://www.thehindu.com/news/national/arunachal-archers-with-stapled-visas-prevented-from-leaving-for-china/article5226118.ece. Last accessed on 19 May 2015.

Dooren, V. T. 2015. 'A Day with Crows: Rarity, Nativity, and the Violent-Care of Conservation'. *Animal Studies Journal* 4, no. 2: 1–28.

Down to Earth. 2008. 'Disquiet in Dibang'. Available at http://www.downtoearth.org.in/coverage/disquiet-in-dibang-4539. Last accessed on 24 October 2015.

Duffy, R. 2010. *Nature Crime: How We're Getting Conservation Wrong*. New Haven: Yale University Press.

Dutt, B. 2004. *Biodiversity, Livelihoods and the Law: The Case of 'Jogi-Nath' Snake Charmers of India*. New Delhi: Wildlife Trust of India.

Dutta, A. P. 2008. 'Reservoir of Dams: Arunachal Pradesh'. *Down to Earth* 16, no. 24: 32–9.

Eilenberg, M. 2012. *At the Edges of States: Dynamics of State Formation in the Indonesian Borderlands*. Leiden: KITLV Press.

Elwin, V. 1959. A Philosophy for NEFA. Itanagar: Director of Research, Government of Arunachal Pradesh.

Elwin, V. 1964. *The Tribal World of Verrier Elwin: An Autobiography*. New Delhi: Oxford India.

Erb, M. 2012. 'The Dissonance of Conservation: Environmentalities and the Environmentalisms of the Poor in Eastern Indonesia'. *The Raffles Bulletin of Zoology* 25: 11–23.

Erb, M., and G. Acciaioli. 2006. 'Conservation with and against People(s)'. In *Biodiversity and Human Livelihoods in Protected Areas: Case Studies from the Malay Archipelago*, edited by N. S. Sodhi, G. Acciaioli, M. Erb, and A. K. Tan, 143–52. New York: Cambridge University Press.

Erni, C. 2000. 'Indigenous People's Self-Determination in Northeast India'. In *Indigenous Affairs: Self-Determination*, edited by C. Erni and M. Jensen, 56–66. Copenhagen: International Work Group for Indignenous Affairs.

Fa, J. E., R. W. Burn, and G. Broad. 2002. 'Bushmeat Consumption and Preferences of Two Ethnic Groups in Bioko Island, West Africa'. *Human Ecology* 30, no. 3: 397–416.

Faier, L., and L. Rofel. 2014. 'Ethnographies of Encounter'. *Annual Review of Anthropology* 43: 363–77.

Fei, X. 1980. 'Ethnic Identification in China'. *Social Sciences in China* 1, no. 10: 94–107.

Fletcher, R. 2010. 'Neoliberal Environmentality: Towards a Poststructualist Poliltical Ecology of the Conservation Debate'. *Conservation and Society* 8, no. 3: 171–81.

Foale, S., and M. Macintyre. 2005. 'Green Fantasies: Photographic Representations of Biodiversity and Ecotourism in the Western Pacific'. *Journal of Political Ecology* 12, no. 1: 1–21.

Frank, D. J., A. Hironaka, and E. Schofar. 2000. 'The Nation-State and the Natural Environment over the Twentieth Century'. *American Sociological Review* 65, no. 1: 96–116.

Franklin, A. 2002. *Nature and Social Theory*. London: Sage Publications Ltd.

———. 2006. *Animal Nation: The True Story of Animals and Australia*. Sydney: Universty of New South Wales Press.

Gadgil, M., and R. Guha. 1995. *Ecology and Equity: Use and Abuse of Nature in Contemporary India*. London: Routledge.

Gadgil, M., and K. C. Malhotra. 1998. 'The Ecological Significance of Caste'. In *Social Ecology*, edited by R. Guha, 27–41. Delhi: Oxford University Press.

Gao, D. 2015. 'Railways and the Issue of Inner Line Permit in Arunachal Pradesh: Can the Two Function Together?' *Economic and Political Weekly* 50, no. 8. Available at http://www.epw.in/journal/2015/8/reports-states-web-exclusives/railways-and-issue-inner-line-permit-arunachal-pradesh. Last accessed on 7 October 2016.

Gartlan, S. 1998. 'Every Man for Himself and God against All: History, Social Science and the Conservation of Nature'. *Bulletin Series, Yale School of Forestry and Environmental Studies* 102: 216–26.

Ghimire, K. 1992. *Forest or Farm? The Politics of Poverty and Land Hunger in Nepal*. Delhi: Oxford University Press.

Ghosal, S., V. R. Athrey, J. Linnell, and P. O. Vedeld. 2013. 'An Ontological Crisis? A Review of Large Felid Conservation in India'. *Biological Conservation* 22, no. 11: 2665–81.

Gissibl, B., S. Hohler, and P. Kupper. 2012. *Civilizing Nature: National Parks in Global Historical Perspective*. New York: Berghahn.

Government of India (GoI). 1994. *The Indian Wildlife Protection Act, 1972 (as Amended Upto 1993)*. Second edition. Dehradun Natraj Publishers.

Goldman, M. J., P. Nadasdy, and M. D. Turner. 2011. *Knowing Nature: Conversations at the Intersections of Political Ecology and Science Studies*. Chicago: Universty of Chicago Press.

Gopi, G. V., Q. Qureshi, and Y. V. Jhala. 2014. *A Rapid Field Survey of Tigers and Prey in Dibang Valley District, Arunachal Pradesh*. Technical report, National Tiger Conservation Authority, New Delhi; Wildlife Institute of India, Dehradun; and Department of Environment and Forests, Government of Arunachal Pradesh, TR-2014/001.

Govindrajan, R. 2018. *Animal Intimacies: Interspecies Relatedness in India's Central Himalayas*. Chicago: University of Chicago Press.

Greenough, P. 2003. 'Pathogens, Pugmarks, and Political "Emergency?": The 1970s South Asian Debate on Nature'. In *Nature in the Global South: Environmental Projects in South and Southeast Asia*, edited by P. Greenough and A. Tsing, 201–30. Durham & London: Duke University Press.

Griffin, P. B., and M. B. Griffin. 2000. 'Agta Hunting and Sustainability of Resource Use in Northeastern Luzon, Philippines'. In *Hunting for Sustainability in Tropical Forests*, edited by J. G. Robinson and E. L. Bennett, 325–35. New York: Columbia University Press.

Guha, R. 1997. 'The Authoritarian Biologist and the Arrogance of Anti-Humanism'. *The Ecologist* 27, no. 1: 14–20.

———. 1999. *Savaging the Civilized: Verrier Elwin, His Tribals, and India*. Chicago: University of Chicago Press.

Guite, J. 2014. 'Colonialism and Its Unruly? The Colonial State and Kuki Riads in Nineteenth Century Northeast India'. *Modern Asian Studies* 48 no. 5: 1188–232.

Guyot-Rèchard. B. 2017. *Shadow States: India, China and the Himalayas, 1910–1962*. New York: Cambridge University Press.

Hacking, I. 1990. *The Taming of Chance*. Cambridge, UK: Cambridge University Press.

Hage, G. 1998. *White Nation: Fantasies of White Supremacy in a Multicultural Society*. Annadale, NSW: Pluto.

Hall, S. 1991. 'The Local and the Global: Globalization and Ethnicity'. In *Culture, Globalization and the World-System: Contemporary Conditions for the Representations of Identity*, edited by A. D. King, 19–41. Hamsphire: Macmillan.

———. 1996. 'Introduction: Who Needs Identity?' In *Questions of Cultural Identity*, edited by S. Hall and P. DuGay, 1–17. London: Sage.

Hamilton, A. 1912. *In Abor Jungles: Being an Account of the Abor Expedition, the Mishmi Mission and the Miri Mission*. London: Eveleigh Nash.

Hardiman, D. 1987. *The Coming of the Devi: Adivasi Assertion in Western India*. Delhi: Oxford University Press.

Hardin, G. 1968. 'The Tragedy of the Commons'. *Science* 162, no. 3859: 1243–8.

Hardman, C. 2000. 'We, the Brothers of Tiger and Bamboo: On the Notions of Person and Kin in the Eastern Hills of Nepal'. In *Culture, Creation and Procreation: Concepts of Kinship in South Asian Practice*, edited by M. Böck and A. Rao, 53–80. New York: Berghahn Books.

Heatherington, T. 2012. 'Remodeling the Fortress of Conservation? Living Landscapes and the New Technologies of Environmental Governance'. *Anthropological Forum* 22, no. 2: 165–85.

Heriot, L. 1979. *The First Martyrs in Arunachal Pradesh: The Story of Frs. Krick and Bourry Foreign Missionaries of Paris*. Bombay: Asian Trading Corporation.

Hilaluddin, R. Kaul, and D. Ghose. 2005. 'Conservation Implications of Wild Animal Biomass Extractions in Northeast India'. *Animal Biodiversity and Conservation* 28, no. 2: 169–79.

Hornborg, A., and M. Kurkiala. 1998. *Voices of the Land: Identity and Ecology in the Margins*. Part of the series *Lund Studies in Human Ecology*, volume 1. Sweden: Lund University Press.

Howell, Signe. 1982. 'Chewong Myths and Legends'. *Malaysian Branch of the Royal Asiatic Society* 11: 136.

———. 1984. *Society and Cosmos: Chewong of Peninsular Malaysia*. Singapore: Oxford University Press.

Igoe, J. 2004. *Conservation and Globalization: A Study of National Parks and Indigenous Communities from East Africa to South Dakota*. Belmont, CA: Wadsworth.

Ingold, T. 1980 *Hunters, Pastoralists and Ranchers: Reindeer Economies and Their Transformations*. London: Cambridge University Press.

———. 1986. *The Appropriation of Nature: Essays on Human Ecology and Social Relations*. UK: Manchester University Press.

———. 1994. 'From Trust to Domination: An Alternative History of Human–Animal Relations'. In *Animals and Human Society: Changing Perspectives*, edited by A. Manning and J. Serpell, 1–22. London and New York: Routledge.

———. 1996. 'Hunting and Gathering as Ways of Receiving the Environment'. In *Redefining Nature: Ecology, Culture and Domestication*, edited by R. Ellen and F. Katsuyoshi, 117–56. Oxford: Berg.

———. 2000. 'From Trust to Domination: An Alternative History of Human–Animal Relations'. In *The Perception of the Environment: Essays on Livelihood, Dwelling and Skill*, edited by T. Ingold, 61–77. London and New York: Routledge.

International Union for Conservation of Nature (IUCN). *The IUCN Red List of Threatened Species*. Available at www.iucnredlist.org. Last accessed on 19 November 2014.

Jacob, J. 2011. 'For a New Kind of Forward Policy': Tibet and Sino-Indian Relations', Special issue: Revisiting the China-India Border Dispute *China Report*, 47, no. 2: 135–148.

Jalais, A. 2010. *Forest of Tigers: People, Politics & Environment in the Sundarbans*. New Delhi: Routledge.

Jamieson, D. 2001. *A Companion to Environmental Philosophy*. Oxford: Blackwell Publishers Ltd.

Jhala, Y. V., Q. Qureshi, and A. K. Nayak. 2019. *The Status of Tigers, Co-predators, and Prey in India 2018*. Summary report, TR No./2019/05. National Tiger Conservation Authority, Wildlife Institute of India, Dehradun, India.

Johnsingh, A. J. T. 1982. 'Ecology and Behaviour of Dhole or Indian Wild Dog (*Cuon alpinus* Pallas 1811) with Special Reference to Predator–Prey Relations at Bandipur'. PhD Thesis, Madurai Kamaraj University, Madurai, India.

———. 2013. 'Hunting Out: Poaching in the Mishmi Hills'. *Frontline*, 15 November. Available at https://frontline.thehindu.com/environment/conservation/hunting-out/article5275950.ece. Last accessed on 14 January 2016.

Kabra, A. 2009. 'Conservation-Induced Displacement: A Comparative Study of Two Indian Protected Areas'. *Conservation and Society* 7, no. 4: 249–67.

Karlsson, B. G. 2000. *Contested Belonging: An Indigenous People's Struggle for Forest and Identity in Sub-Himalayan Bengal*. London: Routledge.

Karlsson, B. G., and T. B. Subba. 2006. *Indigeneity in India*. London: Kegan Paul.

Kaul, R., Hilauddin, J. S. Jandrotia, and P. J. K. McGowan. 2004. 'Hunting of Large Mammals and Pheasants in the Indian Western Himalaya'. *Oryx* 38, no. 4: 426–31.

Kaul, S. 2014. *Use Locals to Protect Borders*. *India Today*, 8 August. Available at http://indiatoday.intoday.in/story/sanat-kaul-kiren-rijiju-indo-tibetan-border-shyam-saran-mcmohan-line/1/376048.html. Last accessed on 28 August 2016.

Kaulback, R. 1935. 'Letter from Ronald Kaulback to Col. F.M. Bailey'. Mss Eur F157/252. London: The Birtish Library.

King, B., and J. P. Donahue. 2006. 'The Rediscovery and Song of the Rusty-Throated Wren Babbler *Spelaeornis badeigularis*'. *Forktail* 22: 113–15.

Kingdon-Ward, F. 1913. *The Land and of the Blue Poppy: Travels of a Naturalist in Eastern Tibet*. Cambridge: Cambridge University Press.

Kirksey, S. E., and S. Helmreich. 2010. 'The Emergence of Multispecies Ethnography'. *Cultural Anthropology* 25, no. 4: 545–76.

Knight, J. 2004. *Wildlife in Asia: Cultural Perspectives*. London: Routledge Curzon.

———. 2005. *Animals in Person: Cultural Perspectives on Human–Animal Intimacy*. Oxford and New York: Berg.

Kohn, E. 2013. *How Forests Think: Toward an Anthropology beyond the Human*. Berkeley: University of California Press.

Kothari, A. 2003. 'Protected Areas and Social Justice: The View from South Asia'. *The George Wright Forum* 20, no. 1: 4–17.

Kri, H. 2008. *The Mishmis: An Introduction*. Tinsukia: The City Press.

Kumara, H. N., and M. Singh. 2004. 'The Influence of Differing Hunting Practices on the Relative Abundance of Mammals in Two Rainforest Areas of the Western Ghats, India'. *Oryx* 38, no. 3: 321–7.

Kumar, M. 2014. *PM to Decide on Constructing 2000 Km Strategic Road in Arunachal Pradesh. Daily News and Analysis*, 5 November. Available at http://www.dnaindia.com/india/report-pm-to-decide-on-constructing-2000-km-strategic-road-in-arunachal-pradesh-2032161. Last accessed on 29 August 2016.

Kurian, N. 2014. *India–China Borderlands: Conversations Beyond the Centre*. New Delhi: Sage Publications Ltd.

Lang, R. (朗润芳), and Qianghaduogi (强巴多吉). 2000. *Discussing Dengba People* (小议察隅僜巴人 [*Xiaoyichayu Dengbaren*]). China Tibet (Zhongguo Xizang [中国西藏]) 1: 37.

Laudati, A. 2010. 'Ecotourism: The Modern Predator? Implications of Gorilla Tourism on Local Livelihoods in Bwindi Impenetrable National Park, Uganda'. *Environment and Planning D: Society and Space* 28, no. 4: 726–43.

Lewis, M. 2003. *Inventing Global Ecology: Tracking the Biodiversity Ideal in India, 1945–1997*. New Delhi: Orient Longman.

Lewis, P. M., G. Simons, and C. D. Fennig. 2013. *Ethnologue: Languages of the World*, 17th Edition. Dallas, Texas: SIL International.

Li, J. (李建文). 2008. 'The 57th Minority' (Di Wushiqigi 'Minzu' [第五十七个民族']). *Youth Science (Qingnian Kexue [青年科])* 11: 41.

Li, T. M. 2000. 'Articulating Indigenous Identity in Indonesia: Resource Politics and the Tribal Slot'. *Comparative Studies in Society and History* 42, no. 1: 149–79.

Linggi, M. 2011. *Origin of Idu Mishmi*. Reh Souvenir, Roing.

Lugard, F. 1972. *The Dual Mandate in British Tropical Africa*. Edinburgh and London: William Blackwood and Sons.

Luke, T. 1997. *Ecocritique: Contesting the Politics of Nature, Economy, and Culture*. Minneapolis: University of Minnesota Press.

———. 1999. 'Environmentality as Green Governmentality'. In *Discourses of the Environment*, edited by E. Darrier, 121–51. Oxford: Blackwell.

Lyte, C. 1989. *Frank Kingdon-Ward: The Last of the Great Plant Hunters*. London: John Murray.

MacKenzie, J. M. 1988. *The Empire of Nature: Hunting, Conservation and British Imperialism*. UK: Manchester University Press.

Madhusudan, M. D., and K. U. Karanth. 2002. 'Local Hunting and the Conservation of Large Mammals in India'. *Ambio* 31, no. 1: 49–54.

Mainprice, F. P. 1945. *Tour Diary of F.P. Mainprice, ICS, Assistant Political Officer, Lohit Valley, Nov 1943–May 1945*. Mss Eur D1191/3. London: The British Library.

Manning, A., and A. James Serpell. 1994. *Animals and Human Society: Changing Perspectives*. London: Routledge.

Marcus, G. E., and D. Cushman. 1982. 'Ethnographies as Texts'. *Annual Review of Anthropology* 11: 25–69.

Marx, K. 1979. *Capital: A Critique of Political Economy*, volume 1. London: Penguin Books.

Mascia, M. B., J. P. Brosius, T. A. Dobson, B. C. Forbes, L. Horowitz, M. A. McKean, and N. J. Turner. 2003. 'Conservation and the Social Sciences'. *Conservation Biology* 17, no. 3: 649–50.

McAfee, K. 1999a. *Biodiversity and the Contradictions of Green Developmentalism*. PhD thesis, Department of Geography, University of California at Berkeley, USA.

———. 1999b. 'Selling Nature to Save It? Biodiversity and Green Developmentalism'. *Environment and Planning D: Society and Space* 17, no. 2: 133–54.

McDuie-Ra, D. 2012. *Northeast Migrants in Delhi: Race, Refuge and Retail*. Amsterdam: Amsterdam University Press.

McKibben, B. 1989. *The End of Nature*. New York: Random House.

Mathur, V. B., A. K. Nayak, and N. A. Ansari. 2019. 'Fourth Cycle of Management Effectiveness Evaluation (MEE) of Tiger Reserves in India, 2018'. Report by National Tiger Conservation Agency, Wildlife Institute of India, Ministry of Environment, Forests and Climate Change, Government of India.

Melucci, A. 1980. 'The New Social Movements: A Theoretical Approach'. *Social Science Information* 19, no. 2: 199–226.

Mene, T and S. K. Chaudhuri. 2019. *Change and Continuity among tribes: The Idu Mishmis of Arunachal Pradesh*. New Delhi: Rawat Publications.

Mene, T. 2011. *Suicides among the Idu Mishmi Tribe of Arunachal Pradesh*. PhD thesis, Department of Anthropology, Rajiv Gandhi University, Itanagar.

——. 2013. 'Understimation of Suicide: A Study of the Idu Mishmi Tribe of Arunachal Pradesh'. *Economic and Political Weekly* 48, no. 52: 129–33.

Menon, V., and A. Kumar. 1997. *Signed and Sealed: The Fate of the Asian Elephant*. A report by the Asian Elephant Conservation Centre, Wildlife Protection Society of India.

de Merode, E., K. Homewood, and G. Cowlishaw. 2004. 'The Value of Bushmeat and Other Wild Foods to Rural Households Living in Extreme Poverty in Democratic Republic of Congo'. *Biological Conservation* 118, no. 5: 573–81.

Mills, J. P. 1952. 'The Mishmis of the Lohit Valley, Assam'. *The Journal of the Royal Anthropological Institute of Great Britain and Ireland* 82, no. 1: 1–12.

Mishra, C., M. D. Madhusudan, and A. Datta. 2006. 'Mammals of the High Altitudes of Western Arunachal Pradesh, Eastern Himalaya: An Assessment of Threats and Conservation Needs'. *Oryx* 40, no. 1: 29–35.

Misra, P. K. 2012. 'J. H. Hutton and Colonial Ethnography of North-East India'. In *North-East India: A Handbook of Anthropology*, edited by T. B. Subba, 57–78. New Delhi: Oriental BlackSwan.

Mitchell, J. F. 1883. *Report (Topographical, Political, and Military) on the North-East Frontier of India*. Calcutta: Superintendent of Government Printing.

Mitchell, T. 1995. *Ecological Identity: Becoming a Reflective Environmentalist*. Cambridge: MIT Press.

Ministry of Environment, Forests and Climate Change (MoEF). n.d. *List of Tiger Reserves Core and Buffer Areas*. Available at www://projecttiger.nic.in/content/109_1_ListofTigerReservesCoreBufferAreas.aspx. Last accessed on 31 March 2015.

Miri, M. 2010. 'Quickwitted Anno and other Tales on Idu Mishmi Folktales of Arunachal Pradesh'. Roing: RIWATCH.

Monahan, F. J. 1899. '*Massacre at Mitaigaon, a Khamti Hamlet, and Proposals for an Expedition against the Bebejoya Mishmis*'. 432 For./3332 P. Itanagar, Arunachal Pradesh: State Archives Office, Directorate of Research.

Moore, D. S., J. Kosek, and A. Pandian. 2003. *Race, Nature, and the Politics of Difference*. Durham and London: Duke University Press.

Morris, B. 1982. *Forest Traders: A Socio-Economic Study of the Hill Pandaram*. Monographs in Social Anthropology, no. 55. London: London School of Economics.

———. 1998. *The Power of Animals: An Ethnography*. Oxford: Berg.

———. 2000. *Animals and Ancestors: An Ethnography*. Oxford: Berg.

———. 2004. *The History and Conservation of Mammals in Malawi*. Malawi: Kachere Series.

———. 2014. *Anthropology, Ecology, and Anarchism: A Brian Morris Reader*. Oakland, CA: PM Press.

Mullin, M. 1999. 'Mirrors and Windows: Sociocultural Studies of Human–Animal Relationships'. *Annual Review of Anthropology* 28: 201–24.

Myers, N., R. A. Mittermeier, C. G. Mittermeier, G. A. B. da Fonseca, and J. Kent. 2000. 'Biodiversity Hotspots for Conservation Priorities'. *Nature* 403, no. 6772: 853–8.

Naess, A. 1989. *Ecology, Community and Lifestyle: Outline of an Ecosophy*. New York: Cambridge University Press.

Narayan, K. 2012. *Alive in the Writing: Crafting Ethnography in the Company of Chekhov*. Chicago: University Of Chicago Press.

Needham, J. F. 1896. *Report by the Assistant Political Officer, Sadiya, on the Relations with the Frontier Tribes for the Year 1895–1896*. Assam Secretariat Proceedings, State Archives, Directorate of Research, Itanagar.

Negi, D. S. 1996. *A Tryst with the Mishmi Hills*. New Delhi: Tushar Publications.

Neumann, R. 1998. *Imposing Wilderness: Struggles over Livelihood and Nature Preservation in Africa*. Berkeley and Los Angeles: University of California Press.

Nijhawan, Sahil; (2018) *Human-animal relations and the role of cultural norms in tiger conservation in the Idu Mishmi of Arunachal Pradesh, India*. PhD Thesis, University College London, United Kingdom.

Nijhawan, S and A. Mihu (2020). Relations of Blood: Hunting Taboos and Wildlife Conservation in the Idu Mishmi of Northeast India. *Journal of Ethnobiology*, 40(2): 149–166.

Oma, A. 2010. 'Between Trust and Domination: Social Contracts between Humans and Animals'. *World Archaeology* 42, no. 2: 175–87.

Ostrom, E. 1990. *Governing the Commons: The Evolution of Institutions for Collective Action*. Cambridge: Cambridge University Press.

Pandit, R. 2014. *Army Kicks Off Raising New Mountain Strike Corps agianst China. Times of India*, 9 January. Available at http://timesofindia. indiatimes.com/india/Army-kicks-off-raising-new-mountain-strike-corps-against-China/articleshow/28571907.cms. Last accessed on 20 January 2015.

Paudel, N. S. 2005. 'Protected Areas and Reproduction of Social Inequality'. *Policy Matters* 14: 155–69.

Paudel, N. S., P. Budhathoki, and U. R. Sharma. 2007. 'Buffer Zones: New Frontiers for Participatory Conservation?' *Journal of Forest and Livelihood* 6, no. 2: 44–53.

Peet, R., P. Robbins, and M. Watts. 2011. *Global Political Ecology.* London and New York: Routledge.

Peluso, N. L. 1993. 'Coercing Conservation? The Politics of State Resource Conrol'. *Global Environmental Change* 3, no. 2: 199–217.

Perelman, M. 2007. 'Primitive Accumulation from Feudalism to Neoliberalism'. *Capitalism Nature Socialism* 18, no. 2: 44–61.

Phadnis, U. 1989. *Ethnicity and Nation-Building in South Asia*. New Delhi: Sage Publications Ltd.

Pimbert, M. P., and J. N. Pretty. 1997. 'Parks, People and Professionals: Putting 'Participation' into Protected Area Managment'. In *Social Change and Conservation*, edited by K. Ghimire and M. P. Pimbert, 297–330. London: Earthscan Publications Limited.

Pomeroy, C. 1995. 'Review of Ecological Identity by Mitchell Thomashow'. *Journal of Political Ecology* 2, no. 4: 47–51.

Pratt, M. L. 1991. 'Arts of the Contact Zone'. *Profession* 91: 33–40.

Rahman, M. Z. 2014. *Territory, Tribes, Turbines: Local Community Perceptions and Responses to Infrastructure Development Along the Sino-Indian Border in Arunachal Pradesh*. New Delhi: Institute of Chinese Studies.

———. 2017. 'Bridges and Roads in North-East India May Drive Small Tribes away from Development'. *The Conversation*, 6 July. Available at https://theconversation.com/amp/bridges-and-roads-in-north-east-india-may-drive-small-tribes-away-from-development-78636. Last accessed on 23 November 2019.

Ramakrishnan, P. S. 1998. 'Ecology and Traditional Wisdom'. In *The Cultural Dimension of Ecology*, edited by B. Saraswati, 56–67. New Delhi: Indira Gandhi National Centre for Arts.

Rangarajan, M. 1996. *Fencing the Forest: Conservation and Ecological Change in India's Central Provinces, 1860–1914*. New Delhi: Oxford University Press.

———. 2009. 'Striving for a Balance: Nature, Power, Science and India's Indira Gandhi, 1917–1984'. *Conservation and Society* 7, no. 4: 299–312.

———. 2015. *Nature and Nation: Essays on Environmental History*. New Delhi: Permanent Black.

Rangarajan, M. 2012. 'Environment and Ecology Under British Rule'. In *India and the British Empire*, edited by D. M. Peers and N. Gooptu, 212–230. UK: Oxford University Press.

Rao, M., T. Myint, T. Zaw, and S. Htun. 2005. 'Hunting Patterns in Tropical Forests Adjoining the Hkakaborazi National Park, North Myanmar'. *Oryx* 39, no. 3: 292–300.

Rashid, O. 2015. 'Maharashtra Gets "State Butterfly"'. *The Hindu*, 22 June. Available at: https://www.thehindu.com/news/national/other-states/maharashtra-gets-state-butterfly/article7342955.ece. Last accessed on 26 July 2016.

Redford, K. H. 1991. 'The Ecologically Noble Savage'. *Orion* 9, no. 3: 24–9.

———. 1992. 'The Empty Forest'. *Bioscience* 42, no. 6: 412–22.

Rehmani, A. 2011. 'State Species: Need to Go Beyond Symbolism'. *Journal of the Bombay Natural History Society* 108, no. 2: 1–2.

———. 2014. 'Symbolism *Par Excellence*'. *Journal of the Bombay Natural History Society* 111, no. 3: 159–60.

Reuters. 2015. 'China Protests over Japan's Comments on Border Dispute with India'. *Reuters*, 19 January. Available at http://in.reuters.com/article/2015/01/19/china-japan-india-idINL4N0UY303201501192015. Last accessed on 15 November 2015.

Rina, T. 2012. 'Namdapha Tiger Reserve under Threat: PCCF Bears the Brunt of Poacher's Ire'. *Arunachal Times*, no. 17 (March): 1.

Robb, P. 1997. 'The Colonial State and Constructions of Indian Identity: An Example on the Northeast Frontier in the 1880s'. *Modern Asian Studies* 31, no. 2: 245–83.

Rosaldo, R. 1989. *Culture & Truth: The Remaking of Social Analysis*. Boston: Beacon Press.

Routledge, B. H. 1945. *'Tour Diary of B.H. Routledge, Sadiya Frontier, Dec 1945–Dec 1946'*. Mss Eur D1191/2. London: The British Library.

Roy, E., and F. Katsuyoshi. 1996. *Redefining Nature: Ecology, Culture and Domestication*. London: Bloomsbury Academic.

Roy, A. 2018. *Swidden, Hunting and Adi Culture: Highland Transitions in Arunachal Pradesh, India*. PhD Thesis, Manipal Academy of Higher Education, Karnataka, India.

Saberwal, V. K., and A. Kothari. 1996. 'The Human Dimension in Conservation Biology Curricula in Developing Countries'. *Conservation Biology* 10, no. 5: 1328–31.

Saberwal, V. K., M. Rangarajan, and A. Kothari. 2001. *People, Parks and Wildlife: Towards coexistence*. New Delhi: Orient Longman Private Limited.

Salazar, N. B. 2012. 'Tourism Imaginaries: A Conceptual Approach'. *Annals of Tourism Research* 39, no. 2: 863–82.

Sarma, K., M. Krishna, and A. Kumar. 2014. 'Fragmented Populations of the Vulnerable Eastern Hoolock Gibbon *Hoolock Leuconedys* in the Lower Dibang Valley District, Arunachal Pradesh'. *Oryx* 49, no. 1: 133–9.

Sarma, Rashmirekha. 2015. Disappearing Dialect: The Idu-Mishmi Language of Arunachal Pradesh (India). *International Journal of Intangible Heritage* 10: 62–72.

Schwartz, K. 2006. *Nature and National Identity after Communism: Globalizing the Ethnoscape*. Pittsburgh: University of Pittsburgh Press.

Saikia, P. J., and P. Gogoi. 2018. 'Bhupen Hazarika Setu and the Politics of Infrastructure'. *The Wire*, 28 February. Available at https://thewire.in/government/bhupen-hazarika-setu. Last accessed on 1 December 2019.

Selvan, K. M., G. G. Veeraswami, B. Habib, and S. Lyngdoh. 2013. 'Losing Threatened and Rare Wildlife to Hunting in Ziro Valley, Arunachal Pradesh, India'. *Current Science* 104, no. 11: 1492–5.

Sethi, N. 2013. 'Hunting on Hackneyed Ideas'. *The Hindu*, 20 August. Available at http://www.thehindu.com/news/national/other-states/hunting-on-hackneyed-ideas/article5072086.ece. Last accessed on 25 January 2014.

Sethi, N. 2014. RSS turns Arunachal tribals towards Hinduism. 01 May. Available at *https://www.business-standard.com/article/elections-2014/rss-turns-arunachal-tribals-towards-hinduism-114042900231_1.html*. Last accessed on 13 March 2015.

Seton, E. T. 1966. *Wild Animals I Have Known*. New York: Shocken.

Shahabuddin, G., and Rangarajan, M. 2007. *Making Conservation Work: Securing Biodiversity in This New Century*. New Delhi: Permanent Black.

Sharma, A. 2014. 'Chinese Troops Training Pak Army near India–Pakistan Border, BSF Tells NSA Ajit Doval'. *Economic Times*, 3 December. Available at http://articles.economictimes.indiatimes.com/2014-11-15/news/56115065_1_bsf-chinese-troops-border-security-force. Last accessed on 24 January 2015.

Sharma, M. 2012. *Green and Saffron: Hindu Nationalism and Indian Environmental Politics*. Ranikhet: Permanent Black.

———. 2017. *Caste and Nature: Dalits and Indian Environmental Politics*. New Delhi: Oxford Univesity Press.

Sharma, R. 2015. 'Modi in China: A High-Octane Reception Muddied by CCTV's Map of India'. *Firstpost*, 19 May. Available at http://www.firstpost.com/world/modis-china-visit-high-octane-reception-muddied-cctv-map-2245418.html. Last accessed on 31 December 2015.

Sharpes, D. 2006. *Sacred Bull, Holy Cow: A Cultural Study of Civilization's Most Important Animal*. New York: Peter Lang Publishing, Inc.

Sillitoe, Paul. 2009. 'Hunting for Conservation in the Papua New Guinea Highlands'. *Ethnos* 66 (3): 365–93.

Simoons, F. J., and E. S. Simoons. 1968. *A Ceremonial Ox of India: The Mithan in Nature, Culture, and History*. Madison: University of Wisconsin Press.

Singh, B. 2014. 'Arunachal Pradesh Now on Railway Map, Train Reaches Naharlagun, a Town near Capital Itanagar'. *Economic Times*, 12 April. Available at http://articles.economictimes.indiatimes.com/2014-04-12/

news/49080232_1_harmuti-railway-map-arunachal-pradesh. Last accessed on 12 July 2014.

Singh, B. P. 1987. 'North-East India: Demography, Culture and Identity Crisis'. *Modern Asian Studies* 21, no. 2: 257–82.

Singh, D. K. 2010. 'Arunachalis' Self-Perceptions: Assertion and Reconstruction of Identity and Ethnic Nationalism'. In *Stateless in South Asia*, edited by D. K. Singh, 180–220. New Delhi: Sage Publications.

Singh, P. K., R. K. Singh, A. Biswas and V. R. Rao. 2013. 'High Rate of Suicide Attempt and Associated Psychological Traits in an Isolated Tribal Population of North-East India'. *Journal of Affective Disorders* 151, no. 2: 673–8.

SN. 2014. Fieldwork report titled 'The Role of Cultural Norms in Wildlife Conservation in Arunachal Pradesh'. First Phase: December 2013–June 2014. Available at http://21tiger.zslsites.org/assets/21tiger/Project_PDFs/India/TigersDamsandTribalCulturesArunachalPradeshInterimReport2014.pdf. Last accessed on 21 December 2014.

Songster, E. 2004. 'A Natural Place for Nationalism: The Wanglang Nature Reserve and the Emergence of the Giant Panda as a National Icon'. PhD thesis, Department of History, University of California, San Diego.

Spillet, J. J. 1966. 'General Wild Life Conservation Problems in India'. *Journal of the Bombay Natural History Society* 63, no. 3: 616–29.

Stewart, J. 2006. *Spying for the Raj: The Pundits and the Mapping of the Himalayas*. Phoenix Mill: Sutton Publishing Limited.

Talukdar, B. K. 2000. 'The Current State of Rhino in Assam and Threats in the 21st Century'. *Pachyderm* 29: 39–47.

Tanner, A. 1979. *Bringing Home Animals: Religious Ideology and Mode of Production of the Mistassini Cree Hunters*. New York: St. Martin's Press.

Tiger Task Force. 2005 *Joining the Dots: The Report of the Tiger Task Force*. New Delhi: Ministry of Environment and Forests, Government of India.

The Indian Express. 2013. Two tigers in a boat to say nothing of the 900 km'. 13 October. Available at https://indianexpress.com/article/news-archive/web/two-tigers-in-a-boat-to-say-nothing-of-the-900-km/. Last accessed on 8 June 2016.

The Indian Express. 2018. 'Tiger in the Snow: The Big Cat Now Roars in the High Altitudes of Arunachal Pradesh'. 5 December. Available at https://indianexpress.com/article/opinion/editorials/royal-bengal-tiger-snow-arunachal-pradesh-dibang-valley-5478728/. Last accessed on 21 July 2020.

Thomas, J. A. 2009. 'The Exquisite Corpses of Nature and History: The Case of the Korean DMZ'. *Asia Pacific Journal (Japan Focus)* 7, no. 43 (October): 1–17.

Times News Network. 2013 'Protest against Chinese Incursion in Arunachal Pradesh'. *Times of India*, 28 August. Available at http://timesofindia.

indiatimes.com/city/guwahati/Protest-against-Chinese-incursion-in-Arunachal-Pradesh/articleshow/22110499.cms. Last accessed on 4 November 2015.

Times of India. 2015. 'India to Fortify Defence Along China Border, 54 New ITBP Posts Being Planned in Arunachal'. Times of India, 24 October. Available at http://timesofindia.indiatimes.com/india/India-to-fortify-defence-along-China-border-54-new-ITBP-posts-being-planned-in-Arunachal/articleshow/36353494.cms. Last accessed on 24 October 2015.

Tsing, A. 2005. Friction: *An ethnography of global connection.* Princeton University Press, Princeton and Oxford.

———. 2012. 'Unruly Edges: Mushrooms as Companion Species'. *Environmental Humanities* 1 (November): 141–54.

———. 2013. 'More-Than-Human-Sociality'. In *Anthropology and Nature,* edited by K. Hastrup, 27–42. New York: Routledge.

Tsing, A. L., J. P. Brosius, and C. Zerner. 2005. 'Introduction: Raising Questions about Communities and Conservation'. In *Communities and Conservation: Histories and Politics of Community-Based Natural Resource Management,* edited by J. P. Brosius, A. L. Tsing, and C. Zerner, 1–34. Walnut Creek, CA: Altamira Press.

Van Schendel, W. 1992. 'The Invention of the "Jummas": State Formation and Ethnicity in Southeastern Bangladesh'. *Modern Asian Studies* 26, no. 1: 95–128.

Van Schendel, W., and I. Abraham. 2005. *Illicit Flows and Criminal Things: States, Borders, and the Other Side of Globalization.* Bloomington & Indianapolis: Indiana University Press.

Van Schendel, W., and E. de Maaker. 2014. 'Asian Borderlands: Introducing Their Permeability, Strategic Uses and Meanings'. *Journal of Borderlands Studies* 29, no. 1: 1–9.

Velho, N., K. Karanth, and W. F. Laurance. 2012. 'Hunting: A Serious and Understudied Threat in India: A Globaly Significant Conservation Region'. *Biological Conservation.* doi:10.1016/j.biocon.2012.01.022.

Vertzberger, Y. 1982. 'India's Border Conflict with China: A Perceptual Analysis'. *Journal of Contemporary History* 17, no. 4: 607–31.

Vidyarthi, L. P. 1963. *The Maler: A Study in Nature-Spirit-Man Complex of a Hill Tribe in Bihar.* Calcutta: Bookland Private Limited.

Waller, D. 1990. *The Pundits: British Exploration of Tibet and Central Asia.* Lexington: The University Press of Kentucky.

Walter, R. K., and R. J. Hamilton. 2014. 'A Cultural Landscape Approach to Community-Based Conservation'. *Ecology and Society* 19, no. 4: 41–50.

West, P. 2006. *Conservation Is Our Government Now: The Politics of Ecology in Papua New Guinea.* Durham and London: Duke University Press.

Wijkman, A., and J. Rockstorm. 2012. *Bankrupting Nature: Denying Our Planetary Boundaries*. New York: Routledge.

Willerslev, R. 2007. *Soul Hunters: Hunting, Animism, and Personhood among the Siberian Yukaghirs*. Berkeley: University of California.

Williams, R. 1976. *Keywords: A Vocabulary of Culture and Society*. New York: Oxford University Press.

———. 1980. *Culture and Materialism: Selected Essays*. New York: Verso.

———. 1983. *Towards 2000*. Harmondsworth: Penguin.

Williams, D. R., W. P. Stewart, and L. E. Kruger. 2013. 'Place-Based Conservation: Advancing Social Theory and Practice'. In *Place-Based Conservation: Perspectives from the Social Sciences*, edited by W. P. Stewart, D. R. Williams, and L. E. Kruger, 3–28. New York: Springer.

Williamson, N. 1910. Report of Mr. Williamson, APO in Connection with His Work Carried Out in 1909–1910 in the Digaru-Miju Bridle Path and of His House in the Mishmi Hills to the Border of South-Eastern Tibet. F/20 P of 1910. State Archives of Arunachal Pradesh, Itanagar.

Wilson, P. 2007. 'Agriculture or Architecture? The Beginnings of Domestication'. In *Where the Wild Things Are Now: Domestication Reconsidered*, edited by R. Cassidy and M. Mullin, 101–21. Oxford and New York: Berg.

Wright, B. 2010. 'Will the Tiger Survive in India?' In *Tigers of the World: The Science, Politics, and Conservation of Panthera Tigris*, edited by R. Tilson and P. J. Nyhus, 87–100. UK and USA: Elsevier Inc.

Xaxa, V. 2010. "'Tribes', Tradition and State'. *The Newsletter: International Institute of Asian Studies* 53 (Spring): 18.

Yeh, E. 2009. 'Greening Western China: A Critical Review'. *Geoforum* 40: no. 7: 884–94.

———. 2012. 'Transnational Environmentalism and Entanglements of Sovereignty: The Tiger Campaign across the Himalayas'. *Political Geography* 31, no. 7: 408–18.

INDEX

ABOUT THE AUTHOR

Ambika Aiyadurai is an anthropologist of wildlife conservation with a special interest in human–animal relations and community-based conservation. Her ongoing and long-term research aims to understand how local and global forces shape human–animal relations. Ambika is trained in both natural and social sciences with master's degrees in wildlife sciences from Wildlife Institute of India (Dehradun, India) and in anthropology, environment and development, from University College London (UK), funded by Ford Foundation's International Fellowship Programme. Ambika is now assistant professor (anthropology) in Indian Institute of Technology, Gandhinagar, India. She completed her PhD thesis in anthropology from the National University of Singapore in 2016. She received the Ananda Rajah award for the best PhD thesis in social sciences. In 2017, she was awarded the Social Science Research Council (SSRC) Trans-regional Research Junior Scholar Fellowship. She was affiliated with the Global Asia Initiative, Duke University (North Carolina, USA), as a visiting scholar in 2018.